RING SHOUT, WHEEL ABOUT

KATRINA DYONNE THOMPSON

Ring Shout, Wheel About

THE RACIAL POLITICS OF MUSIC AND DANCE IN NORTH AMERICAN SLAVERY

UNIVERSITY OF ILLINOIS PRESS

URBANA, CHICAGO, AND SPRINGFIELD

© 2014 by the Board of Trustees
of the University of Illinois
All rights reserved
Manufactured in the United States of America
1 2 3 4 5 C P 5 4 3 2 1

∞ This book is printed on acid-free paper.

Library of Congress Cataloging-in-Publication Data
Thompson, Katrina Dyonne.
Ring shout, wheel about : the racial politics of music and dance in North American
slavery / Katrina Dyonne Thompson.
    pages cm
Includes bibliographical references and index.
ISBN 978-0-252-03825-9 (hardback) — ISBN 978-0-252-07983-2 (paperback) —
ISBN 978-0-252-09611-2 (e-book)
    1. Slaves—Southern States—Songs and music. 2. Slaves—United States—Social
life and customs. 3. Race in the theater—United States—History. 4. Theater and
society—United States—History. 5. African American dance—History. 6. Slavery—
United States—Justification. 7. Plantation life—United States. 8. Racism in popular
culture—United States—History. I. Title.
    E443.T49   2014
    390'.250973—dc23   2013032131

For Leri, Otis, Christee, Matthew, and Alexia

In Memory of Ruth Galmon

Contents

Acknowledgments

"They brought her down here and sold her you see they have them on a big block . . . and make them stand up and act a certain way . . . if they think you good they buy you . . . you didn't act right they wouldn't buy you." These were the words of my great aunt Ruth Galmon who, at age 105, still retained a clear memory of her mother's and grandmother's stories of slavery and encouraged me to research the intricacies of the lives and culture of my history. I have been fortunate to have an amazing family, friends, and colleagues who continually encouraged and supported me throughout writing this book.

I wish to thank my colleagues in the History Department and African American Studies at Saint Louis University who have provided support for my work since I joined the faculty in 2008. As a graduate student, I had the privilege of receiving support from the History and Africana Studies Department at Stony Book University, the W. Burghardt Turner Fellowship, the History Department at Roanoke College, the Erskine Peters Fellowship, and Africana Studies at the University of Notre Dame. My advisor from Stony Brook University, Floris B. Cash, was always encouraging and supportive, as were other members of my committee. I would also like to extend thanks to Richard Pierce of the University of Notre Dame for his continual guidance. To Dexter J. Gabriel, Silvana Siddali, Karla Scott, George Ndege, Heidi Ardizzone, Wilbur Miller, and Nancy Tomes, I am eternally grateful.

Ring Shout, Wheel About was immeasurably improved by the insightful comments of those who meticulously read the manuscript. I would like to gratefully acknowledge my mentor and colleague at Saint Louis University, Lorri Glover, for her time, encouragement, and guidance. In addition to reading every word of this manuscript several times, Lorri made me feel that I could successfully accomplish this goal, and for that I am forever in her debt. To all friends and colleagues that offered any words of encouragement during my young career: thank you.

Support came from a variety of other sources, such as the archivists at the Schomburg Center for Research in Black Culture, Fisk University, Houghton Library at Harvard University, Library of Congress, University of New Orleans, University of North Carolina, Duke University, Northwestern State University of Louisiana, Louisiana State University, New York Public Library for the Performing Arts, National Maritime Museum, and U.K. Parliamentary Archives. There were also countless librarians and archivists who helped me access materials that were indispensable to this project. Also, I would like to thank my peers from the Association of Black Women Historians and Association for the Study of African American Life and History who have committed their lives to history of the African Diaspora.

To my family and friends I extend deep feelings of gratitude. First, I want to thank my parents, Leri Thompson Mouton and Otis Thompson for their constant love and support. Thanks also to my personal cheerleader, sister, and best friend, Christee Lewis, and brother Matthew Thompson, whose heart is pure gold. I send my love to my niece Alexia Lewis: you truly are my sunshine. To my friend Renae (Image) Baker and her beautiful girls, Loren and Lailah Rose: thank you for your constant love. To Apostle Tony and Prophetess Ina Westley, I am truly appreciative for the support and spiritual guidance you have provided throughout my life. Finally, I would like to thank the strong women in my family, Iola Duncan, Earlene Banks, Rosielee Frank, and Kathy Gordon. I am extremely fortunate to be from a city full of history, culture, and love: New Orleans—we will continually stand.

RING SHOUT, WHEEL ABOUT

Introduction

"They don't sing as they used to," a white Georgian in the early twentieth century lamented of Southern blacks. "You should have known the old darkeys of the plantation. Every year, it seems to me, they have been losing more and more of their carefree good humor . . . I don't know them any more. . . . .and I'm free to say I'm scared of them!"[1] In the aftermath of the 1906 Atlanta race riot, journalist Ray Stannard Baker traveled throughout the South with the desire to "make a clear statement . . . of the Negro in American life." Believing that he would "look at the Negro, not merely as a menial, as he is regarded in the South, nor as a curiosity, as he is often seen in the North, but as a plain human being," Baker toured throughout the South, interviewing people of all races and observing race relations.[2] Revealing the sentiment of a local white female resident, Baker exposed what by the turn of the twentieth century had become a common American nostalgia for an imagined Old South in which blacks were happily docile and whites held power and dominance.

The fears of the rising "New Negro" at the turn of the century only encouraged the persistent stereotype that affiliated black innate docility with propensity for the performing arts of music, song, and dance. Baker assumed that the "temperament of the Negro is irrepressibly cheerful, he overflows from his small home and sings and laughs in his streets; no matter how ragged or forlorn he may be good humour sits upon his countenance, and his squalor is not unpicturesque. A banjo . . . an exciting revival, give him real joys."[3] Many white Americans at the turn of the century shared Baker's biases, which derived from nostalgia of an "Old South" that never truly existed outside of folklore and imagined memories. In typical trope, an Alabama newspaper, the *Independent Monitor*, in 1869 charged: "Negroes, as bondsmen, were happier. . . . We never hear the ringing horse-laughs, the picking of banjoes, beating of tamborines . . . that formerly marked their *sans souci* existence."[4] Though Baker was attempting to approach his project in an unbiased manner that differed from the perspective of earlier writers who continually propagated the idea that most Southerners longed for the plantation slavery system, the idea that blacks were innately musical persisted in his writings. Also, Baker assessed that blacks who were singing, dancing, and performing for or in the presence of whites were happy and submissive, content in their offering of entertainment and amusement. Scholar George Frederickson expressed in the groundbreaking work *The Black Image in the White Mind* that the scientific racism that developed in the United States evolved from the association of the performing arts with blacks.[5] He revealed a popular American belief: "even in their . . . unfulfilled state," blacks have a "light-heartedness," a "natural talent for music," which equated to their "willingness to serve."[6] However, music and dance held much more complex and conflicting roles in the lives of many African Americans.

Since the late nineteenth century, African Americans have been able to gain wealth, popularity, and acceptance through recognized talents in the performing arts of music, song, and dance. Their contributions to American culture have been well documented and have acquired international recognition. From spirituals and jazz to blues and hip hop, African Americans have continually contributed distinct sounds and prolific performers to the world. However, music and dance, while offering an avenue for achievement, have also contributed to the persistent degradation of black culture and people through the stereotypes associated with African Americans and entertainment. Music and dance in the black community has a multiplicity of meanings that for centuries advanced a paradoxical dynamic of agency, masquerade, and subjugation. The conflicting role of music, dance, and song was a part of the "double consciousness" that W. E. B. Du Bois introduced in *The Souls of Black Folk*: "double-consciousness, this sense of always looking at one's self through the eyes of others, of measuring one's soul by the tape of a world that looks on in amused contempt and pity. One ever feels his twoness,— an American, a Negro; two souls, two thoughts, two unreconciled strivings; two warring ideals in one dark body, whose dogged strength alone keeps it from being torn asunder."[7]

The double consciousness within black performing arts is related to the persistence of race as an aspect of entertainment. Harlem Renaissance writer Langston Hughes captured the multiplicity of music and dance within African American culture in his 1932 poem "Black Clown":

> I am the fool of the whole world.
> Laugh and push me down.
> Only in song and laughter
> I rise again—a black clown.
> Strike up the music.
> Let it be gay.
> Only in joy
> Can a clown have his day.
>
> Three hundred years
> In the cotton and the cane,
> Plowing and reaping
> With no gain—
> Empty handed as I began.
>
> A slave—under the whip,
> Beaten and sore.
> God! Give me laughter
> That I can stand more.
>
> God! Give me the spotted
> Garments of a clown
> So that the pain and the shame
> Will not pull me down.
>
> Cry to the world
> That all might understand:
> I was once a black clown
> But now—
> I'm a man![8]

Hughes's poem directly reflects the rise of the "New Negro" during a time when whites throughout the world were flocking in droves to the "black Mecca" of Harlem to witness the distinctly black genres and styles of music, dance, and singing of black performers.[9] Although his poem illustrates the progress of African Americans from minstrel in popular culture to "man," a recognized individual contributing to the world, the negative racial stereotypes continued to linger in the American entertainment culture. Historian Karen Sotiropoulos argues in *Staging Race* that "African Americans were hyperconscious of how much their self-presentation on stage would be read through stereotype and how a modern sensibility required distancing oneself from pervasive black imagery."[10]

For the majority of America's existence, blacks have been vulnerable to negative representations in the entertainment public sphere. Racism, as part of the American psyche and culture, is continually recognized in the political and social systems of this country, but it often goes unnoticed when manifested in popular culture. African Americans have made great strides to reverse racism in the last half-century, but underlying systems of bias remain. These lingering, fundamental remnants of white supremacy and black degradation have consistently influenced popular culture, appearing in many forms of amusement that exist today. Several scholars trace the origins of American entertainment culture to the beginning of blackface minstrelsy in the nineteenth century. In 1992, Donald Bogle's historic work, *Toms, Coons, Mulattoes, Mammies, and Bucks*, chronicled black representations in mass media, specifically film.[11] He argued that American popular entertainment initiated with the misrepresentation of blacks as caricatures in the minstrel show. Robin Means Coleman in 1998 explored black representations in mass media, specifically radio and television, from its beginning to its present state.[12] She also traced the source of negative racial imagery in popular culture to the emergence of the American minstrel show in the 1830s, concluding that a new era of minstrelsy has developed as a trend in today's mass media. Coleman presents several pointed questions that her work directly addresses: "Why is it that images of Black people in popular culture and mass media are so often reduced to racial stereotypes? Where did this 'Other' as object, as exotic, and as spectacle for public consumption and amusement come from?" She further probes, "The current popularity and prevalence of pro-slavery, 'happy darky' misrepresentations aside, what implications do these early generations of distortions have for contemporary mediated representations?"[13] Though Coleman's suggestions that minstrelsy and modern mass media stereotypes of African Americans emanated from slave folklore are correct, the larger historicity of the topic has yet to be fully addressed. Simplifying the "happy darky" into a stereotype that Southerners created to disguise the abuses of slavery obscures the multilayered role and influence of music and dance in the construction of race, gender, and the experiences of blacks in America. Similarly, John Strausbaugh, in his book *Black Like You* (2006), states that American entertainment resonates with the legacy of blackface minstrelsy, which initially rose to popularity in the 1830s.[14] Blackface minstrelsy often has been credited as the source of many of the negative black stereotypes that exist in American popular culture. Intending for his book to serve as cultural commentary, Strausbaugh reviews the history of blackface minstrelsy as the main form of entertainment in the United States and postulates that it only became politically incorrect with the advent of the civil rights movement during the 1950s and 1960s. He argues that black-face minstrelsy has been newly reincarnated in the twenty-first century, concluding that blacks and whites "mock and mimic one another, are by turns attracted to and repulsed by one another. . . . It is a culture . . . [and] all this will continue for as long as America is America."[15] While this argument has brought to the forefront the prevalence of racist ideology in mainstream entertainment, it has also seriously neglected the historical significance of these events.

In this book, *Ring Shout, Wheel About: The Racial Politics of Music and Dance in North American Slavery*, I challenge the commonly accepted belief that the minstrel show was the first American entertainment genre. Instead, I delve further into earlier misrepresentations of blacks, positing that the slave society fostered the first American entertainment venue. The history of blacks in entertainment, or more specifically blacks as entertainment, contributed significantly to the construction of race and identity for African Americans. Scenes of enslaved blacks performing music, song, and dance for the amusement of white spectators represented the first major American entertainment setting, long before minstrel shows appeared. Thus, negative black stereotypes in entertainment reach much further back in history than current scholarship acknowledges. Eric Lott, in his groundbreaking work *Love and Theft*, recognizes that the minstrel show has "been so central to the lives of North Americans that we are hardly aware of its extraordinary influence."[16] Similarly, numerous scholars, including Dale Cockrell, Sam Dennison, Mel Watkins, and Michael Rogin, have recognized the influence that blackface minstrelsy had on race, gender, and popular culture.[17] Indeed, its importance is undeniable; however, in the work that follows, I am concerned with the manner in which African Americans and stereotypes were shaped and influenced in the centuries before the rise of the blackface minstrel show. *Ring Shout, Wheel About* also examines slavery holistically to fully reveal how centuries of blacks performing for white audiences in a political, social, and cultural institution such as slavery contributed to the foundation of American entertainment.

The history of slavery in the United States is filled with stories that depict a Southern setting with blacks tirelessly toiling in the fields under the authority of white masters, the music of the slaves all the while providing the scene's score. The public memory of slavery in the United States is filled with these scenes and has continually manifested in popular culture, contributing to a somewhat distorted view of the complicated nature and experiences of enslaved black men, women, and children. Ex-slave and abolitionist Frederick Douglass recalled in his autobiography, "Slaves are generally expected to sing as well as to work."[18] Music, song, and dance were intertwined into every aspect of a slave's life. *Ring Shout, Wheel About* contributes new perspectives on race, gender, stereotypes, and popular culture through the use of richly detailed, firsthand accounts that illustrate a common occurrence throughout the American plantation society, enslaved blacks performing for white audiences. This work unveils the process by which racial stereotypes about blacks developed and were perpetuated. It recognizes the dual significance of African American performance during slavery; on one hand, these forced performances were key in constructing white stereotypes of blacks, but on the other, they served as a means for blacks to construct their identity and retain their cultures.

The belief that African Americans have an innate ability in these arts represents a stereotype that has endured throughout American history. William Van Deburg, in *Slavery and Race in American Popular Culture*, wrote, "For black Americans, the character and the overall effect of these opinions have been especially important. . . . As outcasts in a white-dominated society, blacks alternately were portrayed as feeble-willed noble savages, comically musical minstrel figures, and dehumanized brutes."[19] These stereotypes of blacks reveal whites' anxieties and their desire to control black bodies while justifying a deplorable institution of racial slavery. Unsuccessfully, African Americans throughout the years have attempted to combat the erroneous stereotyping that developed during America's formative years. Whites assessed the character of blacks during the initial contact between Europeans and West Africans. The unfavorable first impressions resulted in the (convenient, financially advantageous) positioning of blacks as outcasts in the New World society. Blacks were categorized as savages who were oversexualized, immoral, and intellectually and culturally underdeveloped. These misconceptions contributed to the emergence of negative racial images that became infused into the culture and history of America.

For more than two centuries, the performance of music, song, and dance was an integral part of every aspect of the Southern slave experience.[20] Ethnomusicologists, historians, and folk scholars have explored the dance movements and song lyrics of the enslaved community, recognizing that these traditions were adaptations of West African cultures that contributed to the creation of distinct African American communities.[21]

However, this book explicitly recognizes that music and dance were not simply relics; instead, these scenes hosted the development of culture and choreographed ideals of race while also framing a space in which masters and slaves continually negotiated power. These scenes of blacks performing for white audiences will be viewed as representing multiple roles in both the black and white communities. For blacks, performing constituted a way to gain agency, cope, entertain within their own community, and rebel. For the white community, these performances affirmed their dominance, served as a form of amusement, supported their ideals of paternalism, and veiled their constant fears of rebellion. Music, song, and dance became both resoundingly positive and negative aspects of life for both groups. *Ring Shout, Wheel About* will problematize this tension in detail. More explicitly, the book will unpack these performance scenes to explore what are termed *onstage* and *backstage* performances. The central question I answer is: How did black music and dance affect the cultural development of blacks and whites? Also, did these music and dance scenes contribute to a distinctly American culture? Especially salient to the novelty of this project is my expanded treatment of cultural exchanges throughout the Southern slave communities, recognizing the influence that blacks and whites had on each other's cultures and racial perceptions.

Ring Shout, Wheel About illustrates that the first form of American entertainment was the music, song, and dance performed by enslaved blacks for the amusement and under the coercion of whites on the Southern plantation. These performances became a popular pastime for Southerners as well as Northern and European visitors. For men and women held in bondage, however, performances signified resistance, power, and cultural autonomy. Slaves performed for themselves as well as for white audiences—their music and dance was, then, a complex, often contradictory piece of stagecraft. Race was a theatrical performance in which whites and blacks contributed to a cultural script. The chapter titles reflect this staged performance of race and power.[22]

Chapter 1, "The Script: *Africa was but a blank canvas for Europe's imagination*," examines European and American travel journals to reveal the manner in which they portrayed West Africans in order to create the moral and social justifications for slavery and racial stereotypes. Several scholars have recognized the importance of understanding American slavery's foundation through the initial engagements in West Africa.[23] Ira Berlin in *Many Thousands Gone* and Michael Gomez in *Exchanging Our Country Marks*, just to name a few, have examined African American cultural development and the slave experience from an African Diaspora perspective.[24] The present work recognizes that European travelers often ignored the ritualistic purpose of West African music and dance and instead reduced West Africans to servants, prostitutes, and entertainers, as recognized by Peter Fryer in *Staying Power*.[25] These societal positions were developed on the premise of European hegemony and aimed to create an African commodity. Throughout West Africa, music, song, and dance were important cultural expressions. However, from the sixteenth to nineteenth centuries, European and American travelers distorted these expressions in order to project and fulfill their own desires. Travel narratives presented the identity of West Africans as malleable and capable of being shaped according to the desired purpose of the gazer. Mary Louis Pratt famously demonstrated in *Imperial Eyes* that what spectators saw when gazing upon the "other" within travel narratives was representative of the gazer more so than those being observed.[26] Reviewing European travel journals in the era of slavery reveals the multifaceted intentions and perspectives of the travelers, as well as the foundation of American race.

The creation of the innate dancers and singers that reverberated in travel journals contributed to the subjugation and reconfiguration of the black body through its neglect of the actual culture and tradition of the performing arts. Europeans often interpreted the dance style prevalent among West African women as evidence of their innately oversexualized, lewd nature, thereby demoting both the dance style and the black bodies that participated.[27] At the same time, music, song, and dance were understood as manifestations of Africans' natural intellectual, moral, and social inferiority. These ideals contributed to a perverted understanding of West African cultures and assisted in the commodification of the African body. The misrepresentation of African cultures helped to establish the setting required to foster an institution centered on human chattel.

Chapter 2, "Casting: *They sang their home-songs, and danced, each with his free foot slapping the deck*," explores the manner in which African captives were forced to perform music, song, and dance during the Atlantic voyage. Within the Middle Passage, white slavers brought the slaves on deck for airing. While on deck, the slavers drenched the captives with salt water, inspected them for any hint of disease, and, ironically, made them sing and dance. Historically, music and dance during the Middle Passage were viewed as a form of exercise used to preserve the human cargo. This chapter analyzes those scenes to illustrate the transformation of the top deck of the ship into a stage upon which race and gender roles were prescribed and performed.[28] European and American ideals of Africanness were forced upon the captives in order to transition the diverse populations into chattel. The coerced performances on the slave ship distorted the normally sacred or ritualistic meanings of music, song, and dance. To white slavers, these performances represented that their captives were innately happy and willing subjects.

However, the performing arts allowed West Africans to preserve their distinct cultures and enabled them to conceal rebellions, retain homeland traditions, and encourage their spirits. White slavers often collected native African instruments for the voyage, thereby allowing cultural artifacts to extend into the New World; furthermore, an exchange occurred in which European instruments were performed with an African beat. Within the past decade, the topic of international slave trade has resurged within historical scholarship. Eric Robert Taylor's 2006 *If We Must Die* offers the first in-depth analysis of slave-ship insurrections throughout the Atlantic voyage.[29] Several historians, including Emma Christopher in *Slave Ship Sailors and Their Captive Cargoes* and Stephanie Smallwood in *Saltwater Slavery*, introduce to the conversation on the trade a novel way in which to examine the relationships and exchanges between the international groups that came together within this Atlantic medium.[30] Studying slave-ship logs, slaver and travel journals, and testimony before the British Parliament reveals the significance of music and dance to the exchanges that took place in the Middle Passage. The top deck of the slave ship was a stage upon which African captives were forced to perform their new racialized and sexualized role. The slave ship was the medium between Africans' cultural history, white sailors' traditions and perceptions of their human cargo, and the black bodies' adaptation to their horrific condition, all of which contributed to the development of a social construction of race and racism in North America.

Music, song, and dance in the Middle Passage continued onto America's shores. Performance scenes are the cornerstone of the next two chapters. Chapter 3, "Onstage: *Dance you damned niggers, dance*," examines this continued order by white slave masters throughout plantation communities, small farms, and some urban communities. Slave narratives, travel journals, planter's writings, and publications reveal how the erroneous perceptions of race in the United States were staged within the performing arts. It was the duty of slaves both to labor and to entertain. Although the peculiar institution varied according to region, crop, and population, the music, song, and dance performances were shared experiences that affected the black community. The classic works of Winthrop Jordan (*White Over Black*) and George Fredrickson provide a background on the foundation and development of racism in the United States. Such works offer the initial attitudes of whites toward blacks and the manner in which white perception influenced the development of scientific and intellectualized racism. Building upon this scholarship, my work offers a novel perception of examining the way racial stereotypes were created and forced upon African Americans.

Masters often invited guests to their plantations to show off their performing slaves and would even bet on or challenge their slaves against slaves from other plantations in the performing arts. I examine the manner in which these onstage performances veiled white fears while portraying a paternalistic society to Northerners, European observers, and abolitionists. Ironically, whites continually asserted negative racial stereotypes concerning music and dance while constantly forcing the slaves to perform. The racial imagery within these public performances exhibited blacks' role as submissive in society while whites, the audience, remained superior.[31] However, music, song, and dance played wildly different roles within the enslaved black community.

Chapter 4, "Backstage: *White folks do as they please, and the darkies do as they can*," reveals the façade of the dancing, happy slave to expose the private world of bondsmen and bondswomen. Slaves used the performing arts to gain agency and autonomy, create family and community bonds, and preserve homeland cultures while their own unique traditions emerged. This chapter reviews how music, song, and dance contributed to the development of a dual world that blacks continually straddled, one side representing entertainment and subjugation and the other symbolizing resistance and an emerging culture. Reading slave narratives and autobiographies makes evident that blacks manipulated the negativity of the performing arts, transforming their performances into an expression of power. This backstage chapter exposes the secret world of slaves that contributed to their autonomy, resistance, and distinct cultural development.[32]

Chapter 5, "Advertisement: *Dancing through the Streets and act lively*," reviews the common order for bondsmen and women to dance, act lively, and smile in one of the most traumatic experiences in the institution of slavery, the domestic slave trade. Early on, Frederic Bancroft's *Slave Trading in the Old South* and Michael Tadman's *Speculators and Slaves* offered groundbreaking analyses of the internal trade for a more general audience. Soon after, Walter Johnson introduced a detailed analysis of the New Orleans slave market in *Soul by Soul*, which also examined each party involved in the slave trading experience. Steven Deyle's more recent work *Carry Me Back* examines the domestic slave trade as a whole and comprehensively analyzes the origins, economic influences, long-term effects, and each perspective within the trade to restore the internal trade as an important aspect of the overall institution of slavery.[33] In my work, I break down the coffle, slave pen, and auction block experiences in order to clarify the reasons why music and dance often were incorporated into the complex system of the domestic slave trade. The coffle, an active part of the slavery system, served as an organized transportation network of slaves to the auction block within the interstate slave trade. The slave coffle was a public event in which black slaves were forced to travel, often by foot, throughout many towns and states in the United States. While en route, the slaves could be seen "dancing through the streets" with the direct order to "act lively" for white spectators and potential buyers. This was an exhibition that whites would often watch with fascination and curiosity. In many ways, these performing coffles were public advertisements for not only planters but also those hoping to achieve planter status. In this chapter, I focus on the manner in which these singing and dancing coffles positively promoted the institution of slavery to non-slaveholders. Dance and music also publicly presented the racial hierarchy of the time. These slave coffle scenes represented to whites a justification of their enslavement of blacks. Ironically, however, these forced performing arts also represented an avenue of agency for blacks. Through lyrical and musical expression, enslaved blacks were able to veil hidden messages from the white witnesses. Regardless, the misrepresentation of black culture through the performing arts was endemic to the auction block. At the heart of this study lies a tension between the enslaved black performers and the white spectators.

These images contributed to the development and infiltration of racial stereotypes that manifested into the popular culture. Chapter 6, "Same Script, Different Actors: *Eb'ry time I wheel about, I jump Jim Crow*," focuses on the emergence of a distinct American entertainment culture, specifically recognizing that these scenes of blacks performing music and dance for whites directly influenced popular culture through the blackface minstrel show, fiction literature, travel narratives, and Southern folklore. These distorted images were recreated and further developed on the Northern stage through the rise of the American blackface minstrel show in the 1830s. I reveal that white men performing in blackface in minstrel shows were mimicking black slaves while black slaves were presenting a façade of black culture that was forced upon them by white masters. Beyond the development of the blackface minstrel show as a major form of entertainment, scenes of enslaved blacks performing became the staple setting for popular fiction and proslavery and antislavery texts.[34] This project recognizes that blackface minstrelsy represented whites imitating Southern white ideals and images of blackness. Fully understanding how race was staged in the long ordeal of slavery requires breaking the fourth wall and appreciating the production that underlies the performance.

1   The Script

*"Africa was but a blank canvas
for Europe's imagination"*

Eager to publish in one of the most popular media outlets of his time, Jean Barbot, in 1688, was busily preparing his writings on his experiences and adventurers in West Africa. The Frenchman was attempting to contribute an illustration of Africa and its inhabitants to an inquisitive European and North American audience. As a slaver and author, he well understood how to create a sellable product. He wanted to entertain, thrill, and educate his readers. In order to attract a publisher and potential readers, he added rich detail and vivid scenes to his travel narrative. Purposely attempting to entice an audience, Barbot openly states to his readers, "Sir, I have told you as much as I can about the customs, temperament, occupations and way of life of the peoples of Gold Coast, in general. . . . I shall now satisfy your request by entertaining you with their dances."[1] Music, song, and dance, cultural traditions often presented in travel narratives, provided not only amusement but also insight into the beliefs and practices of the region.

As the *National Geographic* of their day, travel narratives often revealed more than simple observations of distant lands and foreign peoples; they also critiqued those societies, and Barbot's writings followed that trend. The slaver richly detailed a scene of music, dance, and debauchery in his narrative, describing men and women "leaping and stamping their feet" while continually "running against each other, breast to breast, knocking bellies together very indecently . . . and uttering some dirty mysterious words." The Frenchman described the participants as "more like devils than men" who danced in "strange postures . . . as if they were possessed." The entire horrid affair ended as perversely as it started with "someone being murdered," which was only an expression of the lack of "respect" West Africans had toward "their lives" and, analogously, to their morality, according to Barbot.

Music and dance served as more than artistic traditions; in colonial-era travel narratives such as Barbot's those expressions revealed the morality, character, and intellectual capabilities of an exotic people. The repetitive nature of music and dance scenes throughout these writings from the sixteenth through the nineteenth centuries played a significant role in creating an inauspicious impression of West Africans for Western audiences. This caricature probably comforted many readers; it confirmed the unfavorable assessments of previous writers while supporting the burgeoning racial ideology of Western Europe and North America.

Barbot's description of West African music and dance exists as one example of a larger ideological maneuver in which the white male traveler's perspective contributed to the shaping of blacks as oversexual, immoral, intellectually deficient entertainers fit for enslavement. [2] In this sense, Barbot acted as the spectator who viewed and relayed the customs, physiology, daily activities, and morals of West Africans, according European readers his perspective. His viewpoint subjugated West Africans, categorizing African or black attributes as inferior, especially in comparison to whites. Barbot, similar to his contemporaries, contributed to the cultural trend of objectifying West Africans and distributing their hegemonic perspective through travel literature. The act of Western Europeans and North Americans recording and publishing travel journals about the state of Africa and its inhabitants illustrated the authoritative stance of these writers and allowed readers to gain influence and superiority as they gazed by proxy. Both the producers and the consumers of travel narratives were able to assume dominance within these tales, continually placing themselves as superior to the West African subjects intellectually, morally, and socially.

The intent for visiting the region often contributed to the view reflected within the travel publications. Barbot traveled throughout Africa for his business: slave trading. Barbot's travel narrative, like his trade, was constructed as a commodity, appealing to the longing for human labor, sexual desire, and power through the commodification and eroticization of African bodies. Barbot and his European contemporaries who entered the field of travel writing in the sixteenth century joined a centuries-long legacy of writers using this genre to sculpt their personal ideals, aspirations, and imaginations. These travel journals reveal how Europeans (and, later, North Americans) frequently mischaracterized Africans in order to justify purging their land of resources, converting them to Christianity, or ultimately enslaving them. This pattern persisted through the colonization of the Americas, and even into the nineteenth century.

Because these writings constructed West Africans for public consumption as the "other," their cultures, physiology, skin color, and language were belittled as uncivilized and dysfunctional.[3] Psychologist Perry Hinton argues that three main components assist in defining and understanding the creation of the "other" in society.[4] The first is that a group of persons must be identified by specific characteristics, such as skin color or hair texture. Europe had a long history, prior to the Renaissance era, of associating the color black with evil and other negative attributes. Thus, the skin complexion of Africans set them apart as other or different by European standards. The second element involves developing a set of additional characteristics for the out-group. The traits of savagery, cannibalism, depravity, innate musical and dance abilities, and heathenism were only a few of the characteristics constructed by Europeans to fulfill this component. The last component entails identifying all persons in the out-group as having the assigned characteristics.[5] Hinton recognizes these three factors in the "other;" however, his elements must be furthered to recognize that the "other" may be constructed simply by establishing the controlling society as normal. Europeans situated themselves as the standard, infusing themselves with authority and power over any groups that they determined as different from and therefore subordinate to themselves.

European and, later, North American reports on Africans often were limited to descriptions of their observable physical and cultural characteristics.[6] Music and dance were important cultural expressions throughout West Africa that the majority of Western Europeans and Americans visiting the region witnessed. Travel writers consistently discussed music and dance as a shared cultural expression and also to provide interesting and entertaining scenes within their narratives. As well, the fluidity of music and dance in the region allowed most visitors to witness a performance. And finally, the expression was malleable. The performing arts, if properly understood, can assist in understanding the cultures, lifestyles, and histories of foreign persons. The performing arts held a functional role throughout West Africa. Music and dance were interrelated aspects of West African societies. Together they served recreational purposes or were utilized in the performance of ceremonies or rituals. Although Western Europeans may not have recognized the pivotal and complicated role the performing arts held, they entered the region with contradictory opinions about music and dance. Music, song, and dance being an aspect of every society, including Western Europe, it was a recognizable cultural expression that the readers could relate to and understand. However, by depicting West Africans by their music, song, and dance as exotic, writers distanced themselves and their readers from their African subject.

Seventeenth- and eighteenth-century European travel narratives describing West Africans as an exotic other that still possessed human qualities represented an evolution from earlier travel narratives. Earlier Europeans had a history of describing the others, whether West Africans or any other foreign populations, as inhuman or animalistic. For example, Herodotus of Halicarnassus, a Greek researcher and storyteller from the fifth century BCE, was the first to record observations on the interior of Africa. Herodotus was known as the "Father of History" but equally deserved the title of "Father of Travel Literature."[7] Although his writings have been proven erroneous, they were still quite influential in establishing a basic understanding of the Western perspective of Africa and its inhabitants. Herodotus wrote that Africans "eat locusts and snakes, share wives, and speak no human language, but rather screech like bats."[8] He further claimed that wild animals inhabited Africa, "men who had 'dogs' heads, and those with no heads [had] eyes . . . in their chests." [9] The Roman compiler, Gaius Plinius Secundus, also known as Pliny the Elder, uncritically received these fantastic descriptions and continued the mythical images in the first century CE.[10] He contributed to the exoticism of the African that "hath a cloven foot. . . . His muzzle or snout turneth up: his taile twineth like the bores."[11] These statements prevailed throughout classical works; Africans were not simply exotic but often depicted with nonhuman characteristics. In a similar vein, third-century geographer Gaius Julius Solinus described Africans with "long snouts" and others who possessed "no noses, no mouths, and still others, no tongues."[12] The writings of these three early explorers offered fallacious tales that depicted Africa and its inhabitants as monstrous, mythical creatures. Although erroneous, these tales supplied the groundwork for many longstanding cultural assumptions.[13]

Outside the Greek and Roman sphere, the Islamic world also immensely influenced the image of Africa. A tenth-century traveler, Mutahar Ibn Tahir al Maqdisi, continued the classical tradition with a significant difference: Africans were no longer depicted as inhuman but instead cast as intellectually and morally inferior. "There is no marriage among them; the child does not know his father, and they eat people . . . they are people of black color, flat noses, kinky hair, and little understanding or intelligence."[14] For medieval Islamic writers, West Africa afforded a fertile ground for fallacious stories and self-serving ideologies. Music and dance may be seen in these early travel accounts as being a cultural expression that was manipulated to illustrate the deficient and immoral nature of the "others." In the fourteenth century Ibn Khaldun assessed that Africans "are found eager to dance . . . due to expansion and diffusion of the animal spirit." [15]

By the fifteenth century, Western Europeans and, later, North Americans replicated many of these Arab and medieval patterns. They ventured to West Africa for three main reasons: missionary pursuits, scientific exploration, and economic interest. Underlying each were entrenched, fallacious stereotypes of Africans' barbarism. Economic and technological advances in Portugal, England, Spain, the Netherlands, France, and other nations spurred their exploration and colonization of the Americas and enslavement of Africans. The Portuguese began to travel to Africa in the fifteenth century, primarily for commercial enterprises and missionary work.[16] They set the standard for the manner in which Europeans would interact with Africans, and they greatly influenced the development of the Atlantic slave trade that continued and flourished in the New World. The Portuguese claimed various regions on the continent "in the name of God, the pope, and the king."[17] As early as 1441, Portuguese adventurer Antam Gonçalvez enslaved a Berber and his West African servant, returning to his homeland with them as gifts.[18] The following decades fostered the capture of hundreds of Africans for servitude in Portugal and Spain. As Catholics, the Portuguese insisted that their pursuits in West Africa were religiously based. Portuguese missionaries recognized slavery as a legitimate and acceptable Christianizing process that permitted Africans to make the transition from "immoral heathens" to Christians. Portugal's dominance in the slave trade lasted throughout the sixteenth century until the Dutch entered the region and became the principal slave traders in the early seventeenth century. England soon entered the Atlantic trade, gaining dominance over the competing nations of France and Spain by the early 1700s. The slave trade was the dominant reason for Western Europeans and North Americans to enter West Africa; however, some of the earlier travel narratives were written by those ostensibly interested in spreading Christianity. The travel accounts of these explorers mischaracterized African music and dance in order to justify purging the land of resources, converting the people to Christianity, and, ultimately, enslaving them. Therefore, their publications consistently supported their religious aspirations.

Travelers who ventured to Africa to spread religious ideology often depicted Africa as savage and pagan in order to support their pursuits.

One of the most significant publications that best symbolizes the Christian indoctrination and ideology in the African context was written by Al-Hassan Ibn-Mohammed Al-Wezaz Al-Fasi, commonly known as Johannes Leo Africanus.[19] Although born in the last Muslim stronghold of Granada, Spain, Africanus was raised and formally educated at the University of Al-Karaouine in Fes (or Fez), one of the largest cities in Morocco. He traveled throughout Maghreb and West Africa on diplomatic missions while also taking his El-Hajj, or pilgrimage to Mecca, which was a part of his religious tradition. Due to his extensive travels and education, when captured by Spanish pirates in the early sixteenth century, Africanus was brought to the Vatican. Under Pope Leo X, he studied and converted to Catholicism and was baptized in the Basilica of Saint Peter in 1520. Encouraged by the Pope, this new convert began recording his experiences and observations throughout Africa, specifically the Ghanaian city of Timbuktu. (Africans who were captured and converted to Christianity often were used as guides for Europeans traveling throughout the region.) In 1526, Africanus's travel narrative was published in flawed Italian and later re-released in proper Italian in 1550; with the translation by John Pory in 1600, an English version appeared under the title of *A Geographical Historie of Africa*.[20]

The values of Leo Africanus are relayed through his writings; however, English translator John Pory added text to relate culturally to a European reading public. Not surprisingly, his narrative discusses the performing arts culture of the region. Designating music and dance as insignificant amusements, he assessed that Africans "addict themseues to nought else but delights and pleasure, feasting often & singing lasciuious songs." Africanus's perspective asserted that Africans had a "corrupt and vile disposition," which caused them to assert "unlawful and filthie lust" as expressed through their music and dance.[21] Africanus's work reflected a culture that was instilled within him based upon European superiority and the desire to support religious and economic pursuits in the region.

A Geographical Historie of Africa offered to the reader a savage land with imprudent inhabitants whose music and dance displayed their overtly sexual and deviant manners. His work was used widely until the eighteenth century in England, well after the initial contact between Africans and Europeans had taken place.[22] At the time of Africanus's travels, music and dance were discussed and debated actively through numerous publications and among religious figures throughout Europe. In 1582, for example, Christopher Fetherston published *A Dialogue against light, lewde* [sic] *and lascivious dancing* to assert the dangers of dancing. According to Fetherston, "If dancing were a recreation of the body then it should refresh . . . it should make nimble the joints and strengthen the legs . . . but dancing is so far from refreshing the body from being weary that it maketh the same more weary." For Fetherston, dancing harms not only the physical body but also the work ethic of the community. He further questions the dangers of dancing by asking, "How many men's servants being set to work do after their dancing days lie snoring in hedges because they are so weary they cannot work, whereby their masters do reap but small gains." According to Fetherston, dance was improperly abused by the public and therefore resulted in physical pain, deformities, and sluggishness. His pamphlet warned against the dangers of excessive dancing and represented the negative commentary present throughout Western Europe on the vices of this social amusement. Also, this morality tract was an elite perspective intended to warn against the more overt, less restrained dancing of the lower classes and commoners of Western Europe. Fetherston identified that "those which have danced one half day for pleasure" are guilty of "sluggishness."[23] Africanus's assessment that African music and dance were an immoral pleasure used to express a lascivious nature paralleled the burgeoning debates and publications in Europe.

European and, later, North American travel narratives exerted tremendous influence thanks to new developments within printing that allowed for the widespread dispersal of knowledge.[24] The sixteenth century was an age of transformation in European life; the rise of the Atlantic slave trade, European colonial pursuits, and the desire to assert Eurocentric hegemony collided with the new technological revolution of printing.[25] The method by which records were duplicated, knowledge transmitted, and information stored and retrieved all directly shaped perceptions of African cultures. In some instances the advances in printing technology directly and fundamentally affected the formation of outside cultures and histories. The printed page narrowed the dimensions of reality, thus causing a more lasting effect on the reader.[26] The printing revolution created a rise in the availability of reading materials, thus exposing a larger audience to these myths. The transition from an elitist society in which few people had access to books to a broader general public's having open access to a variety of literature caused a change in writing style. Writers tried to appeal to the masses with interesting, sometimes mythical stories. In addition, travel journalists in particular desired to produce narratives that validated their personal pursuits in West Africa, including slavery, missionary work, and colonization. The culturally arrogant and ethnocentric observations of these explorers were immortalized in Western culture by the printed page and accepted by an ever-growing reading public.[27]

The rise of the printing revolution and its effect on the European world (and later North America) fueled growing literacy during the sixteenth century. In 1533, half of England was semi-literate to literate.[28] As travel journals spread an erroneous image of Africa to the literate, other media, including art and theater, reached the semi-literate and illiterate. The illiterate populations heard remnants of the propaganda of travel journals through their oral folk culture in music, stories, and art. For example, in 1493, a painting titled *The Archers' Festival in the Garden of Their Guild* displayed a black musician performing for Europeans, and a 1529 painting, *Drummer at the Entrance of the Emperor*, portrayed a black-skinned drummer.[29] Such images of Africans as performing musicians were actively disseminated among the populace. Travel journals, folklore, and artistic displays continually associated West Africans with music, song, and dance.

Beginning in the sixteenth century and continuing to the nineteenth century there were similar descriptions of West Africans, and the frequent translation and publication of travel narratives allowed for a corresponding perspective of blacks throughout the West. Travel narratives were textual entertainment of the time that promoted the traveler's gaze and were a propaganda technique to support their personal pursuits. The gaze as described by scholar Jonathan Schroeder "signifies a psychological relationship of power, in which the gazer is superior to the object of the gaze."[30] The gaze functioned in travel writings as a means by which to assert Europeans and North American whites as dominant and Africans or blacks as passive and subordinate. Within travel narratives, black bodies became malleable objects shaped to serve the purposes of the writer. The characteristics of West African men, women, and children were manufactured into serviceable goods for white consumers. The textual commodification of black bodies allowed the writers to garner power to subjugate and sexualize.[31] Their journals were the means by which West Africans transformed into commodities with assigned traits supporting this role.

The controversial role of music and dance in Europe was applied to the travel writers' evaluation of West African music and dance. For Jean Barbot, a French Huguenot, dance held a controversial role due to his religious beliefs, which was evident in his comment that West Africans have "dancing schools for the young people. . . . where they are taught many indecent postures. . . . It is no wonder that dancing-schools should make women unchaste there, since we see them to produce the same effect in England."[32] Western European readers would not have been surprised by this comparison, as dance was an aspect of their society that was restricted and restrained, especially among the women. Since the Middle Ages, the Church regulated music and dance. European society represented the standard to which West African customs were compared.[33] Africa was rendered the subject of Europe's projections, positive or negative. The similarities that existed between the two societies allowed for the narrator, or European travel writer, to show when West Africans conformed to the "appropriate" standards.[34] Variations from European traditions were depicted as evidence of immorality and barbarism. Both images reflected the personal feelings of superiority between the conqueror and the conquered, the spectator and spectacle.[35]

Such attitudes pervaded travel narratives. Frenchman Jean-Baptiste Labat characterized West Africans in his late-seventeenth-century narrative, saying that they "only love their pleasures . . . are excessively lazy, flee work as if it were the worst thing in the world; if hunger did not force them, they would never cultivate their land. . . . They love to dance."[36] This French, Dominican priest denigrated blacks as lazy while inadvertently placing them as frivolously indulgent only in the pleasure of dance. Calling them "lazy" also reflected the European belief publicized earlier by Christopher Fetherston and other social commentators that social dancing resulted in the overexertion of the physical body and a lack of attention to labor. As a Catholic priest, Labat was aware that using the term *lazy* would suggest to many in the West a cardinal sin that stood in direct opposition to a Christian lifestyle. Also, his reference to "pleasure" implied that dance was a profane amusement and that blacks were immoral because they wanted only sexual indulgences, quite similar to the description offered a century earlier by Africanus. For missionaries, the dance customs relayed by Labat represented the wicked culture within West Africa, which signified the necessity of asserting Western Christianity within the pagan region. His travel narrative promoted Western hegemony and supported the need for the continuation of missionary pursuits, while also contributing to the development of blackness as immoral and deviant.

Religion afforded Europeans a powerful tool for ostracizing Africans and denigrating their cultural traditions. The depictions of West Africa often reflected the motives of the respective European explorer. For many missionaries, "the heathen was his target, and of all human groups, the Africans were believed to be the most heathen."[37] Missionaries from Britain and the Netherlands brought Protestant religion to Africa. Catholic missionaries came from France, Spain, and Portugal.[38] The Portuguese and Spanish were the first Europeans to connect their exploration activities to converting people to Catholicism. Missionaries were some of the most influential visitors, often learning local languages to assist them in their pursuits. Their travel narratives emphasized the need to Christianize Africa and also served as a public decree that Christianity was superior, as they believed that Christianity would liberate the African and could save him from the "bondage of sin, fear, and superstition."[39] Africa was depicted as a place with "human sacrifice, highly sexual religious ceremonies, wicked excess of polygamy, and lascivious dances with a childlike ignorance"; these criticisms of African religion, social customs, and institutions caused condemnation of the music and dance as representative of the "barbarous superstition" of the region.[40]

Designating West Africans as heathens supported not only missionary pursuits but also the developing racial system in the New World as black bodies were commodified.[41] Many Europeans believed that it was their duty to assert "order, self-discipline, self abnegation, sexual restraint, and Christianity."[42] One slaver stated he was "instrumental in the salvation of more souls than all the missionaries in Africa" through the placement of Africans into slavery.[43] The formation of race, blackness, and whiteness depended on identifying the differences between the two groups.[44] Englishman Thomas Winterbottom, in the late eighteenth century, commented on the European travel narratives' common affiliation between West African music and heathenism. "No wonder then that the imagination of strangers, just landed upon an unknown coast, aided by the power of superstition, should attribute these uncouth noises to invisible spirits."[45] Constructing music and dance scenes as some form of pagan celebration was common within English and North American accounts. One eighteenth century writer, William Bosman, claimed, "They feast at graves, and if they should see their Country in Flames, would cry out, let it burn, and not suffer it in the least to interrupt their Singing, Dancing and Drinking."[46] Europeans also used stories about music and dance to show the supposed lack of human emotion among Africans. This sentiment reverberated through numerous publications and across the North American colonial era. As a slaver who visited the Western Coast of Africa at the early age of sixteen and was later appointed over the Dutch slave castle Elmina, Bosman's journal was seen as possessing insight into the land and its people. Beyond paganism, Bosman told his Dutch and English readers that West Africans lacked emotional and mental capacities. He adamantly states that West Africans "are equally insensible of Grief or Necessity, sing till they die, and dance into the Grave."[47]

Although slight variations divided the perceptions of travelers, depending on nationality and the period in which they wrote, similarities outnumbered those differences. French-American explorer Paul du

Chaillu, in the mid-nineteenth century, claimed that in West Africa "each family has a huge idol, to whose temple all that family gather at certain periods to worship. This worship consists of rude dances and singing."[48] Through a continual emphasis on the "sacrilege" of the music and dance ceremonies with common mention of "charms," "talismans," and "fetiches," Western readers saw blacks as heathens.[49] To support the race-based slavery system in the West, music and dance were used as evidence of the heathenism of Africans and contributed to their classification as the subjugated other and therefore supported their enslavement from the sixteenth century though the nineteenth.

Europeans and later North Americans scrutinized music and dance in order to place West Africans into the roles of servant, prostitute, and entertainer.[50] Whites needed to create and believe in the subordinate state of the Africans for two reasons: to commodify Africans and to justify whites' pursuits of colonies and people under the power of the European monarch. Through their own Western gaze, these writers transformed African music and dance performances into sexualized scenes of intellectual and cultural inferiority for the consumption of a primarily white, male audience. These travel narratives sculpted African bodies for the Atlantic slave trade and Christianizing expeditions. First, all West Africans were innately related to music and dance, a stereotype that served as a mechanism for creating racial difference. Early in the European exploration of West Africa there were several references to blacks having a natural inclination to music and dance, without recognition of the cultural significance. In one popular travel journal, *The Golden Trade*, Richard Jobson in 1623 supported the well-known belief that "there is, without doubt, no people on the earth more naturally affected to the sound of musicke then these people."[51] The belief that blacks were "naturally affected" to the performing arts resulted in Africans' being identified by specific characteristics that reasserted their otherness in European society. The innate attribute of music and dance assigned to Africans contributed to their placement as entertainment and amusement. More than a century later, Thomas Winterbottom ventured to West Africa as a physician and abolitionist. After spending four years in residence in Sierra Leone from 1792 to 1796, this Englishman's account of West Africa determined that "[a]mong the chief amusements of the [Africans] . . . must be reckoned singing and dancing." Such designations reduced them to physical rather than intellectual beings.[52]

In fact, music and dance were, for West Africans, varied and complicated cultural expressions. Music and dance revealed one's profession, the natural resources of the region, spiritual beliefs, or the folklore/history of that populace. For example, the environment and main occupations of the inhabitants of the area contributed to the execution of dances. According to traditional West African dance scholarship, the dances of the forest and coastal regions in particular focused on the lower portions of the body protruding. Dance scholar Alphonse Tiérou states that hunters and gathers in mainly forest areas often dance "near the ground," while the dance movements of those closer to the coast and those who were fishermen often "comes from the equilibrium which makes [their] legs flexed."[53] Western travel accounts often neglected and dismissed the customs associated with music and dance in order to depict Africans as indifferent to anything other than physical desires, as simply animalistic. To make the sweeping statement that all West Africans, no matter how different in their traditions and appearances, were generally predisposed to singing and dancing allowed for a heterogeneous people to become homogenized, at least textually. The majority of travel narratives that surveyed West Africa recognized the importance of the performing arts tradition; however, casting it as a natural or innate inclination took away from the craft of musicians and dancers.

One example of this attempt at denigration and homogenization can be seen in the very language of musicianship. In West Africa, the most common term for a musician was *griot*. However, playing an instrument or singing was only one role of the griot, who held multiple roles in West African societies as a historian, advisor, mediator, interpreter, and composer. Although the term "griot" was recognized in numerous travel journals as "the name the negroes gave to musicians and drummers of this county," the complexity of this position in West African communities was not fully understood.[54] For example, Andre Alvares d'Almada, in 1594, referred to griots as "importunate beggars" comparable to "gypsies." Gypsies in Western European society were outsiders who lived in an unconventional, often unacceptable manner within the lower rungs of society. In another instance, slaver Barbot compared the music and dance performance he witnessed to the "dances of the Filox" which was a term used for "villain, thief, sharper," or pickpocket and was viewed as being a part of the lowest sort in France.[55] In an effort to appeal to a European audience, Almada (and almost a century later Barbot) used identifiable language to denigrate West African cultures. Many writers used European moral standards and cultural signifiers to illustrate to their reading public the status of West Africans; this was especially evident in the evaluations of women's music and dance culture.

Although many patterns persisted across the three centuries, the seventeenth century witnessed a rise in publications that discussed the proper role of music and dance in society. In 1650, John Playford published *The Dancing Master*, one of the first manuals on how to perform country dances.[56] These English country dances were social performances from the folk culture, while the other primary types of dances were restricted to court dances of the nobility and theater performances. England was not the first European country to publish a formal dance guidebook; in 1623, a descriptive manual, *Apologie de la dance*, appeared in France.[57] However, the English instruction manual on dance became an annual publication that lasted until 1728, thus influencing dance and music trends throughout Western Europe and North America for several decades.[58] These dance manuals created a degree of uniformity within the dance practices throughout Western Europe, especially in England and France.

Dance manuals detailed precisely how dance should be performed. The style varied according to region and whether the dances were country, court, folk, or theater. However, a common set of postures used throughout England can be deduced by examining these publications. For example, there was a dance movement known as the limping hop, "wherein the dancer hopped on one foot and held the other in the air, bringing it down after the beat as though going limp."[59] Similar to the limping hop, the "cadenza" involved the dancer jumping continuously with feet parted. Dance manuals primarily regulated leg movements, often allowing for some autonomy in arm movements.[60] As one dance instruction manual stated, "The Correspondence of the Legs and Arms in Dancing is a Point of so nice a Nature that any Awkwardness or improper Movements therein would destroy the Beauty of the whole."[61] As dance became more regulated, the movements of the arms, shoulders, legs, and feet became a structured part of guidebooks. The controlled postures and limited allowances within the dance culture of England were an aspect of Western society that contributed to the denigration of the improvisational dance style throughout West Africa.

The seventeenth-century philosophies on music and dancing further developed in the eighteenth century to focus on the style of the performance and the gender of the performers. In 1711, a newsletter titled *The Spectator* began publication in England under the leadership of Joseph Addison and Richard Steele with the stated purpose to "enliven morality with wit, and to temper wit with morality."[62] The newsletter aimed to prevent "vice and folly; in which the age is fallen" through public discourse, which often was aimed toward the immorality of dance and dancing, especially among females.[63] In a letter addressing youth dances throughout England, the writer states, "The Moral of this Dance, I think very aptly recommend modesty and Discretion to the Female Sex."[64]

"Impudent and lascivious" movements that "crept into this Entertainment" of dance often were described as moral flaws in female dancers, though male performers were not held to the same standards, according to numerous writings within *The Spectator*. Women's dance and dancing were always considered as "liable to corruptions."[65] Throughout Western Europe, dance and dancing were continually regulated in order to conform to proper social standards. From the seventeenth to nineteenth century, dance was a contentious topic of debate that held influential power throughout Western Europe and North America. Publications on dance often were translated and readily available for a reading public, thus contributing to a congruent perspective of dance that created a common language and bias of the white male traveler in Africa and other foreign lands. This description of dance is not meant to simplify or generalize the varying cultures and histories throughout Western Europe and North America; rather, it is to show that ideological similarities existed among Western societies that contributed to the assessments of West African dance and, later, to black female dance.[66]

The Western ideals of dance varied slightly according to the region of origin, religion, and personal experiences of the explorer and reader. However, as evident with the array of Western European (and later North American) publications, dance, especially among women, was always controversial. Women's bodies and their dance represented symbiotic borders that defined the moral and immoral aspects of society.[67] Several accounts of European explorers categorize non-European women as oversexualized, a wanton characteristic evident in their dance style. In 1681, Jan Janszoon Struys, in an account of his world travels, stated, "there were several Persian Whores and Prostitutes who came to seek their Game, singing and dancing after a very lascivious fashion."[68] His comment contains strong language that positioned Persian females as the "sexualized others" that produced sexual services through their "lascivious" dance. The white male gaze that directed travel narratives commonly positioned music and dance as a form of sexual entertainment. Another example can be seen in Paul du Chaillu, a North American citizen of French birth who explored the western coast of Africa near the Gaboon River in the mid-nineteenth century.[69] According to du Chaillu, "Anyone who has seen a Spanish fandango, and can imagine its lascivious movements tenfold exaggerated will have some faint conceptions of the postures of these black women."[70] Du Chaillu's reference to Spanish dancing, specifically the fandango, illustrated that Western Europe and North America tended to offer negative critique of the dance style and culture of the "others" they encountered during their pursuits. The fandango, a popular dance and melody that first appeared in Spain during the early eighteenth century, later became quite popular throughout Europe.[71] It was well known among the French and English and often was used to represent the exoticism of the Spanish. In 1756, French writer and philosopher Voltaire stated, "Spain is a country that we do not know better than the most savage regions of Africa and that is not worthwhile knowing."[72] The Spanish, similar to West Africans, often were asserted as the Other within travel literature of many Western European countries, specifically France and England, and the fandango was critically described with little reference to the cultural meaning or choreographed style of the performance. In the statement comparing Spanish and African dance, du Chaillu not only demonstrates his awareness of the exotic reputation of this Spanish dance, but he also displays his belief that the reading public would understand his illustration, indicating that travel literature was generally well dispersed. Du Chaillu's assertion that black women displayed ten times the exoticism in dance of the Spanish was similar to the observations of other travel writers, even when separated by time and nationality, who uniformly set apart black female dancing as the greatest exemplum of immorality and savagery when compared to other cultures.

Writers also warned that the dance of black female bodies, by displaying lustful sensual desire, attracted and even intoxicated white travelers. In his discourse on black women, Barbot shows his personal interest in the "genteel persons of that sex" that he described as "not only curious and rich in their dress, but extraordinary good-humour'd, merry and diverting."[73] In his narrative, Barbot seems barely able to conceal his attraction to African women he encountered in his travels; however, he continually transfers his own sexual desires onto them, casting black women as sexual pursuers who entice through their dance. Barbot's account illustrates the constant internal conflict within these travelers' narratives. On the one hand, black female dance was viewed as lewd, immoral, and uncivilized, yet simultaneously, these white male critics found it alluring, exotic, and a genuine, authentic expression of culture. Western travelers routinely attributed immoral behavior to West African women. In his account, Barbot recognizes that "generally speaking, both sexes much love dances"; however, the women were identified as more prone to perform "[as] soon as they hear someone singing and playing any instrument."[74] To Barbot, black women's predisposition to performing turned their bodies into pornographic scenes. Barbot constantly compliments black women as "handsome . . . well-shaped" with their beauty doing "much to attract the eyes," while he simultaneously denigrates their morality. Twenty years later, a French naval officer, Abraham

Duquesne, would continue the gaze toward dancing females by stating, "[T]he women . . . above all things love dancing."[75]

Yet these accounts overemphasized African women's role within dance in order to contribute to black females' being identified as immoral and lascivious. Possessing a "lustful disposition" characterized Africans regardless of gender, but women's bodies often were used as the demarcation between civilized and uncivilized, moral and immoral, self and other.[76] Establishing black women as libidinous directly affected the construction of race and the experiences of these females throughout the New World slavery system. Gender was not considered more important than race when developing difference. Rather, race became interlaced with gender when making distinctions regarding the nature of the Other. Travel writers used music and especially dancing not only to subvert African cultures but also to sexualize black females. In travel literature, black women served as the emblem for black sexuality in general; if black women were immoral and oversexualized, then blackness embodied those traits as well.

Certainly, in traditional West African dance culture, ceremonies existed that required mainly female performers. However, women and men both were active in the dance culture, with neither group having a dominant role. As sexual displays constituted part of the cultural milieu, dance could be used to express flirtations or fertility. Yet such expression did not necessarily dominate the performances presented for white male travelers. According to Africanist dance scholar E. E. Evans-Pritchard, "Boys and girls come to the dance to flirt . . . but society insists that neither the one nor the other shall be indulged in blatantly . . . [except] as they occur with discretion and moderate concealment."[77] The modesty expected among West African youth dances mirrored Western European and North American cultural decorum; however, travel narratives propagated the prevailing conviction that blackness represented the antithesis of the progress achieved by white men and women throughout the West. The dance culture of the region enforced rules of conduct and order that regulated the dance style and upheld community values. Although Europeans often misunderstood, either intentionally or inadvertently, West African dance cultures, they were accurate in their assessment that dance was an active element of many of the society's traditions.

The freedom allotted to black women within dance, and within society overall, differed starkly for women's proper behavior and roles in European societies. Richard Jobson who journeyed throughout the Gambia River valley in 1620–21 in search of gold in West Africa described West African women dancing, noting that with "crooked knees and bended bodies they foot it nimbly," and "if there be any licentious libertie [*sic*], it is unto these women." [78] With this first English travel narrative, published in 1623 prior to the emergence of England's dominance in the Atlantic slave trade, Jobson contributed to the lure of West Africa. Emphasizing their "licentious libertie" may have advertised black women's sexual potency while also revealing that they possessed power over their own bodies. Du Chaillu spoke on the independence of West African women by stating that they "have great freedom and an intriguing spirit."[79] However, this compliment was soon followed with a warning that this freedom has the "consequence . . . that a faithful wife is an unheard of thing."[80] To du Chaillu, black women's autonomy signified the corruption of West African societies. Similar to Jobson, du Chaillu was fascinated with black women. But he too associated black women's autonomy in dancing with deviant sexuality. This perspective may have been a result of the writers' asserting their ethnocentrism—or, more specifically, a European form of patriarchy—as superior. Although patriarchy was not unknown in West African societies, du Chaillu and Jobson indicated through their language that black women were sexually unrestrained because of West African men's inability to control them, unlike in Western European societies. The depiction of the male *other* as feminine and weak was a method of subjugating the culture and people of foreign lands.[81] This was a tactic used within numerous travel accounts that addressed the autonomous yet detrimental nature of black womanhood. These descriptions of gendered blackness, pervasive from first contact through the early nineteenth century, offered critical character assessments that contributed to Western Europeans' and, later, North Americans' justifications for their economic pursuits within the region.

European explorers often used the physical postures of black female dance as evidence of the females' sexual deviancy. Naval officer Abraham Duquesne published, initially in French and later in English, an account of his adventures throughout West Africa from 1690 to 1691.[82] While voyaging throughout the Senegal and Gambia regions, Duquesne documented the body positions of dancing women. Unlike du Chaillu and Jobson, Duquesne does not broadly apply sexuality to these women; instead, he specifically identifies how dance postures created an overt sexuality within the performance. According Duquesne, black women danced with "Hand on their Heads, and other behind, advancing the upper part of the Bodies, and clapping their Feet on the Earth: their Postures are lascivious and infamous."[83] He does not specifically discuss how the dances were "infamous," but travel narratives about the region, the active Atlantic slave trade, and communal dialogue may have contributed to the distribution of this information. The journal was published while England had a stronghold in the Atlantic slave trade, and the reputation of West African women as sexualized was an inducement to continue that traffic and the violence perpetuated against these women within the system. Duquesne's description exposed his gaze upon these women while transforming them from passive to active figures. He assessed that West African women "value Beauty as much as we, and particularly in the Eyes, Mouth, Lips and Nose."[84] Duquesne furthers his assessment by stating that "there are Negresses as handsome as any of our European ladies."[85] His rhetoric may have surprised his French and English readers; comparing the beauty of West African and European women was not common in seventeenth-century travel narratives. His attitude toward black women revealed that blackness as the antithesis of whiteness was not definite and clear cut, although it must be noted that Duquesne's writings were more liberal than other works at the time. Within his narrative, Duquesne claimed that these women desired the "Caresses of white Men," and "they will not offer several Favors for nothing, although their Husbands consent to their Debaucheries."[86] Black womanhood was transformed into a sexualized commodity, but within this text, the females themselves prostituted their own bodies. The description suggested to readers that black women were attractive, lascivious, and willing participants in the slave and sex market.

The description of black women as active participants in their sexualization and commodification was repeated in other narratives. A century after Duquesne's travels, Scottish explorer and physician Mungo Park entered the region intent on genuinely surveying the cultures and people of West Africa.[87] Park was a member of the London-based Association for Promoting the Discovery of the Interior Parts of Africa, known as the African Association, a group organized in 1788 specifically for scientific explorations of the African continent.[88] This group consisted of aristocrats and wealthy businessmen who professed devotion to an unbiased, scholarly view of the interior of West Africa.[89] In December 1795, while visiting in a region he called "Dramanet" in the interior of West Africa, Park witnessed "a great crowd surrounding a party who were dancing. . . . The dances, however, consisted more in wanton gestures than in muscular exertion. . . . The ladies vied with each other in displaying the most voluptuous movements imaginable."[90] Park's account thus claims that black women used sexual overtures within their dance with the competitive objective of being the most lascivious. His reference to "muscular exertion" may be directly related to the European belief that dance should serve the purpose of physical exercise. Park postured the dances of black women as a form of erotic exhibition that contained strong visual and sexual overtones. He was not an inactive observer. His narratives shaped the identity of black women while his gaze assessed their behavior, inscribing their place in the human hierarchy. Similar to Duquesne, Park aggressively interposed his ideology while shaping black women into willing objects capable of satisfying the sexual desires of white males. Park's perspective of blackness may have had a stronger effect than that of his predecessors due to the guise that his inquiry was scholarly and unbiased. But he did not otherwise diverge very much at all from the stories told in the sixteenth century.

Like black women, black men also were described as overly sexual. Explorer Barbot highlighted the lascivious performance of men and women in his narrative: "When young men or boys dance with maidens, or women, both sides always made abundance of lascivious gestures." Beyond the "lascivious" postures, the nudity present among West Africans contributed to their performing arts being viewed as immoral or savage in the eyes of the European reading public. As early as the sixteenth century, English merchant Henry Hawks referred to nudity in West Africa: "The wild people go naked, without anything upon them."[91] However, partially clad black women were not the only ones recognized in travel narratives. David Livingstone, in the early nineteenth century, described the male performers in the dance he witnessed in a remarkably similar vein: "The dance consists of the men standing nearly naked in a circle" while the women "stand by, clapping their hands." He negatively evaluated this performance, noting that if "witnessed in a lunatic asylum it would be nothing out of the way." The nudity and style of dance placed black men and women as libidinous savages radically different from English men and women, whether the white author wrote in the sixteenth or the nineteenth century.

Travel narratives' descriptions of music and dance scenes illustrated that the black body was used for amusement and sexual pleasure, thus supporting and justifying the intentions of those who wanted to exploit Africa's resources and enslave African people. In this relationship between Africans and Europeans, a growing disparity in power was created, and, consequently, Africans' true culture, history, and traditions were hidden from the Western world. The misrepresentation of African culture paved the way for the establishment of the institution of slavery and centuries of mistreatment of Africans by Europeans and Euro-Americans. Through records that testified to the Africans' "nature," European travelers created a negative image of blacks that ultimately laid and perpetuated across time the foundation for racial hierarchy. This hierarchy placed whites safely at the top as a physically, intellectually, and morally superior race, while relegating blacks to the bottom. Travel journals seriously harmed the reputation of blacks, and eventually this power transferred from the written page to physical control. Travel writers were not writing merely about music and dance; they were ascribing how blacks ought to be perceived and treated. The first stage of racial development in public ideology was to turn West African men, women, and children into commodities.

The era, while pervaded by such white-created narratives of African people, offers very few accounts from the African themselves. Due to the limited number of firsthand accounts from the captives and the diversity of music and dance cultures among West Africans, references to the performing arts are few yet significant. Music and dance held a dialectical relationship within the African captives' experience in the slave economy. While performances held cultural importance throughout many West African societies, they also were used continually as a form of torture and degradation. However, ironically, one of the most influential African writers in the eighteenth century, Olaudah Equiano, wrote a simple yet complex statement in his personal narrative, "We are almost a nation of dancers, musicians and poets."[92]

Published in 1789, Olaudah Equiano's firsthand account of his capture, enslavement, and ultimate freedom was widely popular and successful in Europe and America.[93] Equiano was born in the West African region he identified as the kingdom of Benin, located in present-day Nigeria. Equiano's life story took place within the largest social and economic enterprise in the modern world, the Atlantic slave trade. Captured into slavery at age eleven, the abolitionist approximates that it was 1756 when he was kidnapped from his homeland. Following a pattern similar to many of his unfortunate countrymen and women, he was first sold to the English colony of Barbados, later found himself in the colony of Virginia as a plantation slave, and finally was bought by British naval officer Michael Henry Pascal. Under this master, Equiano ventured throughout the English colonies, later settling in England and purchasing his own freedom in July 1766. Upon obtaining his freedom, Equiano became actively involved in the growing antislavery movement, which was the purpose for his writing. The abolitionist expressed that his personal narrative was written to "excite . . . a sense of compassion for the miseries which the Slave-Trade has entailed on my unfortunate countrymen."[94] Appealing to the sympathies of a Western European and North American reading public, his story was a part of the continually growing abolitionist movement; however, Equiano also wanted to combat the rationalizations for slavery. Equiano's motivation for writing his narrative went beyond serving the antislavery movement; this African-born abolitionist wanted to establish and defend himself and his fellow countrymen.

Within the narrative, Equiano wanted to clearly inform his readers that music and dance served a functional and ceremonial purpose, which contradicted the typical view offered in publications at the time. Defending his homeland's customs, he informed the narrative readers that in some West African societies, "every great event, such as a triumphant return from battle, or other cause of public rejoicing is celebrated in public dances, which are accompanied with songs and music suited to the occasion."[95] Music and dance were interrelated aspects of many West African societies, used either for recreational purposes or, as Equiano described, for a specific ceremony or ritual. The specific role of the performing arts varied according to group association; however, the abolitionist's assessment of the functionality of music and dance may be applied to several indigenous populations caught within the slave trade.[96] For example, music and dance were used as diversionary tactics to outwit enemies in times of battle, for marriage ceremonies and royal rituals, as spirit mediums, and to commemorate births.[97] The emphasis on the functional role of music and dance was especially apparent in Equiano's description of a marriage ceremony that was "accompanied with music and dancing."[98] Within his text, he continually constructed identity. Positioning music and dance as functional aspects of society, he publicly established the validity of traditions while simultaneously countering the ideology that music and dance were evidence of the innate inferiority, immorality, and sexualized nature of inhabitants of West Africa and black people in general. This point, one of Equiano's most trenchant, emphasizes the importance of music and dance in society while also offering a recognizable cultural reference to English and American readers. In his personal narrative, Equiano's references to the performing arts culture of West Africa was a strategic effort to counter the racist ideologies in Western society that supported and justified a race-based slavery system.

Equiano countered the dominant racial ideologies that were based on difference by exploring similarities. As he repeatedly asserted in his narrative, the languages of different nations throughout West Africa did "not totally differ, nor were they so copious as those of the Europeans, specifically English."[99] The ideology that set West Africans and Europeans so firmly apart was based on both traditions' being diametrically opposed. However, Equiano's assessment attempted to reconcile this antagonistic relationship by illustrating the parallels between the two societies. In an effort to illustrate the complexity of the performing-arts culture,

Equiano emphasized the diversity and complexity of the music culture by stating, "We have many musical instruments, particularly drums of different kinds, a piece of music which resembles a guitar, and another much like a stickado. These last are chiefly used by betrothed virgins, who play on them on all grand festivals."[100] Equiano revealed fundamental aspects of his indigenous culture. First, the instrumental music had a systematic structure, with particular individuals—in this case female musicians—designated to play particular instruments. Women and men customarily played prescribed instruments in both European and African societies. Although English tradition was more restrictive for women in music than that of West Africa, the sixteenth century witnessed a rise in female instrumentalists.[101] Also, with his reference to "betrothed virgins," Equiano was directly addressing the assessment of West African women as oversexualized. Earlier in the same section of the narrative, the abolitionist adamantly challenges this ideology by emphasizing that adultery was a punishable offense enforced "throughout most of the nations of Africa." He reinforced the point by emphatically stating that marriage was "so sacred among them," completely contradicting the prevalent image of the immoral African.[102] Speaking directly to slavery advocates, earlier travel accounts, and the overbearing ideology of the period, Equiano emphasized the virtuous nature of black women, and coincidently black men, as an important aspect of many West African societies. In a continuous effort to publicly challenge the negative reputation of West Africans, and furthermore blacks of the African Diaspora, Equiano's personal narrative was more than simply an antislavery text; it was an attempt to correctly define blackness.

To further his case, Equiano illustrated the complexity of West African music and similarities between African and European instruments. Equiano's reference to his homeland having an instrument similar to the "guitar" intentionally paralleled English society. The guitar, which had Spanish origins, eventually spread to Western Europe and had become one of the most popular instruments in England by the seventeenth century. Equiano's narrative was not the first to compare the European guitar to instruments used in Africa. Equiano's claims in the eighteenth century were supported by earlier travel accounts. For example, al-'Umari, in 1337, referred to the guitar as having been played in Africa by a local king after returning from a journey. Similar to the guitar, the lute was quite popular throughout both West Africa and Western Europe. The lute, which varied in sound and number of strings, was one of the most popular instruments in the world; Equiano's reference to this instrument connected the two regions.[103] Such juxtaposition of musical instruments was also employed by the African-born Sitki, later named Jack Smith.[104] Identifying his birthplace as an "interior country of western Africa," Sitki was later captured initially into the internal slave trade "at the age of four or five" and later caught within the Atlantic economy, which brought him to North America. Similar to Equiano, Sitki took the time to describe the cultures and people of his homeland, with specific references to the music culture: "They blew horns of ivory, beat drums, sang and played on harps, banjos & guitars. I remember seeing an instrument that looked like a piano."[105] Sitki was referring to one of many keyboard instruments prevalent in West Africa, Western Europe, and America. In the mid-eighteenth century, the piano was one of the most popular instruments in the West; therefore, the intended reading audience would immediately identify with this reference.

Equiano's, and subsequently Sitki's, use of comparative words such as "resembles" and "like" illustrates the similitude that exposed the society's disparate cultures and the manner in which this African in the West negotiated his identity. As an African living in England, Equiano experienced a duality of vision, which was both a gift and a burden.[106] In 1759, he was sent to a school in London to learn how to read and write. While receiving this formal education, he was "baptized in St. Margaret's church, Westminster in February." Equiano was inundated by this culture, which was evident in his statement, "I now not only felt myself quite easy with these new countrymen, but relished their society and manners. I no longer looked upon them as spirits, but as men superior to us . . . and I had the stronger desire to resemble them."[107] Socially and culturally, Equiano was certainly more English than African; however, his black complexion relegated him as subordinate and kept him on the periphery of European society. This mental conflict between his desire to "imitate" English "manners" and his need to negotiate his identity as an African was a constant struggle.[108] Every society has some form of musical expression; therefore, the parallels he drew could have created some sense of cultural solidarity. However, while such parallels existed between societies, music and dance still held distinct characteristics in each region.

As a part of the oppressed and exploited population, Equiano sought to illustrate the similarities between Africans and the English in order to emphasize the humanity of blacks. Comparing the music traditions of both societies served as a method by which to validate West Africa, its people, and Equiano himself. Musicians in West Africa held a variety of roles in society external to the world of music, which was not the case in England. From the sixteenth to eighteenth centuries, the role of music and musicians in English society underwent major changes. Music became a marketable good, with musical instruments and sheet music becoming readily available commodities. Music also changed in direction, with secular music for the first time surpassing sacred music in popularity. With the availability of music in Europe, Equiano's intended audience would have seen music as recognizable and relatable subject matter. In fact, with the professionalization of music in England and the availability of sheet music, a standardized sound permeated Europe. Also, as music was such an important cultural expression throughout West Africa, it would have been a part of Equiano's homeland memory while remaining an active part of life among blacks (slave and free) in the colonies. [109] Interestingly, music in England acted as an art form but was not necessarily as expressive of emotions or customs as in West Africa. Music was an important element of social and national identity; it was manipulated within popular writings of the time to show the degenerate and animalistic nature of blacks, perceptions Equiano wanted to counter.[110]

Interestingly, the one instrument that connects Equiano and Sitki is the drum. This instrument, an important aspect of many West African traditions, gained prominence as it traveled to the New World through the Atlantic exchange. In West Africa, drums had a long, rich heritage and held an important role in society, as evidenced by Equiano's emphasis on "particularly drums."[111] There were dozens of drums types used throughout West Africa, the varying in shape, the method of assembling the body, the playing technique, and the player. Traditionally, drums were associated with special occasions, each rhythm having a purpose, a time, and a place. For example, drums were played at infant naming ceremonies, circumcisions, agricultural ceremonies, religious ceremonies, coming-of-age rituals, and other cultural rites, as well as for entertainment and communication.[112] With respect to the drum's importance as a form of communication among persons in the community, the drum and drummer were able to send messages among those who understood the language of the "talking drums"[113] to communicate warnings of danger or war, peace arrangements, and other information that assisted with survival. In stark contrast, drums were not an active aspect of music in English culture, where percussion instruments were not used in sacred music, nor were they given a role in many of the secular musical compositions of the time. Therefore, the reference to drums served more as a reflection on West African culture than as a direct attempt to draw parallels between the two societies. While Equiano recognized the coinciding traditions of music, he still wanted to emphasize the distinct cultures present in his homeland.

Equiano countered the ideological tactics that assigned racial identities, and therefore power, by justifying the customs of West Africa as comparable to English customs. This technique was not utilized in descriptions of dance. Instead, Equiano offered information about the cultural relevance of dancing in his homeland, detailing that dance specifically "represents some interesting scene of real life, such as a great achievement, domestic employment, a pathetic story, or some rural sport."[114] In West Africa, dance was an expression used in a variety of events from birth until death,[115] an essential and sacred component of the social, political, religious, and aesthetic life of West Africans. Marriage, birth, death, puberty, fertility, rain, sun, prayerfulness, hopes for a plentiful harvest, good hunting, the welcome of visitors, the recognition of leaders, and many other events were heralded with dance and musical ceremonies. The complexity of dance in West Africa did not coincide with the dance cultures throughout Europe.

The standardization of dance in England contributed to Equiano's description of the precise movements of a dance ceremony. In his autobiography, the former slave and abolitionist described in great detail a particular dance ceremony: "The assembly is separated into four divisions, which dance either apart or in succession, and each with a character peculiar to itself. The first division contains the married men, who in their dances frequently exhibit feats of arms and the representation of battle. To these succeed the married women, who dance in the second division. The young men occupy the third; and the maidens the fourth." Dances in West African societies represented a complex, ritualistic expression that held a functional role.[116] The multiplicity of performing arts cultures that existed throughout West African societies is too complex for a brief explanation, but a survey of the common characteristics of dance throughout the area is possible. Dance performances throughout West Africa were physical, artistic, cultural, psychological, economic, social, communicative, and political.[117]

Equiano was quite accurate in his assessment of the importance and variety of West African dances, countering the European propaganda that their dances were simply expressions of a lascivious, immoral culture. African dance was first a physical endeavor, requiring the use of the human body as an instrument. Culturally, African dance styles and purposes reflected the traditions, customs, and mores of the performers. For example, the birth of a child in one region was celebrated by elaborate, choreographed dance movements related to that event, but the performance style and participants may have differed drastically according to the traditions of a particular district. Socially, dance was performed in public and represented a nonverbal relationship between the dancer and the spectator. Interpretations of the performance differed according to the viewer's traditions, attitude about the body, and personal emotion elicited by the dance.[118] As a psychological behavior, dance involved emotions and feelings signifying a variety of communal and personal ideals. Economically, many dancers received payments to perform at various ceremonies. Professionally trained dancers performed throughout West Africa, although lay people also danced. Politically, dance could be used to reinforce a person's leadership role. Military and political leaders often had their own dancers and musicians who traveled with them to battle or were used for ceremonial purposes. The dance method and purpose varied greatly according to the indigenous group, while the movements often were prescribed by their tradition and function.[119] Also, the profession of the dancer contributed to the style and structure of the performance. Dances in West African societies represented a complex, ritualistic expression that held a functional role.[120]

Dance throughout Equiano's homeland was a structured aspect of society; however, improvisation was expected within the performance. Early European visitors often neglected to recognize the artistic nature of these performances, which were always interrelated with the environment and culture. Equiano emphasized this point by illustrating that dances were performed according to "the subject," which was continually changing according to the "recent event" which was "therefore ever new." The adaptive nature of dance contributed to it being viewed as unorganized to the European and American spectator. To further emphasize the artistic importance of his homeland dances, Equiano proudly boasted the expressive customs of the performance: "This gives our dances a spirit and variety which I have scarcely seen elsewhere."[121] For Equiano, this statement was personal. Although this tactic did not dominate the text, Equiano asserted that his homeland cultures were not only different but were also better than certain customs found in Europe. West African dance style reflected rituals, customs, professions, geography, and emotions. In contrast, dance in England became somewhat generic through publications on dance and restrictions on movements. Equiano recognized the freedoms allowed in dance throughout West Africa; it was spontaneous and autonomous in many ways. The expressive freedom present in West African dance distinguished it from the dance seen in English and North American society. In Western Europe, dance often was discussed from the standpoint of social utility, but the cultural significance frequently was neglected. In the burgeoning New World, continuous debates raged that either opposed dance altogether or attempted to enforce restrictions on dance and dancing. In 1684, Increase Mather wrote the first major treatise on dancing in America, "An Arrow against Profane and Promiscuous Dancing," which soon was followed by his son Cotton Mather's treatise in 1700, "A Cloud of Witnesses."[122] These writings asserted that dance and dancing distracted the mind from work and God. Also, dancing between men and women was automatically associated with promiscuity; therefore, Increase Mather believed that this form of the sexes coming together was "utterly unlawful" and should not be "tolerated."[123] The strong opinions against dance did not stop with the Puritans. In 1798, John Phillips's pamphlet "Familiar Dialogues on Dancing, between a Minister and a Dance" explored the potential vices of dance and was addressed to "Christians of every Denomination." Although the eighteenth century witnessed a rise in secular music and dance in England, Equiano must have been aware of the precarious position this secular expression held, which was not the case in West African customs. The movements, styles, and intentions of the African dancers throughout the West were scrutinized continually in public discussions.[124]

Africanist scholar Dunduzu K. Chisiza stated that within West African dance, "[W]e nod our heads, rock our necks, tilt our heads and pause. We shake our shoulders, throw them back and forth, bounce breasts. . . . We rhythmically hefty shake our rear ends, our tummies . . . while our feet perform feats."[125] Certain basic motifs and postures of West African dance persisted for centuries.[126] Equiano seemed both to celebrate and berate the autonomous nature of dance.[127] While recognizing the "spirit and variety" of West African dance as positive, he remained influenced by the numerous publications and debates on the morality of dance. However, Equiano's references to West African music and dance were intentional attempts to enter the public conversations and to influence developing ideologies that supported and justified a forced, race-based slavery system.

Equiano's narrative represented a singular voice of millions, exposing a world that was fallaciously described and a people who were viewed by Europeans as minimally more than animals. He utilized a typological approach to validate the customs of West Africa and in turn developed counter-images in order to fight against the Atlantic slavery system. He adamantly declared throughout the narrative, "I hope the slave trade will be abolished," therefore using his firsthand experience in the burgeoning antislavery movement. Equiano also had an internal compulsion to write the narrative. As a Europeanized African living within a society that downgraded and demonized blackness, Equiano needed to reconstruct that perception. He understood the negative view of Africans as "uncivilized and even barbarous," but instead of denouncing Europeans as incorrect in their assessment, he placated English supremacy. Equiano had to manipulate the paradox of being considered part of a conceived degenerate race while simultaneously seeking acceptance as an intelligent and capable individual. One way in which he garnered support and unlaced this paradoxical dilemma was by conceding contemporary Eurocentric notions: "Did Nature make them inferior to their sons? And should they too have been made slaves? . . . No. Let such reflections as these melt the pride of their superiority into sympathy for the wants and miseries of their sable brethren."[128] In the beginning of his narrative, Equiano establishes himself as an African through his birth and experiences; however, his perspective and identity change as his story progresses. As he obtained the opportunity to learn and live in England and her colonies, he became a cultural insider, a loyal subject to the history, religion, and traditions of the West. Equiano embraces English ideals while attempting to expunge the demarcations between white/black, superior/inferior, and civilized/savage, presenting himself as representative of the potential, in European terms, of the black race. His writing constructs West Africans and their descendents as infantile rather than savage, and he counters the ideological tactics that assigned racial superiority while he reasserts other unfavorable attributes to his countrymen. With music and dance, he did not completely placate or succumb to Western ideology; instead, Equiano illustrated the culture as an important aspect that was misunderstood and slightly unprogressive.

"There is merit in this narrative," Equiano told his readers. "If any incident in this little work should appear uninteresting and trifling to most readers, I can only say, as my excuse for mentioning it, that almost every event of my life made an impression on my mind and influenced my conduct."[129] Equiano was correct in his assessment of the parallels; more important, he illuminates the differences in music and dance in the two regions that contributed to the unfavorable impression Europeans had of West Africa. But that understanding did not prevail in the worldviews of missionaries and slave traders. Instead, they clung to their interpretations of music and dance as being a public display of African natural intellectual, moral, and social inferiority. The misconstrued culture of West African music and dance greatly contributed to the plight of blacks in the New World.

"We are almost a nation of dancers, musicians and poets," Equiano professed in an effort to acknowledge the millions of Africans for whom rich cultural history was distorted and subjugated. In a society in which

Africans and their descendants were confronted with prevailing social and cultural arguments of their inferiority, Equiano intentionally opposed those ideals in his narrative. Although he spent many chaotic years outside of Africa, Equiano's memory of his native land revealed insights into the music and dance traditions brought within the bowels of the slave ship onto the shores of North America. The perceived nature and culture of the region's music and dance were solidified in the American slavery system and contributed to the perception and treatment of West Africans for centuries.

2 Casting

*"They sang their home-songs, and danced,
each with his free foot slapping the deck"*

"The bitch is sully," testified shipmate Stephen Devereux. These were the apparent words of Captain John Kimber to the shipmate concerning a young African girl who was, at the time of the conversation, hoisted by a leg and suspended above their ship's deck.[1] "I am almost certain he gave her a slap on the face," and then "Captain Kimber flogged her," attested Devereux in the 1792 trial of slaver and accused murderer John Kimber. About two hundred leagues from the ship's destination in Grenada, West Indies, this young African girl was reportedly murdered after weeks, maybe months, of torture aboard the *Recovery*. According to testimony, slave surgeon Thomas Dowling and shipmate Devereux were the only witnesses to the malicious murder of the young girl that was enacted "feloniously" and "willfully." They testified that "the girl would not get up to dance with the other girls and women, which I suppose to be the cause of suspension," which eventually led to her death. Based in Bristol, the *Recovery* landed in one of the most active ports of the English trade, the Calabar River region on the coast of West Africa, for "the purpose of procuring slaves." In this Atlantic system, ships docked for several weeks or even months to negotiate the purchase of African captives for the oceanic voyage. For almost four months, small boats brought African men, women, and children to fill the bowels of the *Recovery*. The young girl who would later die aboard the slave vessel is accounted for in the ship surgeon's log: "In this cargo there was a

Illustration made by abolitionist to illustrate the events aboard the slave ship *Recovery* of Captain Kimber flogging the young female captive for her refusal to dance. (Cartoons Prints, British, Prints & Photographs Division, Library of Congress, LC-USZCN4–254.) Courtesy of Library of Congress.

negro girl about fourteen or fifteen years of age." She entered the ship in a "diseased state" with a "very severe" case of gonorrhea, which according to the ship's surgeon caused "a lethargy or drowsy complaint." [2]

Several members of the female cargo were infected with sexually transmitted diseases spread by various members of the ship's crew. According to the testimonial evidence of other shipmates, the anonymous girl contracted the venereal disease from Thomas Dowling prior to departing the Calabar region. Two other female captives, Venus and Jack Amacree, suffered from "venereal infection" that they contracted from white slavers; however, the ship's surgeon, Dowling, was "careful to restore them," therefore allowing them to be sold with the rest of the human cargo in Grenada.[3] These afflicted women most likely endured pain in the vaginal and abdominal regions, with extreme cases causing severe soreness in the throat, mouth, eyes, and anus.[4] Due to their physical and mental state, many of the sick women resisted the white slavers' demands concerning their daily sustenance. The young victim's sickness "prevented her from eating her victuals so heartily," along with other females who refused to eat "on account of the venereal disease," according to the ship's surgeon.[5] It appears that the young victim's only major offense that stood out from those of the other captives and was specified by witness Devereux was her unwillingness to dance.

"The bitch is sully" referred to the girl's defiance against performing her role as the sexual amusement for the white slavers. Her indolence represented more than her deteriorated state; she threatened white authority in the tumultuous space of the top deck. This anonymous girl did not conform to the racial script in which she was the willing, subordinate dancer for the dominant, choreographing white slavers. Her refusal to dance resulted in her being "frequently flogged" and "suspended by one hand, and then another." After continuous beatings, she received "several mortal wounds and bruises . . . on the back, sides, arms, legs, and other parts of her body," filling her final days with suffering and pain, according to the trial records.[6] Other factors might have shaped the abuse. Perhaps the captain was attempting to straighten her leg, which was "bent" due to her sickness and to her contorted position in the holds, or simply to a birth deformity. Or perhaps the captain was abusive to the young girl because her sullenness greatly exceeded that of the other captives. Nevertheless, the only reason specified for her torture and ultimate death was her refusal to dance. "The bitch is sully" was a callous statement that, along with the conditions of the supposed murder, may have left the jury aghast. However, the spectacle was not just the suspension but the dancing.

The tradition of dancing the captives, interlaced with violence, rape, and subjugation, was a cruel but common act that took place for 150 years of the Atlantic slave trade.[7] Captain John Kimber was "honorably acquitted" in the trial, with the jury determining the character of the two witnesses, Devereux and Dowling, "unworthy of credit."[8] New charges of "willful and corrupt perjury" were brought against the two witnesses. Defense attorney Mr. Pigot asked Shipmate Dowling if the spectacles aboard the *Recovery* drew "a great deal of attention, discussion, and observation" among the other shipmates. "No sir," he responded, "such things are customary on board slave ships."[9]

It has been well documented that music and dance were active elements of the Middle Passage. As recognized in the trial, slavers used dance "for the purpose of keeping up a due circulation, and to prevent the muscles from becoming more contracted than they already [were]."[10] But that was hardly the only purpose of the practice. On the *Recovery*, Devereux and Dowling were "dancing with the women" as a source of entertainment, sexual stimulation, and an expression of power. African captives were transformed into commodities and sexual objects within the jumping and melodies of the Middle Passage.

Ironically, the transcripts of Captain John Kimber's trial were published in order for "the public" to "judge for themselves" the "humanity" of the slave trade.[11] What went unrecognized in this trial was that the malevolence enacted on the *Recovery* and interposed throughout the Middle Passage occurred on every fair-weather day, when African men, women, and children were brought top deck to perform. During the voyage from West Africa to the New World, the erroneous ideology of travel journals was applied, and, under the crack of the whip, music and dance became tools of subjugation. The transformation of West Africans into Atlantic commodities began with the initial capture, and music and dance soon followed.

Similar to the *Recovery*, the *Neptune* left England, specifically Liverpool, with a crew of fourteen headed to the Calabar River region of southeastern Nigeria.[12] In 1774, the ship arrived in the port that housed several other slaving vessels: three ships from Liverpool, one from Bristol, and one from France. This assortment was common, as the Atlantic slave trade represented an international enterprise. Coastal regions throughout West Africa often hosted several European nations that ventured to the region for trade, according to slaver Henry Schroeder aboard the *Neptune*. Slaver Jean Barbot chronicled the Atlantic exchange in his narrative, stating that "the Dutch have the greatest share in the trade; the English next, and after the Portuguese from Brasil . . . all together export thence a great number of slaves yearly to America."[13]

This international competition for slaves had a long history. In the fifteenth century, the Portuguese first arrived on the Guinea coast to engage in a trade that included slaves. Portugal and Spain were the primary operators, with both countries mainly using West Africans as domestic servants. With the establishment of colonies in the Americas, African slaves gradually became the main source of labor. From the fifteenth century to the early eighteenth century, the Spanish, Portuguese, French, and Dutch competed in the Atlantic trade. In 1672, the Royal African Company emerged and was granted a monopoly in the English empire over the African slave trade, allowing England to gain dominance in the economic system. By the end of the seventeenth century, the monopoly ended, allowing other English merchants into the trade and causing a dramatic increase in the number of African slaves transported on English ships. By the early eighteenth century and throughout the nineteenth century, Britain and America dominated the long-established triangular trade system.[14] The fervor for "black gold" intensified over the centuries, resulting in an estimated 12.4 million African men, women, and children eventually boarding slave ships.[15]

Upon arriving in the Calabar River region, the *Neptune* was boarded by local "traders and chiefs, with their wives," who entered the ship to discuss the procurement of African captives for the ship's cargo. These traders negotiated with the captain and informed him that "they were going to catch slaves; most probably by making war on some unarmed villages," according to a member of the crew.[16] This manner of acquiring human chattel involved warfare and the enslavement of the defeated. At other times, raiding parties kidnapped individuals into the trade. After capture, African men, women, and children were bound together and forced to walk within a coffle for miles, sometimes several hundred miles, while confined by ropes, wooden restraints, and chains. Slave traders captured Africans from different ethnic groups with varying languages and cultures. White slavers rarely traveled inland; therefore, slave catchers normally were West Africans who traveled extensively throughout the regions to collect a multiethnic group to sell on the coast. These slave traders took many precautions to prevent the rebellion or escape of their cargo. As South Carolina slave trader Joseph Hawkins commented on his experiences in the Sierra Leone, the African captives "were tied to poles in rows, four feet apart; a loose wicker bandage round the neck of each, connected him to the pole, and the arms . . . they had sufficient room to feed, but not to loose themselves, or commit violence."[17] Due to the furtive nature of the slave trade, the African slave catchers needed their captives to be restrained and silent in order to maintain order and prevent family and friends from assisting in their escape. Captured African Olaudah Equiano spoke of the manner in which his kidnappers "in a moment seized" him and "without giving us time to cry out, or make resistance, they stopped our mouths, and ran off with us into the nearest wood."[18] The captives often lacked proper food and water during their long trek to the shore.

After reaching the shore, African captives often were housed in barracoons or factories, where slave ships with their crews awaited them. In these coastal regions, ship crews remained quite active while preparing their vessels for the coming journey. The area between decks was prepared for the anticipated cargo, and the interior of the slave ship often was divided by partitions into two or three sections that would separate the male and female captives. Slave ships varied in size; often, ordinary merchant vessels were converted into slave ships, especially in the eighteenth century, when the economic profitability of the slave trade burgeoned.[19] In 1854, Theodore Canot, an Italian-born American slave trader, described his ship, the *Areostatico*, as an "extremely small" schooner that lacked a "slave deck; accordingly, mats were spread over the fire-wood which filled the interstices of the water casks . . . for our cargo's repose."[20] Along with preparing the ship for the African captives, the ship's crew often removed the cargo they brought to be sold to the local communities. When the ship was prepared, members of the crew often were able to go ashore and interact in the local towns, barracoons, and factories. While on the coast, some slavers, such as Henry Schroeder, ventured throughout the local regions to "make more observations than [one] otherwise could have done."[21] Slavers more deeply involved in collecting African captives entered the region to review the slave factories and inspect potential cargo.

These coastal regions became the scene of the first major engagement between white slavers and the potential human commodities of the Atlantic economy. In the fifteenth century, the Portuguese established factories or structures on the shore to stow not only supplies and goods but also slaves awaiting purchase by slavers. As the trade continued, commercial enclaves developed, with Western Europeans, Americans, and Africans establishing new settlements throughout the coastal regions. These towns grew up around trading hubs such as Elmina Castle and the Calabar River region and were populated with brokers within the trade of the Atlantic economy. Historian Ira Berlin described a population he referred to as "Atlantic creoles" as the children of European men who took "wives and mistresses among African women."[22] Many slavers' accounts referenced this burgeoning population. Slaver Theodore Canot's memoirs mentioned an Atlantic Creole active in the trade. He described "Mr. Ormond," who "was the son of an opulent slave-trader from Liverpool, and owed his birth to the daughter of a native chief on the Rio Pongo."[23] Ormond, often referred to in Canot's journal by his "country-name" of "Mongo John," seemed to be well respected by European and American sailors. Mongo John received some education in England, traveled throughout the Atlantic as a sailor, and, in the early nineteenth century, took charge of a slave factory in the Rio Pongo region. Mongo John and many other Atlantic Creoles were multilingual and displayed an array of merged customs and traditions. As in the case of Mongo John, they often served as middlemen for the slave trade.

Atlantic creoles were a part of the polyethnic communities that grew and prospered due to the Atlantic slave trade. These communities often catered to the needs and desires of the slave ships that docked on their shores. While the Italian-American slaver Canot was visiting Mongo

John's factory, he illustrated in his journal the manner in which he was entertained in what he referred to as the "penetralia of his harem." In this facility, "a whirling circle of half-stripped girls danced" in a "semi-savage" manner for the amusement of themselves and for the European guest. Canot's appraisal of this experience, especially his reference to the location of the performance as a "harem," shows that he truly believed that West African women performed dance as a form of sexual invitation toward white visitors. Canot openly stated that it was his "duty to mingle in the bounding thong" and that the "barbarians should have a taste of Italian quality!"[24] While watching the women dance, Canot "leaped from the hammock" and "seized the prettiest of the group by her slim, shining waist, and whirled her round and round."[25] Within the narrative, he blamed intoxicating liquor that "fermented" his brain as the cause for his sexually aggressive behavior toward the female dancers. However, it was not only the liquor that influenced Canot's actions but also the oversexualized reputation of black women stemming from their dance expression.[26] As seen with Canot's sexually aggressive behavior with the dancing females, the early travel writers perpetuated myths that influenced their perception and treatment of the West Africans they encountered. Local Mongo John verbally disciplined the Italian-American slaver for his "uproarious manner" toward the dancers.[27] The Atlantic Creole reminded the slaver that, while "there's no harm in dancing," he was expected to abide by the manners and rules of conduct of the region.[28] As a slaver, Canot would gain control over African men and women on the slave ship, but in this middle ground, West Africans still held some power over their bodies. Although Canot revealed his perception of West African music and dance, especially among the women in the Atlantic community, he was unable to express power over these women. This exchange between the slaver and the local inhabitant illustrates the misperceptions of European and American sailors while also displaying the associations that music and dance conjured for foreign visitors. The negative reputation associated with music and dance in West Africa would affect the experiences of the captives throughout the Middle Passage experience; however, within the coastal regions, power was still being negotiated. Upon the ship, slavers gained authority and their assertions upon West Africans transformed to less observation and more power and control.

The process of transforming Africans into commodities began textually in travel narratives and continued with the manner in which they were processed for the journey. In preparation for the voyage, African men, women, and children were examined thoroughly to determine the quality of the products. As Canot reported, "An African factor of fair repute is ever careful to select his human cargo with consummate prudence, so as not only to supply his employers with athletic laborers, but to avoid any taint of disease that may affect the slaves in their transit."[29] Either within the barracoons or upon reaching the ship's deck, the captives were stripped naked, mainly due to the belief that "perfect nudity, during the whole voyage, is the only means of securing cleanliness and health."[30] Men and women often were shaved as another way to prevent the spread of infectious disease among the cargo. Then, "the ship's surgeon would carefully examine every bit of their anatomy," according to one French slaver.[31] Next, many of the captives would be branded with "irons hot in a fire . . . between the shoulders" as a part of the process of transforming people into commodities.[32] Almost ceremoniously, the white slavers informed their captives, either verbally or physically, that they were no longer individuals representing various ethnic groups and cultures; they had become commodities. The exposure of naked men, women, and children, the branding of their bodies, and the public examinations were all elements of a strategic process of humiliation designed to promote the mental and physical subjugation of the African captives. As slavers continued to gather the cargo, Africans already on board were placed into the confines of the ship. The male captives (and sometimes the female captives as well) were coupled together in iron chains and held below the ship's deck. According to antislavery advocate Thomas F. Buxton, the captives were "frequently stowed so close as to admit of no other posture than lying on their sides."[33] The number of African captives on ships depended on the size of the schooner and slavers' ability to creatively place the human cargo into the ship's bowels. For example, the limited space available aboard *Areostatico* caused Canot to comment that he "could not imagine how this little army was to be packed or draw breath in a hold but *twenty two inches high*!" As a result, he made the captives "lie down in each other's laps, like sardines in a can, and in this way obtained space for the entire cargo."[34] Slaving vessels were drastically different in size; scholar Marcus Rediker identified ships that ranged from 10 to 566 tons.[35] The process of loading the human cargo could take several weeks or months as African men, women, and children were canoed in small groups to the vessel. While ships were still anchored, imprisoned Africans were routinely brought on deck to begin the Middle Passage custom of performing music and dance while still within sight of the shore.

Illustration of African captives crowded on slave ship *Wildfire* on April 30, 1860. (Miscellaneous Items in High Demand Collection, Prints & Photographs Division, Library of Congress, LC-USZ62–19607.) Courtesy of Library of Congress.

The high mortality rate among the African captives during this period of collecting and loading human cargo perpetuated the use of dance because it served as exercise. The surgeon of the *Alexandria* reported that the captives were "jumped up in their irons for exercise."[36] He believed that the "jumping," what often was referred to as "dancing," was "so necessary for their health" that if they refused to perform this activity,

the captives would be "whipped" into submission.[37] In testimony before the English Parliament concerning the Atlantic slave trade, several
slave-ship captains presented evidence that the high mortality rates of
the cargo may have been due to the time they were held in the ports in
West Africa. Captain Thomas Edred, after making three voyages in the
trade, estimated that the majority of slaves did not die from overcrowd-
ing "but from the vessels being long on the Coast."[38] Another ship captain, Robert Norris out of Liverpool, stated that " [the slaves] died on the
coast more than at sea."[39] Slave-ship captains' emphasis on the coastal
deaths also helped to distract from the overcrowded and repulsive nature of the voyage. It was well documented that the prolonged waiting
period on the coast caused many deaths. Many slavers believed that the
exercising or dancing of the captives minimized the mortality rate while
in dock. These scenes of West Africans dancing and singing as they were
processed into commodities were in many ways a rehearsal of the performance expected throughout the journey to the New World.

Upon departure, the responsibility of the white slavers and the tor-
ment of the African captives only increased each day as they traveled
further from Africa. The sexes often were separated, with male captives restrained in iron chains and held below the ship's deck and many
women and children unfettered on the top deck. Within the bowels of
the ship, naked African bodies lay in excrement and filth within tight
spaces that allowed little to no movement. Although slave-ship captains
often claimed that many captives lost their lives while docked on the
African coast, the captives also suffered a high mortality rate at sea.
Tight living quarters, lack of nourishment, physical beatings, mental
anguish, and rampant diseases all contributed to deaths. Scholars vary
in their assessment, but it has been estimated that 1.5 to 1.8 million
Africans died during the Atlantic voyage.[40] The staggering mortality
rate on slave ships made it advantageous for captains to take some
measure to ensure a profitable cargo. One strategy was to employ ship
surgeons, who were active throughout the entire Atlantic experience,
to examine captives on the African coast and care for the human cargo
throughout the Middle Passage.

The "jumping" or "dancing the captives," as it was commonly
termed, was another method used to preserve and promote a healthy
cargo and was a common aspect of the Middle Passage experience. Ship
surgeon Alexander Falconbridge's 1780 account mentioned that "exercise
being deemed a necessary for the preservation of their health, they [slaves
on board] are sometimes obliged to dance, when the weather permit their

coming on deck."[41] This practice began with the early Portuguese slavers and continued on the Spanish, Dutch, English, American, and French vessels. Slaver Robert Norris stated, "The prices which the Negroes sell for are regulated by their Health and good Appearance, and this consideration is an additional Inducement for treating them with every possible care."[42] Innumerable accounts existed of West Africans dancing for the express purpose, according to the white slavers, of exercising or stretching their limbs to preserve their health. For centuries, dance in Europe was considered a physical exercise that assisted in the preservation of health.[43] Although exercise was the expressed purpose of the dancing custom, it served other roles within the Atlantic exchange.

The coerced physical assertion of the captives represented more than the slavers' desire to preserve the human cargo; it also positioned Africans as entertainers while simultaneously situating whites as the audience. Ship Captain Richard Drake stated that every evening the ship's crew "enjoyed the novelty of African war songs and ring dances."[44] Similarly, another slaver, Robert Norris, commented that "musical instruments" often accompanied the song and dance. African captives were consistently forced to sing and play musical instruments within the Middle Passage, essentially extending these scenes of physical exercise into an entertaining performance for the pleasure of the white slavers. Several instances exist of the top deck being referred to as the "stage" and the African captives referred to as the "entertainment" or "amusement" during the Atlantic voyage.[45] In fact, slaver Drake openly commented that "after one of these musical evenings . . . the tired performers were stowed again between decks."[46] Upon the stage of the slave ship, white slavers participated both as audience and choreographers of these performances. As described by historian John Spears, the captives "stood in rows and as the brawny slaver, whip in hand, paced to and fro, they . . . danced, each with his free foot slapping the deck."[47] Dancing the captives was a violent experience for these Africans, who often were bound by chains on their ankles and "flogged" to jump on the slave ship. One slave ship surgeon stated that Africans were "excoriated by the violent exercise;" they were forced to dance with shackles on their ankles that often resulted in "swelling in their legs" that was extremely painful.[48] However, under the forced impetus of the whip, the African captives grudgingly moved their bodies to dance. As evident in John Riland's account of a slave ship experience in 1801, the African captives "shewed no inclination to" dance or sing until "the *cat* was called then, indeed, they began to sing and skip about."[49]

Illustration of the common activity of having African captives dance on the top deck of slave ships as a form of exercise and entertainment during the Middle Passage. (Amédéé Grehan, ed., *La France Maritime*, vol. 3 [Paris, 1837]).

White slavers masked their cruel activities and, perhaps, salved their consciences by essentially ignoring the miserable state of their African cargo. Slave-ship captain Crow commented that captives "were permitted to dance . . . to keep them in good spirits."[50] The white captors wanted to believe that making their captives dance and sing assisted in the happiness of the Africans. One slave-ship captain stated, "We do all we can . . . to promote the happiness of the slaves on board . . . they are encouraged to dance in chains . . . by the application of the whip."[51] The utilization of force was a pervasive element of nearly all displays of music and dance throughout the Middle Passage. Ironically, despite the continual physical abuse used to force song and dance from the captives, the myth persisted that blacks happily enjoyed their musical endeavors. As slave smuggler Richard Drake put it, "Our blacks were a good-natured set, and jumped to the lash so promptly."[52] This language implies that the "good-natured" African captives were inclined to move due to their natural disposition, and the use of a whip was demoted as only a minor impetus to "jump." The slavers on the ship participated actively in the captives' performances. Slavers expected the captives not only to dance but also to reflect a cheerful disposition within every aspect of the performance. One slaver testified before Parliament that during his voyage they taught the captives lyrics that "they are compelled to sing while they are dancing."[53] On one ship, the captives were forced to sing "Meffe, meffe, Mackarida," which translated to "Good Living or Messing well among White Men."[54] In this instance, the slavers took an active role in instructing or choreographing the performance of the African captives. The song placated white slavers' fears of rebellion while also contributing to the growing belief that they were well intentioned and justified.

Throughout the Atlantic voyage, African captives continually showed their discontent at being forced to dance and sing. George Pinckard described that, while dancing, the captives "scarcely moved their feet, but threw about their arms, and twisted and writhed their bodies into a multitude of disgusting and indecent attitudes."[55] The simple acknowledgment of Africans' "indecent attitudes" shows their reluctance and unhappiness throughout these Middle Passage performances. If the music and dance performances were "disagreeable to the Captain" because they showed the human cargo's discontent, then they were "flogged" in a terrible "manner for no other reason than this," one slaver explained.[56] White slavers thus prepared the captives for their new role within the New World society.

Slavers often used music and dance to show the humanity of the system and contentment of the captives. In testimony before Parliament, slaver Robert Norris Esquire stated, "Song and dance are encouraged and promoted . . . for their Amusement . . . every Scheme that can be devised to promote their Health, Cleanliness and Cheerfulness, is practiced."[57] Vice Admiral Edwards testified that the majority of the African captives "appeared cheerful" due to the "dancing and singing" on board.[58] In order to gain public approval while psychologically validating their role within the Atlantic slave trade, white slavers continually attempted to present their captives as happy. Eighteenth-century Liverpool merchant James Penny commanded eleven voyages from West Africa to the West Indies and North America. Throughout his voyages, Penny stated that the captives were "amused with Instruments of Music peculiar to their country," with which he provided them; and "when tired of Music and dancing, they then go to Games of Chance—The women are supplied with Beads, which they make into Ornaments; and the utmost Attention is paid to the keeping up their Spirits and to indulge them in all their Humours."[59] Penny, similar to many white slavers within the Atlantic exchange, determined that music and dance amused the captives, and therefore the human cargos were "perfectly reconciled to their condition, and in Appearance as happy as any of his Crew."[60]

The façade that African captives were treated fairly and possessed a naturally cheerful disposition throughout the voyage became part of the defense of the Atlantic trade when it was challenged in the late eighteenth century. During the 1780s, an antislavery campaign began in England. With the English monopoly on the slave trade, the humanity of the system was of constant concern and contributed to the development of the Committee for the Abolition of the Slave Trade, or the London Committee, in May 1787.[61] One of the main advocates in this group, Thomas Clarkson, along with several other members of the committee, gathered information about the conditions on the slave ship.[62] Due to the London Committee's advocacy, petitions against the slave trade were presented in 1788 to the House of Commons. The House of Commons and House of Lords opened their own inquiries into the slave trade through meticulous interviews with sailors who experienced the Atlantic voyage. Music and dance among the captives was such a common aspect of the Atlantic experience that it became the topic of regular inquiry within the House of Commons. For example, in 1788 the British Parliament asked slave ship surgeon Ecroyde Claxton, "Did the Slaves on board your vessel ever amuse themselves by singing?"[63] Inquiries about the music, song, and dance present during the journey were common in public debates on the slave trade. The arts performed during the Middle Passage introduced images that continued beyond the Atlantic voyage. The question asked of Claxton lacked any recognition that the whip was used to coerce singing aboard the ship. This blind spot may have contributed to the belief that Africans willingly performed music, song, and dance, which confirmed their label as docile and unintelligent. The image of the innate, cheerful black performer and the oversexualized black female were accepted elements of the culture of Africans coming to America. By the time the international slave trade was outlawed in 1807 in Great Britain and 1808 in the United States, music and dance had been a complicated aspect of the Middle Passage experience for two centuries, a practice that was tortuous for the captives but comforting for the white slavers.

Throughout the colonial era, the Middle Passage acted as a stage for performances of music and dance that contributed to the structure of dominance and subjugation in the New World. In shackles and under the direction of the whip, African captives' singing and dancing created an influential image of blackness for whites while physically manifesting the accounts of early travelers. Racial imagery preceded the trade, with illustrations of African behavior, customs, and rank in the human hierarchy distributed through travel narratives. The Middle Passage allowed for Western Europeans and North Americans to enforce their ideal of Africanness on the captives, therefore forcing West Africans to behave in the manner that was scripted for them.

Race was staged through the European and American slavers' assertion of power over the African captives. However, the slave ship was not firmly divided by black and white racial lines.[64] Crews consisted of seamen from various cultural, religious, ethnic, and national backgrounds, often representing a lower class than that of the captain and ship surgeon. In fact, many seamen often were beaten and forcibly recruited into maritime life by the higher-stationed ship captains and shipping companies. They often surrendered their personal freedoms throughout the duration of the voyage, their station somewhat resembling that of the African captives. One New York sailor, William Ray, commented in the eighteenth century that white sailors and slaves were all "bound to sea."[65] Although there was a clear hierarchical system among the white members of the crew, a hierarchical racial divide still existed. In the early eighteenth century, slave-ship captain William Snelgrave instructed the captives "that now they are bought for, that they may be easy in their Minds . . . I then acquaint them, how they are to behave on board; towards the white Men . . . or . . . they must expect to be severely punished."[66] Slavers representing various social classes and regions throughout the New World and Western Europe may not have been clearly identified as white, especially during the initial years of the slave trade. However, these slavers were constructing whiteness, along with the power and dominance associated with that status, upon the slave ship.[67]

Slavers varied according to ethnicity, nationality, and class; however, while on shore, slavers who ventured into coastal regions were forced to follow the rules and customs present in those societies. Once the cargo was collected and the ship undocked, the white slavers gained authority. Early in the trade, the notion of the "white race," similar to the "black race," was not yet fully developed; however, whiteness was apparent throughout the Atlantic experience, although it may have been a temporary condition upon the slave ship that only applied when in direct contact with African captives. Among the ship's crew, a slaver, due to his ethnicity or religion, often was treated and placed in the lower rungs of whiteness. European and American seaman gained whiteness during the Middle Passage, and if they resided mainly in the North American region, they were able to retain their whiteness upon the shore.[68] Ship captains' assertions that "the white men" must be obeyed displayed the unconditional weight of whiteness. Simultaneously, by asserting their whiteness, the slavers were constructing the captives as uniformly subordinate. The occasional presence of black sailors also complicated the unambiguous power of race.[69]

Black seaman, free and enslaved, were not automatically placed in the same category as the slave ship's human cargo. Those West Africans who were used mainly on shore or who voluntarily joined a ship's crew were always vulnerable to enslavement and represented a different group than those who were mainly born in Europe or North America. Men and women of African descent were occasionally a part of the ship's crew, many of them constituting the first, second, or third generation born in the Diaspora, specifically Britain or America. Therefore, their language, religion, and culture resembled the white seamen's more so than that of the African captives. However, the expected role of the captives as subservient and amusing also applied to the black seamen, as they were often slaves themselves. W. Jeffrey Bolster's groundbreaking work on black sailors argues that in the eighteenth century, black mariners' duties often were defined by racial stereotyping; however, aboard ships, many of the multiracial and diverse ethnic population of the ship's crew treated black sailors as (somewhat) equals.[70] Maritime employment was one of the few options for escape for bondsmen and offered great opportunities for free blacks; however, scholarship regarding these men on slaving vessels is limited.[71] Beyond performing the role of cook and steward, black sailors were often aboard as musicians.[72] Maritime culture has always been associated with music and dance. In several instances, those desiring to enter a particular crew were forced to perform music, song, or dance to the amusement of the captain in an effort to gain employment. With the racialized label that blacks were innately related to music, song, and dance, black sailors especially were expected to perform particular roles that often included the performing arts. For example, in 1732 aboard the *Albany*, a "Negro Drummer" named Diamond was on the roster, and another black seaman referred to as Sam and considered a "good drummer and fifer" traveled aboard the *Comet*. In 1741, the log of the Rhode Island ship *Revenge* included Richard Norton, the "Captain's Negro and Drummer."[73] In fact, numerous accounts existed of black sailors purposely being used for their musical abilities. The widespread use of blacks for entertainment through music and dance in the voyages to and from West Africa allowed for race to be scripted and blackness continually associated with amusement for both black seamen and African captives.

The transference of West Africans into docile, childlike creatures that needed and unknowingly wanted the protection and guidance of Western Europeans and North Americans was quite apparent within the Atlantic community. British navy officer Captain Ernest H. Pentecost illustrated this best in his evaluation of the Middle Passage experience: "Mirth and gaiety were promoted . . . while many were dancing and singing and playing together . . . they all seemed to regard the master of the vessel more in affection than fear."[74] He continued, "Our minds, necessarily, suffered in contemplating the degrading practices of civilized beings towards the less cultivated heathen of their species." However, due to the persistence of music and dance, Pentecost assessed that "the comfort and health of the slaves was promoted with every care."[75] This ideology contributed to a developing façade that validated the slave trade through the emphatic testimonies of the humane care given to the captives. Music and dance were used as tangible examples of the respectable nature of the Atlantic economy. At the same time gender was being shaped to allow sexual violence against black women to become a part of the culture of the Atlantic trade.

Female captives normally were kept on the main deck of the ship where they were accessible and vulnerable. Upon boarding the slave ship, female captives often were chosen as sexual "companions" for the crew.[76] In the Report of Lords of Committee of Counsel appointed for the consideration of all matters relating to the slave trade, "it was the general practice with the Captain, on the Receipt of a woman slave, to send her into his Cabin" for sexual purposes.[77] The captain and seamen routinely had sexual intercourse with the black women. One slave ship surgeon, Richard Drake, witnessed the common scene of black women being sexually abused throughout the Middle Passage. He stated, "Once off the coast, the ship became half bedlam and half brothel."[78] The oversexualized nature attributed to African women encouraged the behavior of the white slavers and laid the foundation for relations between black women and white men.

The invariable onslaught of sexual assault toward black women was only heightened by the degradation of forced song and dance. The women were vulnerable, unbound, and continually forced to dance and sing at the slavers' beckoning call. One Dutch slave trader who dined with a slave-ship captain on one of his vessels stated, "When I dined with the Dutch general at the Mine, I saw her (a young, female African captive) there, being brought in to dance before us."[79] The singing and dancing of the female captives not only served as entertainment but also became part of the relentless sexual violence against them. These performances represented a macabre type of foreplay, a prelude for rape that illustrated the white slavers' interest in particular female captives. The slavers "danced with black wenches . . . and lewdness seemed to rule all."[80] The female captives on slave ships who were recognized as good performers often became the main sexual prey of the white slavers. For example, on the *Neptune*, the captain selected two "amongst the female slaves" as his personal companions; "one of them he gave the name of Sarah."[81] Sarah was described as "the best singer and dancer of all the captive train." As one of the women chosen as the favorite for the ship captain, Sarah was continually forced to perform as the amusement on deck while also a concubine within his private quarters.

Slavers often touted the good care they gave the captives and downplayed the sexual vulnerability and abuse of female captives. James Barbot, who sailed off the coast of Guinea in 1698 and 1699, described that "the females being apart from the males and on the quarter deck and many of them young sprightly maidens, full of jollity and good humor, afforded us an abundance of recreation."[82] Barbot purposely omitted any overt reference to sexual abuse forced upon African females and instead described the women as happily willing participants in the sexual, lewd activities engaged in throughout the voyage. Sarah aboard the *Neptune* was continually described as "ever lively" and "ever gay" because of her singing and dancing.[83] Furthermore, she often was referred to as "cheerful Sarah" by the white crewmembers, who were reported as "universally" respecting her upon the ship due to her "sprightliness" that was expressed in her dancing and "African" melodies.

Within the context of the Atlantic voyage, West Africans began to understand their expected role as slaves while always fighting for freedom and autonomy. During the *Neptune* voyage, an "act of hostility" toward the slavers by the African captives occurred. While the captives who had died during the voyage due to disease or starvation were being thrown overboard, several West Africans staged a rebellion by attempting to force members of the ship's crew into the water. After the crew quelled the rebellion, the ship's captain investigated the main insurgents, and the result was that "most of the principal women, together with Sarah . . . were . . . charged with having had previous knowledge of the intended revolt."[84] Although the women claimed innocence, it was determined by the captain that they were a part of the rebellious plan. "Cheerful Sarah's" participation completely contradicts the sailors' belief that she was reveling in the advantages gained from her talents as a performer and her relationship with the captain. Sarah was representative of many of her African peers, male and female, who learned to act in a submissive manner, portraying an image of somewhat willing subordination and cheerfulness while retaining agency. The success of a revolt was enhanced by the white slavers' ignorance of their captives' determination, the belief that music and dance equated to cheerfulness, and the access that women and children were allotted upon the upper decks.[85] The continual presence of music, song, and dance did not suppress the captives' desire for freedom, as many white slavers believed; ironically, it encouraged or assisted in their insurrections.

White slavers were always aware of the potential for insurrections by their human cargo. One shipmate commented on the tenacity of African captives during the Atlantic voyage: "Though weapons of cruelty had mutilated the body, they could not subdue the free-born soul . . . when all appeared tranquil, the most deadly hatred was rankling in the minds of these coerced Africans."[86] Slavers took numerous precautions to prevent potential insurrections, such as engaging in physical and psychological violence, and employing spies and informants who calmed the African captives and acted as translators. The very design of ships, which kept the human cargo separate from the crew, served this purpose.[87] White slavers remained on guard for revolts while also using tortuous methods, such as forced feedings, burning the lips, or breaking the teeth, to prevent subtle resistance by the captives.

Slave resistance during the Middle Passage varied, but two major forms ultimately emerged: subtle resistance and band resistance.[88] Band resistance, as seen on the *Neptune*, included uprisings of African captives who rose together and aggressively attempted to challenge the balance of power by reclaiming their freedom.[89] Subtle resistance of the African captives consisted of "refusing to eat, throwing themselves overboard, or committing suicide."[90] One slave-ship captain, Thomas Phillips of the *Hannibal*, stated that during a particular voyage, "[A]bout 12 negroes did willfully drown themselves, and others starv'd themselves to death." [91] Scholar Antonio Bly has also identified "religious resistance," in which the captives used "prayers, chants and a number of fetishes, charms and other such spiritual icons" that they brought aboard to injure the white slavers.[92] "Slaves silently fought a twofold battle during the Atlantic crossing, one that pertained to their physical resistance and another that concerned their spiritual protest," according to Bly.[93]

African captives gained power within the Atlantic voyage through their songs, which acted as a form of rebellion that often has been ignored in historical texts. Music and dance served as a subterfuge for West Africans to stand between their cultural heritage and an expectation to fulfill myths created by another culture. The performing arts allowed for many West Africans to develop a second sight: first, an understanding of their expected role, and second, the maintenance of a grasp of their own distinct cultures.[94] Although white sailors adamantly proclaimed the happiness of their cargo due to the prevalence of music and dance, every slaver understood that if any opportunity presented itself, the "cheerful" African captives would rebel. French slaver Barbot commented that, aboard the slave ship, the slaves made "plenty of friendly gestures (caresses), and often jest with them and make them play various games, giving them freedom to sing and dance, especially the women."[95]

Ship logs and testimony note that women were the main singers along the journey. The songs of the women allowed to remain on the top deck often expressed a melancholy nature. Slaver James Arnold recognized that, on the slave ship, when "women were sitting by themselves . . . their songs then contained the history of their lives, and their separation from their friends and country. These songs were very disagreeable to the Captain, who . . . flogged them in so terrible a manner for no other reason than this."[96] Numerous accounts exist of women and girls singing lamentations throughout the voyage, even though they often received brutal punishment for this act. These songs represented a form of resistance similar to starvation or throwing themselves overboard; these captives resolved to express their sorrow through song, regardless of the consequence. James Town, a carpenter on the slaving vessel *Syren*, testified on the content of the captives' songs: "I never found it any thing joyous, but lamentations."[97]

While music and dance served as common tools of subtle resistance, they were also incorporated in violent insurrections on the slave ship. In 1804 aboard the Spanish slave vessel *Tryal*, twelve to thirteen African captives attacked the ship's crew violently. The slaves killed eighteen of the Spanish sailors and demanded that the ship be sailed to Senegal, on the coast of West Africa. During the insurrection, several of the female slaves sang a melody "to excite the courage" of the male rebels.[98] Furthermore, there were several accounts of captives, both male and female, using music and dance to either encourage or signal attempts at rebellion, or to distract slavers from plans for such attempts. In 1704 aboard the English slaving vessel *Postillion*, the ship's captain, John Tozor, was encouraged by the Royal African Company to supply "a drum and a banisou" for his human cargo.[99] These musical instruments, indigenous to West Africa, were thought to soothe the fears of the African captives while also providing them entertainment. This practice of gathering musical instruments from their country in order to mollify the Atlantic experience was common on many slave ships. While Captain Tozor and his crew were performing the normal duties required to operate an ocean vessel, the African captives played these instruments below. However, the seamen were unaware that, below deck, the Africans were using the guise of music to suppress the sound of breaking shackles. While the white slavers were comforted and distracted by the music, the African captives attacked, injuring seven crewmembers. The multiplicity of music and dance within West African cultures contributed to the continual onslaught of subtle resistance and violent insurrection against their condition. The custom of having music and dance in the Middle Passage not only provided avenues for resistance but also allowed for the captives to preserve their homeland traditions through cultural possessions carried upon the ships.

White slavers' tradition of collecting musical instruments contributed to the slave ships' carrying more than simply human cargo; it also brought personal belongings and the material culture of West Africa to the New World.[100] The captain of an American slave ship in the late eighteenth century recorded that the captives "were made to exercise, and encouraged, by the music of their beloved banjar."[101] On a British vessel, ship surgeon Alexander Falconbridge attested that the captives aboard his ship danced to the music of "drums" indigenous to West Africa.[102] The drum and various terms used to represent the banjo are mentioned repeatedly as common indigenous instruments that were gathered for the voyage. African cultures traveled on the slave ship into the New World not only in the memories of the captives but also within the material objects gathered for the dancing of the captives. The continuance of the performing arts enabled the captives to preserve their religion, rituals, and customs during the voyage and to transmit them from generation to generation.

For much of the eighteenth and nineteenth centuries, America and Britain dominated the Atlantic trade.[103] One slaver mentioned—and surely others agreed—that the hundreds of slaves on board his vessel represented at least "fourteen different tribes or nations."[104] West Central Africa, Sierra Leone, the Bight of Benin, Senegal, Gambia, the Gold Coast, and the Bight of Biafra were the main regional sources of Africans brought to North America.[105] Music, song, and dance encompassed distinct elements that were unique to each society. The multicultural captives on slave ships boarded with varying dance styles and postures, different languages, a variety of instruments unique to their region, and diverse singing techniques. Their daily activities, professions, and cultural purpose for the dances performed contributed to the style and movements of the dancers. However, within the Middle Passage these dynamics were distorted through the use of the whip, leg fetters, and varying cultures being forced into the performance. On the slave ship, these multicultural traditions temporarily became unified within music and dance performances. Scholar Geneviève Fabre asserts that the Middle Passage dance was a new spectacle that represented an amalgamation of slave ship and bondage quandary as well as memories of Africa.[106]

The forced performances perverted the ritualistic connection between music and dance in the diverse African cultures present on the slave ship. Dancing, for example, consisted of "jumping up and rattling their Chains," according to slaver David Henderson, and was a unifying experience for the African captives. The monotonous "beat of a drum" and the presence of fetters created a shuffling motion that often resulted in the unbound foot slapping the deck.[107] Within these dances, Africans were violently coerced to perform using similar motions and postures due to the fetters and space of the top deck, which allowed for indigenous populations who may have had limited contact with each other in West Africa to stage a uniform performance. It is arguable whether West Africans even considered these forced displays as music and dance. Because the performing arts held such a significant cultural purpose in many societies throughout West Africa, the coerced music and dance of the Middle Passage were representative of physical movements and sounds instead of music and dance. For some African captives, these performances may have altered the cultural meaning of music and dance, expanding the ritualistic association to the performing arts to include humiliation, degradation, and sadness. Regardless, the Middle Passage violently intruded in West African traditions that were associated with music and dance while simultaneously fostering an environment that allowed for the continual presence of homeland traditions.

The multiplicity of music and dance in the Middle Passage was only heightened with the presence of West African native instruments incorporated into the abuse and torture. The dance performances of these diverse populations were accompanied by the musical instruments collected for the voyage, such as the ever-popular drum. In many West African societies, drums were associated with special occasions, each rhythm having a purpose, a time, and a place.[108] In other cultures, drums may not have been used for dancing. The customs and traditions represented by the music of the drums were numerous and possibly conflicting, and they depended on the type of drum brought aboard the particular ship; the style, rhythm, and sound produced by the drum; and the gender and cultural background of the drummer. The complexities of musical instruments in West African societies, drums being only one example, were altered in order to enforce a unified sound. The music aboard the slave ship represented more than a simple beat and rhythm for the dancing; it also showed the simultaneous link and disconnect of West Africans to their homeland. The sound of their native land remained in their memories, but the physical manifestation was altered to subjugate West Africans uniformly into blacks. Beyond musical instruments, the songs also represented a distinct cultural expression. The varying indigenous populations most likely sang songs in different languages or expressed various moans to illustrate sad lamentations, while several songs also may have expressed encouragement and offered peace to the captives. Given the captives' varying languages, their songs served as unifying expressions, whether of lamentations or encouragement. The first syncretic culture formed from the blending of African musical traditions and dance styles aboard the slave ship. These syncretic movements and sounds initiated in the Middle Passage were introduced to North America, making the performing arts of music, song, and dance part of the complicated double consciousness of the developing black cultures in North America. [109]

Music, song, and dance were shared cultural expressions aboard the slave ship that often unified diverse populations of West Africans; however, the notion of a black race was not solidified within the Middle Passage.[110] Quarrels among Africans in the ship's hold were quite common. The extremely tight quarters and minimal victuals contributed to clashes among the captives. Beyond the desire for personal space and basic survival, some of the Africans present within the Middle Passage came from indigenous populations that were in combat against each other. Disputes that began in West Africa between various societies often continued onboard. The Middle Passage was not a "clean break between the past and present" but instead represented a "spatial continuation" between Africa, Europe, and America.[111] West Africans acknowledged their differences, and, while the European and American slavers also recognized the varying traditions and cultures aboard the slave ship, they still unified West Africans as a subjugated lot and forced them to perform. In this space, the performing arts that held sacred, ritual, and cultural meanings in the Africans' homeland were perverted into an entertaining spectacle of sex, degradation, and physical exertion.

In addition to West African instruments aboard the ship, European and American musical instruments also were present. Thomas Phillips aboard the British vessel *Hannibal* described the presence of English instruments. In the evening, when the captives were brought on deck, they danced "for an hour or two to our bagpipes, harp, and fiddle."[112] As active components of maritime and slaving culture, music and dance became so elemental that, on several French slaving vessels, accordion players were hired to play for the dancing of the captives.[113] Playing European-based musical instruments for African captives contributed to a cultural exchange that influenced the development of both the black and white races in the New World. The space between the ship's hold and the captain's quarters represented a public sphere in which culture was being created within the music, song, and dance of the voyage. The first intricate networks of cross-cultural influence were exhibited in this space with the amalgamations of Western Europeans, Americans, and various indigenous groups from throughout West Africa. As a multicultural group of Africans danced to the European-based fiddle and the transnational white sailors danced to the beat of an African drum, their customs were merging and developing into syncretic music and dance that would contribute to the foundation of culture and entertainment in the New World.

The performing arts displayed throughout the journey presented to the outside world a very specific perception of the newly forming population. These scenes were discussed and sketched in the popular literature and developing folklore of the burgeoning New World. The images of travel narratives and stories of the Middle Passage contributed to both sides of the slavery system. For example, in 1797, antislavery advocate Hannah More published a poem entitled "Sorrows of Yamba; or, The Negro Woman's Lamentation." This was one of the most popular antislavery texts, and it focused on the experiences of a slave woman who was separated from her child, experienced the Middle Passage, slavery, and eventually death. In the poem, More narrates an Atlantic voyage scene:

> At the savage Captain's beck,
> Now like Brutes they make us prance;
> Smack the Cat about the Deck,
> And in scorn they bid us dance.[114]

Music and dance were common aspects of the Atlantic voyage and well known to populations throughout Europe and the New World. Although this antislavery poem recognized the brute force controlling these Middle Passage performances, other accounts, such as the results of Parliament's inquisitions, often neglected to mention the power of the whip. With More's account, music and dance performances were seen as a tortuous, inhumane aspect of the Atlantic voyage, but her poem represented the white abolitionist (minority) segment of the population. Those attempting to protect the slave trade viewed the performances of the Middle Passage quite differently. Music, song, and dance were parts of the culture of the Middle Passage that became associated with the African captives. These forced performances entered into the sphere of American entertainment, setting the stage for whites to be amused by blacks, either in person, through stories, or textually.

Englishwoman Hannah More's fictional poem about the experiences of African slaves illustrated two main points: that the performing arts were a recognized aspect of the Middle Passage and that the voices of the captives often were silenced. Few accounts of the slave trade from the Africans' viewpoint exist today. Evidence from the Middle Passage voyages reflected and transmitted the perceptions of white observers. The performing arts displayed throughout the journey thus presented to the outside world an erroneous perception of the newly forming population's culture and ideals. The slave ship was the medium between Africans' cultural history, white sailors' traditions and perceptions of their human cargo, and the black bodies' adaptation to their horrific condition, all of which contributed to the development of a black race in North America. It is important to continually assert Africans' voices, cultures, and experiences within the context of the performance. The Middle Passage stood between history and fiction with the amalgamation of mythical traits and the beginning of racial consciousness. Africans traveled the Middle Passage with a rich legacy from their native land that was tainted for the purpose of humiliation, degradation, and white entertainment, which only continued upon their arrival in the West.

The "dancing and singing of the Negroes on Board" served as advertisement of the merchandise that soon would be available.[115] Any knowledgeable slave-ship captain understood that potential customers desired happy and willing laborers who could be trained easily into their new, subjugated roles. Used to the routine throughout the Middle Passage, the captives jumped and shuffled their feet while singing a melancholy melody, often to the rhythm of a homeland instrument now used for this new purpose. The arrival of the slave ships commenced the next phase within the institution of slavery from the Atlantic to the auction block. "The Negroes usually appeared cheerful and singing," boasted English Vice Admiral Edwards.[116] After the long, tumultuous journey across the Atlantic, it was in the captain's best interests to present human cargo merrily singing and dancing upon their arrival in the West Indies. Slave traders' financial success and reputation depended on the salability of the African captives, and the performing arts became a useful tactic for presenting a happy, healthy lot. The "health and good condition of the Negroes at the time of Sale" was the main concern of the slavers, claimed Captain Robert Norris. The opportunity to earn bonuses beyond their salary encouraged sailors to make sure their human cargo appealed to potential customers.

The slaving vessels from various nations arrived in the West Indies with the ultimate goal of obtaining the optimal profit for the human cargo; the performing arts were an important component in this process. Music and dance numbered among a series of strategies by which slavers attempted to present their African captives as healthy and willing slaves. In preparation for the market, slavers often shaved, washed, and fed fattening foods to the captives to make them appear healthier. In addition, several slave-trading companies set up facilities that "doctored" for the market those captives who had arrived in poor health. The West Indies encompassed several islands, and many slavers would travel from region to region in an effort to dispose of their human chattel. The English slaving vessel *Ruby* ventured to Barbados, St. Vincent, and Grenada in an effort to sell cargo, the sale of which varied according to vessel and region.[117] A London-based slaving vessel, the *Albion-Frigate*, reached port in 1689 and invited local "planters and other inhabitants . . . aboard to buy as many slaves as they have occasion for." Slaver Jean Barbot described that each slave was examined "limb by limb, to see whether they are sound and strong."[118] Another method by which slavers sold their captives was to bring the "sick or refuse slaves" ashore to local taverns or any other venue to host a public auction. Captains who used this technique often would "march their slaves through the town" in coffles as walking advertisements for their merchandise. The slaves would be examined and often purchased, with the obviously sick being sold at reduced prices. Besides sales on the ship and at public auction, one ship doctor, Alexander Falconbridge, stated that the "scramble" method was the most common manner in which slavers sold their cargo. This process involved the captain's establishing a standard price for the captives, "which is agreed upon between the captains and the purchasers before the sale begins." Then, on the appointed day, the African captives were brought to a courtyard, often an enclosed public area, the doors were opened at a predetermined time, and buyers entered to either "instantly seize" slaves, tag them by "handkerchiefs, or collect by rope in order to secure their purchase."[119] The scramble began with the "beat of a drum" signaling the white patrons to rush into the facility to aggressively seize the human commodities.[120] Ironically, the drum throughout the Middle Passage embodied the white slavers' enforcement of performances while also being employed as a tool for communication, encouragement, and obscuring the numerous insurrections of African captives; the drum now set the tone for these seizures, which were, of course, terrifying to the men and women being sold. A stupefied Falconbridge recounted the scene: "The poor astonished negroes are so much terrified by these proceedings, that several of them, on the occasion, climbed over the walls of the courtyard and ran wild about the town."[121] It is no surprise that many attempted to flee, but to escape usually proved unsuccessful. Recaptured slaves were brought back to the public yard or building to be collected by the customers who had prepaid. African captives often journeyed from the ship deck, public coffle, and physical examination to the auction block, a pattern that served as a template for a major enterprise of selling and buying slaves in North America.

As the use of the drum in scrambles conveys, slave traders used music and dance performances as part of the process of preparing captives for the market in the West Indies and North America. A number of the Africans brought to North America also experienced a process known as "seasoning" in the West Indies prior to entering the region. The Bay Islands near the coast of Honduras, like many other locations, boasted an establishment that housed a "slave depot and farm" to which captives from West Africa were brought to be prepared for North American slavery. The slave depot "received . . . blacks and set them at work in agricultural operation and in making good for the African market," reported one American slaver.[122] For the captives, seasoning often entailed an apprenticeship to learn work routines and a rudimentary form of the local language, or at least the ability "to gabble broken Spanish and English," as well as a disciplinary process to subjugate the captives.[123] Another part of the seasoning process for many West Africans involved the continued enforcement of music and dance, tools that slaveholders used regularly to subjugate and humiliate. Part of this process of subjugating the slaves and tempering their attitudes and spirits in order to turn them into more effective laborers involved giving them new names, often Christian or classical Greek and Roman names. However, West Africans were able to manipulate this tool, utilizing the allowance of music and dance to plan insurrections, as evidenced by the eventual outlawing of drums in many islands throughout the West Indies and areas in the New World due to their role in communication and rebellion.[124] Although never succeeding completely in this objective, seasoning attempted to alter the cultural expression of music and dance into a form of public subjugation that would only continue for those West Africans bound for the New World.

3   Onstage

"Dance you damned niggers, dance"

"Dance you damned niggers, dance," Master Edwin Epps shouted to the miserable lot of slaves. With "a slash, and crack and flourish of the whip" he ordered his human property to dance "no matter how worn out or tired" they were after a long day in the cotton fields. He would tolerate "no halting or delay, or slow or languid movements; all must be brisk, and lively, and alert." Slaves worked on the plantation fields from dusk to dawn under the hot sun and with inadequate food and rest; regardless, during the evening hours, they were expected to perform through music, song, and dance for their white masters. Epps demanded the slaves move "up and down, heel and toe" at the unhappy festivities. The tired performers jumped lively and shuffled their feet to the sounds of the violin while Epps and his wife watched with whip in hand, ready to fall on the "wretched souls" who dared to rest for even a moment. It was a scene that could have been witnessed throughout the South, as slaveholders played the role of choreographer, directing the coerced bondsmen and bondswomen to perform a cultural and social script on a plantation stage that held great importance in the Southern community.[1]

From humble origins, Epps continually strived to enter into the planter class. As a driver and overseer on a cotton plantation in Louisiana, he gained a reputation among both blacks and whites, slave and free, as being a "nigger breaker." Well known for his faculty for subduing the "spirit of the slave," Epps freely used the whip to work, to rape, and to dance his slaves. Similar to other Southern gentlemen seeking status in the planter world, Epps used music and dance to publicly assert and legitimize his power. After years of work, Epps was able to lease a cotton plantation in Bayou Huff Power, Louisiana, and acquire a small lot of nine slaves. To further advance his status, Epps invested in the illegally enslaved violinist, Solomon Northup, in the early 1840s.[2] Investing in the performing arts was a custom throughout the South that allowed many whites to publicly display their wealth. For Epps, who often joined his dancing slaves, and for his wife, Mary Elvira Epps, who was "profoundly fond of music," these performances confirmed their status in the community while providing amusement in their daily lives. The violinist was frequently called to the house to play before the family and often was used as entertainment for invited guests. The spectators on Epps's plantation could not contain their laughter upon witnessing the "uproarious pranks" of the entertaining slave community. The music of the violin, the shuffling of feet, and the laughter of slaves were all a part of the atrocities of the plantation society for the enslaved community; however, for Master Epps and many whites throughout the South, this was an expression of authority, potential wealth, and amusement.

"Slaves are generally expected to sing as well as to work," assessed ex-slave and abolitionist Frederick Douglass in his 1855 autobiography, *My Bondage and My Freedom*.[3] Douglass's assessment echoed long-held Western European and American racial expectations: slaves performed music, song, and dance for white audiences. The Southern plantation became a stage, and white slaveholders, overseers, and drivers were the choreographers of the public display of enslaved blacks performing for the appeasement of white desires for dominance. These onstage performances were for the benefit of the white audiences and the slave masters and owners. Within these orchestrated amusements, blacks were not the only performers; whites also performed their desires upon the enslaved community. Master Epps's violence against his slaves in forcing them to sing, play music, dance, and laugh cast him in the role of overseer, planter, and patriarch, displaying for all his power, his domination, and most of all, his whiteness. Furthermore, he intentionally masked the emotions and hardships of the slave community with a pretense of docility and happiness.[4] Coercion and expectation to perform was an important component of the institution of slavery; however, music and dance were well portrayed as innate black qualities. The custom of onstage performances on Edwin Epps's plantation developed over centuries, beginning on the plantations in the West Indies.

A culture of enforcing music, song, and dance in the enslaved community developed early in colonial slavery and quickly became pervasive in the Caribbean. Englishman Richard Ligon believed that the emerging slave population in mid-seventeenth century Barbados brought with it a propensity for the performing arts. "The Negres . . . are fetch'd from severall parts of *Africa,* who speake severall languages," and although Ligon emphasized that they "understands not another," they were able to perform communally.[5] Similar to many of his contemporaries, he believed that the performing arts customs brought from West Africa unified West Africans regardless of their diverse backgrounds. Another Englishman wrote in 1729 that, in the Caribbean, "the Field Slaves . . . divert themselves with Singing, Playing, and Dancing after their several Country Modes."[6] These statements hold some validity. Throughout West Africa, music, song, and dance played significant roles in daily traditions. However, English observers were inaccurate in making music, song, and dance essential aspects of blacks' nature rather than cultural displays. Performing arts customs were not sporadic; rather, they represented particular activities or events. Positioning music, song, and dance as simply instinctual negates the role of whites in the public performances present throughout the plantation society.

Seventeenth-century Englishmen, even those critical of colonial slaveholding, saw the connections between the performing arts and racial power. In the 1660s, English merchant Thomas Tryon traveled to Barbados to witness the atrocities of plantation society, later publishing his observations in the work *Friendly Advice to the Gentlemen-Planters of the East and West Indies.*[7] Tryon openly condemned the institution of slavery, particularly through his fictional conversation between "an Ethiopean or Negro-Slave, and a Christian that was his Master in America." In the theatrical skit, the slave master states, "Come hither, Sambo! You look as gravely to day as a Dog Out-law'd, or a Justice of Peace set in the Stocks; I doubt you have been doing some Rogury; I call'd you to make us some Sport, let us see one of your Dances, such as used in your own Country." The slave responds, "If you will have me Dance upon mine Head, or Caper on the top of the House, I must do it, though I break my Neck; for you are become Lord of both of my Feet, and every part of me."[8] Although Tryon wrote this fictional skit to highlight the rigors of slave life, as evident in the slave's response to the master's request, the antislavery advocate also wanted to expose the reality of plantation life in the West Indies that music and dance were tools of subjugation and sometimes torture used by the slaveholders.

Plantation slavery fostered a custom of onstage performances that began in the British, French, and Spanish colonies throughout the West Indies. Numerous accounts of white planters and travelers in the West Indies detail how blacks "diverted themselves" with music and dance. However, many neglected the role of white planters and overseers in the enactment of these performances.[9] The music and dance observed by whites were a part of the spectatorship of slavery. On a coffee plantation on Saint-Domingue, P. J. Laborie recognized that on "Saturday or Sunday evenings, the negroes are allowed to dance upon the platforms [used for drying coffee]."[10] This plantation contained a dedicated physical space for performance. However, on many plantations throughout the West Indies, any area where slaves presented music, song, and dance in the presence of whites became a stage. Laborie did not specifically call the events entertainment, though the coffee planter did mention the dances as being "lively and swift." "Every nerve is in motion," he said, "every exertion raised to the utmost."[11] In the colonial West Indies, the music and dance of the African population, whenever performed in the presence of white spectators, became a form of amusement for whites, who then exported that tradition to the mainland of North America.

The custom of forcing enslaved blacks to perform music, song, and dance would continue in British North America, as colonies such as Virginia moved toward becoming slave societies.[12] However, the scarcity of early accounts of black music and dance in the seventeenth century has been noted as an interesting phenomenon in this English colony.[13] In 1619, twenty Africans arrived in Virginia on a Dutch vessel, and for the next five decades the African population gradually increased in the colony.[14] These African laborers constituted a small percentage of the diverse indentured servants that included English, Indian, and other European workers. The population of Africans was small because of the limited agricultural development (with tobacco being in its early stages of development as a viable cash crop) in Virginia and the African slave trade being controlled by the Dutch and Portuguese, therefore minimizing British access. Virginia, the first permanent English colony of mainland North America, was the first region to establish in law the master-slave or black-white relationship in the South, with other colonies to follow. Initially toiling as indentured servants alongside Europeans, West Africans soon began experiencing harsher treatment, particularly in the court and legal system. In 1640, all inhabitants of Virginia, "negroes excepted," were expected to bear arms for the security of the colony.[15] During the same year, Virginia courts sentenced a runaway black indentured servant to a lifetime of servitude. Slavery entered into Virginia law in 1661, and an official slave code was established in 1705. With tobacco becoming the first major cash crop of the English colonies, Virginia, and later Maryland, would firmly be instituted as a society based on African slave labor. The minimal population of Africans meant that only fragmentary references to their homeland cultures of music and dance existed. However, due to the continual exchanges between the West Indies and the mainland, it should be recognized that music and dance were an active part of the cultures that the first Africans brought and infused into the New World, especially in the developing plantation societies. The founding of South Carolina in 1663 was directly influenced by Barbadian planters. In 1669, the eight proprietors of the province of Carolina adopted the Fundamental Constitutions of Carolina, which stated, "Every freeman of Carolina, shall have absolute power and authority over his negro slaves."[16] South Carolina was the only mainland colony with slavery from its inception. By the last decades of the seventeenth century, both the Chesapeake colonies and the Carolinas had established political, social, cultural, and economic systems based on racial slavery.[17]

The plantation society that developed in the mainland colonies mirrored the slavery system of the West Indies, including the manner in which whites publicly asserted music and dance as an innate custom of blacks. That link persisted throughout the entire slave era. Strategically, many whites disregarded their direct coercion that forced enslaved blacks to perform music and dance in order to categorize blackness in a manner that benefited whites' status in the slavery system. More particularly, many whites stated that blacks' seemingly innate musical ability was the only positive quality the entire race possessed. Planter Thomas Atwood believed that "the characters of negroes are not so various as one would imagine they would be, from the difference of the country they are brought from . . . the only thing they are remarkable for attaining to any degree of perfection[s], is Musick."[18] Atwood resided in the British West Indies in the late eighteenth century; however, his sentiments regarding the Island of Dominica also resounded throughout North America. Former President and slaveholder Thomas Jefferson assessed the black race similarly. In *Notes on the State of Virginia*, a publication considered to be the most influential work before the 1800s, Jefferson presented the black race as inherently inferior, except in music: "In music they are more generally gifted than the whites with accurate ears for tune and time, and they have been found capable of imagining a small catch."[19] However, to emphasize the mental deficiencies of blacks, he asserted that "whether they will be equal to the composition of a more extensive run of melody, or of complicated harmony, is yet to be proved."[20] Beyond misreading the music and dance cultures of the enslaved communities, whites purposely constructed race to validate their role in society through the degradation of blackness. The Southern plantation society from the late seventeenth through the mid-nineteenth centuries presented music and dance as innate among blacks while ignoring the role whites held in enforcing these seemingly innocent amusements. Traveling throughout the United States in the early nineteenth century, Henry C. Knight wrote to his brother that the black slaves throughout the South performed music and song due to "instinct" rather than external influences.[21]

Slave owners spent more than two hundred years cultivating a public image of cheerful, docile blacks singing and dancing, first in the West Indies and then continuing in the mainland colonies. The onstage performances were not strictly Southern; however, there were significant differences in the evolution of race and power in the Northern provinces compared to those in the South. The public performances of black music and dance significantly influenced the development of race in both regions. Early accounts indicated that blacks congregated on Sundays in the North. In the 1690s, one colonist stated, "Philadelphia's blacks gathered on Sundays and holidays and were seen dancing after the manner of their several nations in Africa, and speaking and singing in their native dialects."[22] Blacks also congregated on Sundays throughout the South. In 1774, English traveler Nicholas Cresswell recorded while in Maryland that "Sundays being the only days . . . [they] have to themselves, they generally meet together and amuse themselves with Dancing to the Banjo . . . a Gourd. . . . Some of them sing."[23] From the colonial era until the end of slavery, blacks, both free and enslaved, gathered on Sunday throughout the United States.

The religious foundation of many of the Northern colonies and the Great Awakening that contributed to the surge of religious sentiment throughout the region caused many colonists to question the music and dance practices of this first generation of Africans in America. White ministers and clergymen in particular were adamantly opposed to blacks gathering on the Sabbath, especially during the colonial era.[24] The Northern region was founded with a strong religious identity; colonists in New England often specifically advocated for civil order and legislation against dance. In 1680, Reverend Morgan Godwin believed that "nothing is more barbarous and contrary to Christianity, than their . . . Idolatrous, Dances, and Revels" in which the black population "usually spend the Sunday."[25] Dancing was an active element of colonial life that was often seen as an immoral practice requiring restriction and restraint. Although most colonists freely enjoyed dance, black dance was seen as more devi-

Illustration of African Americans dancing during a traditional gathering on Sundays, a practice that began in the colonial era and continued until the end of slavery. The image shows whites watching the music and dance festivities; it originally appeared in *The Narrative of the Life and Adventures of Henry Bibb, an American Slave*, in 1849. (Miscellaneous Items in High Demand Collection, Prints & Photographs Division, Library of Congress, LC-USZ62–107750.) Courtesy of the Library of Congress.

ant and immoral. Reverend John Sharpe of New York stated in the eighteenth century that many believed that blacks, due to their "country and complexion," often performed "Heathenish" activities in their dances.[26] Beyond the type of dancing that blacks performed, the day chosen to congregate and dance was seen as a vice among many colonists.

Unlike the Northern regions, the Southern colonies were not founded by religious dissenters but were formed primarily to make a profit. However, many of the qualms about Sunday gatherings in the North were echoed throughout the South. One of the earliest planters in Louisiana, Le Page du Pratz, stated in one of the earliest histories of the region that the newly arrived African slaves continually danced in the public square with little objection from the authorities. Arriving in the region in 1719, Pratz illustrated his disgust of Sunday gatherings by stating in his *Histoire de la Louisiane* that "it were better that they should employ themselves in cultivating that field on Sundays, when they are not Christians, than do worse." He continued by noting that in New Orleans, blacks "assemble together . . . and make a kind of Sabbath."[27] He was not the only one to openly condemn the Sunday custom. George Whitefield, an Anglican minister who spread the religious revitalization of the Great Awakening in Britain and later to the British colonies of North America, addressed the issue of slaves dancing on January 23, 1740. He wrote, "To the Inhabitants of Maryland, Virginia, North and South Carolina, Concerning Their Negroes. . . . I have great reason to believe that most of you, on Purpose, keep your Negroes ignorant of Christianity; or otherwise, why are they permitted thro' your Provinces, openly to prophane the Lord's Day, by their Dancing, Piping and such like?"[28] The atmosphere in the South differed significantly from Northern perspectives on Sabbath gatherings. Many religious leaders morally disagreed with black music and dance in the South. However, the South established a distinct culture in which music and dance were active parts of society for the black and white populations.

The moral degradation of blackness in the North was attributed to classifying these Sabbath performances as innately heathen, while in the South it was a part of casting blacks as inferior; regardless of their conversion to Christianity, blacks were considered immoral and deficient simply due to their complexion. This became evident in the manner by which Christianity was used to create and support a chattel slavery system. Most colonial planters absolutely opposed attempts to Christianize their slaves. The Christianization of the slaves was an issue of debate between religious leaders and slaveholders. Specifically, the Anglican Church had to deal with the issue of whether or not to introduce Christianity to the growing black population and, if so, how they could then morally justify enslaving Christians.[29] A major hurdle for Anglican ministers was slaveholders' fear that introducing Christianity would weaken the institution of slavery. In 1667, Virginia responded by passing an act stating that "baptism does not alter the condition to the person as to this bondage or freedom; masters freed from this doubt may more carefully propagate Christianity by permitting slaves to be admitted to that sacrament."[30] Colonial America in the Northern and Southern provinces contributed to the long process of society production that cast blackness as innately subjugated due to their interpretation of black music and dance.

The culture of slavery caused North America to develop differently by region. However, music and dance were used to define and subjugate blacks even early in eighteenth-century Northern colonies. Negro Election Day in New England and Pinkster Day in New York and New Jersey were both festivals that Northern slaves actively celebrated from the late seventeenth century to the nineteenth century; they represented amalgamations of African and European cultural exchanges.[31] Beginning in 1707, Negro Election Day was filled with music, dancing, and a general coming together in which blacks elected a ruler, king, or governor for the two- to three-day celebration to represent the different regions.[32] Pinkster Day, originally a Dutch tradition in the seventeenth century, was adopted and adapted by blacks, enslaved and free, in the eighteenth and early nineteenth centuries.[33] These festivities not only reveal the inventiveness of the enslaved and free black populations but also illustrate the spectatorship of whites. Historian George S. Roberts explained, "For a week before Pinkster, the inhabitants, black and white, began to make ready for the festival."[34] Also, a 1706 poem on Boston's election-day festivities highlighted that during the celebration the "city swarms with every sort; of black and white . . . of high, low, rich and poor."[35] Although considered to be a "great holiday for the slaves," it was a time during which blacks excitedly performed music, song, and dance as cultural expressions while whites watched, both amused and critical of the public display.[36] White spectators often used words such as "frightful," "lewd and indecent," or simply "savage wildness" to describe the antics of the Africans and their descendants at these celebrations.[37] Regardless of the "horrid manner" the blacks displayed, according to the whites present, these events attracted visitors from throughout the region. For more than a century, whites viewed these festivals as a part of the slaves' "unusual liberty to enjoy themselves."[38]

Although these festivities were autonomous expressions for the internal black community, whites were always present to not only judge and condemn but also to enjoy and participate. White spectatorship of black amusements became a cultural practice that allowed Northern whites to watch, be amused by, and socialize with blacks performing music, song, and dance while always condemning and objectifying their activities as evidence of black "immaturity and childishness."[39] In the colonial period throughout the North, the white spectatorship and fraternization during these festivals was a part of the intrusion of whiteness into black lives that fostered stereotypes and racist ideology.

Similar to the colonial North, watching black music and dance was a pastime throughout the South. However, Southern whites embraced music and dance as a social pastime and as an expression of wealth—and therefore leisure. In 1773, Philip Vickers Fithian ventured from New Jersey to Virginia as a tutor for a wealthy planter family. While in residence, he commonly remarked on the stark differences between New Jersey and Virginia, or rather, the Northerner and the Southerner; dance was one custom that he highlighted.[40] "Virginians are genuine Blood—They will dance or die!" observed Fithian. This Princeton (College of New Jersey)

graduate was quite accurate in his assessment of the affinity many Southerners had for music and dance. Indeed, many wealthy planters hired
dancing masters and music instructors to teach their children, regardless
of gender, in the arts. The ability to hire professional musicians or dancers was considered a privilege in the planter community. Music was a
form of leisure and privilege. In 1818, Thomas Jefferson regarded music,
specifically European music, as a "delightful recreation for the hours of
respite from the cares of the day."[41] As a part of his status as a prominent
planter, Jefferson was a violinist and emphasized music in the education of
his daughters and granddaughters.[42] Although Jefferson never completely
understood the musical contributions of blacks, his references to the importance of music illustrate a major aspect of Southern society. Music
and dance were used to show the status of the white upper class, either
by their own talents in the arts, their ability to hire formal teachers, or
their authority to have slaves exhibit the art forms. Music and dance was
regarded as an intellectual aesthetic skill that was acquired by whites,
and was an aspect of European cultural continuances. Ironically, many
of those whites, in an effort to denigrate the race, considered music and
dance within the black community as innate.

Throughout the South, whites enjoyed performing music and dance
and watching their slaves perform as a favorite pastime. However, music
and dance performances on Sundays were viewed as more than a spectator sport for the white community in the South. White slaveholders also
considered their allowance of music and dance as evidence of their gen-
erosity, and Sabbath gatherings often were used to illustrate that kindness. One South Carolina planter in 1836 stated that his slaves, "upon
their return from church," were employed to dance and sing even though
"some persons will object to this as discretion of the Sabbath."[43] Therefore, Sunday gatherings served as part of the South's defense of slavery
while also contributing to the construction of enslaved blacks as morally
degenerate, docile, and happy.

Visitors to the South consistently commented on the centrality of
slavery to Southern society. In day-to-day life, slavery and slaves were
the "general topic of conversation" throughout the region, as observed
by Josiah Quincy in the mid-eighteenth century.[44] This strict social, cultural, and economic system functioned to keep an emerging population
submissive while simultaneously allowing whites to remain dominant.
As slavery became a staple characteristic of Southern society planters
increasingly invested in every aspect of the daily lives of the enslaved
community. As Charles Woodson explained in the *Farmers* newsletter,
"In a country depending principally upon slave labor," it was important

to create a "system for the general and minute management" of the enslaved population.[45] This system Woodson referred to encompassed planters and overseers enforcing music and dance to gain power and control.
Residents of slave states, regardless of their slaveholder status or stance
on slavery, conformed to a society based on subjugating blacks. The intricate web of dominance was supported and guided by the words and
writings primarily of white men determined to uphold their desires for
a slave community. One Alabama planter stated that the "management
of Negroes," the controlling of slaves, is a subject about which fellow
planters have a similar mutual interest. "For if I mismanage mine, that
mismanagement will be reflected on yours as can be amply shown."[46]

Englishman John Davis traveled throughout the United States from
1798 to 1802 and commented on the cornerstone of the Southern society,
observing that the Southerner who is "without horses and slaves incurs
always contempt. The consideration of property has such an empire over
the mind that poverty and riches are contemplated through the medium
of infamy and virtue."[47] Though an outsider, Davis saw clearly a foun-
dational element of Southern society; possessing slaves was the primary
criterion for success in the economy and for social rank. Southern society
was based on the slavery system. As slavery became a staple aspect of
Southern society, music and dance of the enslaved community became
more an aspect of methodological control and entertainment by whites.
Sunday gatherings or any public display of music and dance by the enslaved community in the South could be transformed as propaganda to
promote the benevolence of white slave masters, validation for black
subjugation, justification for the institution of slavery, or any statement
against the rising abolitionist sentiment of the early nineteenth century.

Planters, overseers, and drivers continually developed strategies to
maintain order and uphold their authority, and music and dance were
powerful tools they often employed. They felt it was their duty to enforce
music and dance within their slave community. Slaves were "like the
plastic clay, which may be moulded into agreeable or disagreeable figures
according to the skill of the moulder," one Virginia planter proclaimed.[48]
As "moulders," white slaveholders, overseers, and drivers throughout the
South adamantly enforced the performance of music and dance among
the enslaved population. "The Negroes are permitted and encouraged
to clap and dance and make merry," proclaimed a Mississippi planter in
the *Southern Cultivator*.[49] Planters throughout the South contributed to
and read from similar newsletters containing agricultural data, information about national events, and advice on maintaining a plantation. In
the postcolonial society, music and dance progressed from pastimes for

white spectators mainly on Sundays to an organized, methodical process of subjugation that was discussed and distributed through planters' exchanges. These publications were meant to influence social life on the plantation and help planters and overseers assert their power over every aspect of enslaved blacks' daily lives, including music and dance. This effort at hegemony was specifically addressed by South Carolina planter N. Herbemont in the *Southern Agriculturist*. In his article "On the Moral Discipline and Treatment of Slaves," Herbemont wrote, "Gentlemen may think it beneath their dignity to interfere in any manner whatsoever with the pleasure and amusements of their slaves." However, the planter emphasized that it was "never thought below the dignity of the sovereign . . . to direct the conduct of their subjects . . . in everything that may lead to their general good."[50] Herbemont insisted throughout the article that the "innocent amusements" of music, song, and dance led to a "path of pleasantness," and every slaveholder should enforce the proper use of such pastimes. Slaveholders throughout the South purposely crafted an atmosphere that induced blacks to perform. In 1860, a Georgia physician and planter believed that all "enjoyments should, as far as possible, be provided for [slaves] at home."[51] They purposely orchestrated performances on the plantation and made music and dance strategically organized aspects of plantation life.

The first step toward using blacks as amusement in the South was the building of stages. Ex-slave James W. Smith, born on the Hallman family plantation in Palestine, Texas, remembered that his master made special arrangements for the enslaved community to publicly dance and sing. In order to facilitate the "dancing and singin'" Smith's owner "had a little platform built for de jiggin' contest" that was a common aspect of Saturday nights on this plantation.[52] Former slave Wesley Jones remembered that his master in South Carolina also "had a platform built." He recalled, "Any darky dat could cut de buck and de pigeon wings was called up to de platform to perform."[53] The construction of stages on plantations throughout the South epitomizes the entertainment aspect of these performances. These physical stages were a part of the setting of the metaphorical onstage performances. The stages, which were built by the slaves, personified the performance aspect of these scenes. The construction of these physical platforms at the direction of slaveholders throughout the South illustrates the importance of music and dance in supporting the slavery system.

On the plantation, slave masters often pitted their slaves against slaves from neighboring plantations in the performing arts and bet on the quality of the performances. The competitiveness of these events only heightened this pastime for many whites, with some whites participating in gambling on cards and horses: risk was part of their culture and signified their wealth and power. Slaveholders often organized and judged dancing contests and provided prizes for those slaves they considered to be the best dancers. A former Virginia slave remembered that the "couple dat danced best got a prize . . . slave owners come o dese parties 'cause dey enjoyed watchin' de dance, and dey 'cided who danced de best."[54] The plantation's best fiddler or dancer often received a heightened status by their master. These contests were specifically choreographed to please the whites and strategically used to offer incentives for prescribed behavior within the black community. One Virginia planter advocated in a Southern agricultural newsletter that rewards for participating in these contests "should also be part of the system whenever there is displayed particular good conduct . . . [as this] goes a great way in their management."[55] Beyond placating their slave community, these events gave white owners the ultimate form of control, intruding on the separate lives and culture that black slaves were attempting to create for themselves away from the plantation regime.

The white slaveholders who intruded into the manner in which blacks danced influenced the style of the performance. If an overseer preferred a fast jig to the ring dance, then he imposed his partiality, which caused many blacks to alter their dance technique while also likely affecting the dances performed privately in that particular slave community. The best dancers were determined not only by the agility of their feet but also by their ability to maintain a continual countenance of happiness while performing, which appeased the white judges. Whites were proud of such slaves and recognized their talent or ability to out-dance or out-fiddle other plantations' slaves as a sign of their own elevated status and benevolence as masters.

Particularly skilled slave musicians also held a central and visible role in white community festivities. Born on a plantation on the Rappahannock River, a bondsman reverently known as "Old Dick" was a musician who acquired his skill through the encouragement of his "young master," who was a "mighty one for music . . . [and] made me learn to play the banjer."[56] These performances, whether on a formal platform, in the main living area of the planter's house, or simply in an open space on the plantation, were vital components of slavery. They occurred anywhere in the United States where the institution of slavery was a part of the social, political, and cultural systems and in any form, whether on a small scale with an audience of only one, or on a large scale with numerous white guests. Former slave Mary Armstrong lived in St. Louis, and while she was a slave, her mistress, Miss Olivia, "used to put a glass plumb full of water" on her head while having her "waltz around the room."[57] Whether large or small, performances were a common form of amusement on the plantation. Marrinda Jane Singleton's master in Virginia would take those who "could dance and sing right kindey good . . . to de big house to entertaining Master and Missus guests."[58]

Beyond building stages and hosting contests, many slaveholders also furnished musicians for this Southern custom. In the mid-nineteenth century, *DeBow's Review* was one of the most popular monthly Southern agricultural newsletters that offered advice on managing the slave community. Several planters boasted in this publication that they purchased musicians specifically for these plantation performances. Slave musicians fetched a higher price on the auction block, and many planters also invested in professionally training their slaves in the performing arts. One Mississippi planter bragged that he bought "a good fiddler" and kept him "well supplied with catgut," and it was the fiddler's "duty to play for the negroes every Saturday night until 12 o'clock."[59] Another planter featured in this publication also proudly bragged that he would "buy the fiddle and encourage it" among his slave population.[60] Purchasing slaves for their musical abilities was a public sign of a planter's wealth. The daughter of a wealthy South Carolina slaveholder, Elizabeth Pringle remembered her father sending "young lads to learn to play the violin every year" for festivities held annually on their plantation.[61] These musicians provided music for the black performances that served as pastimes for the white community. Englishman John Davis, the self-professed "foot-traveller" in America, visited the "house of Mr. MacGregor" while venturing through South Carolina. While there, he witnessed "planters and young women from the neighbouring woods" celebrating the Christmas holiday season.[62] The musician for these Christmas festivities, an "old Guiana negro" named Orpheus, was a popular fiddler in that region. The music for this festival, similar to that used at many cotillions and dances for whites throughout the South, was provided by enslaved black musicians.

Facilitating these onstage performances while advocating the innate relationship between blacks and the performing arts was part and parcel of white slaveholders' attempts to define blackness and slavery, and, in so doing, to ultimately define themselves. Characterizing the black race as "carefree, infantile, hedonistic, and indifferent to their suffering" was an important part of establishing and supporting slavery.[63] Whites' construction of blackness also facilitated the perception of the African American race. Onstage performances contributed to the overarching stereotypes of blacks in the southern United States. They often represented a false reality or façade of race and social relations within the institution of slavery. Thomas Jefferson, the owner of more than one hundred fifty slaves, decreed that blacks, "whether originally a distinct race, or made distinct by time and circumstances, are inferior to the whites in the endowments both of body and mind."[64] Moreover, the architect of the Declaration of Independence used dance to illustrate the lack of reason displayed by the black race. Jefferson assessed in his writings, "They seem to require less sleep. A black, after hard labour through the day, will be induced by the slightest amusements to sit up till midnight, or later, though knowing he must be out with the first dawn of the morning." Although Jefferson wanted to assert that race is "fixed in nature, and . . . real," blackness was constructed within these onstage performances in a scripted manner, at least publicly.[65] While attempting to define the slave community, many white Southerners were supporting the institution. The promotion of these "innocent amusements" served as a central strategy in the slave owner's effort to cultivate contented subjugation while defending black bondage.[66]

The coercion of the whip that forced blacks to perform created a complex dynamic in the plantation society. These "innocent amusements," as they were termed by slavers throughout the South, were neither innocent nor amusing for the unfortunate blacks forced to succumb to their master's violent whims. Although music and dance were often part of the autonomous expression of the enslaved community, performances in the presence of and often at the command of white spectators severely altered the dynamics of this cultural expression. White overseers, drivers, and planters actively involved in the plantation community incorporated music and dance as a means by which to maintain order and productivity. Ex-slave and abolitionist Frederick Douglass recalled that it was common for white planters to order slaves to "make a noise, make a noise" during their labor.[67] This expectation and continual enforcement of black slaves to perform music, song, and dance in the presence of whites was an important element of the onstage performance.

The spectacularization of these orchestrated amusements helped to deflect the vigorous torture and abuse of blacks throughout the South.[68] Onstage performances always included the use of the whip, either literally or figuratively, to make blacks sing and dance. Douglass spoke of the manner in which, during the holidays on Mr. Edward Covey's plantation, the "fiddling, dancing" would be presented within this performance, and while the "singing of 'merry songs'" took place, "once in a while a sharp hit is given" by the slaveholders to the performing slaves.[69] Blacks, coerced either by a physical or metaphorical whip, often were aware that performing music and dance was an enforced expectation of whites in the plantation community, which also seemed to make the very real threat of violence appear theatrical and somehow less than real—at least to white viewers. Music and dance thus became tied to the violence of slavery, turning a form of amusement into one of terror. However, according to many Southern whites, the performing arts also held the power to alleviate black pain.

As one Georgian proudly boasted in the Southern newsletter *American Cotton Planter and Soil of the South*, he encouraged music because it has "positive humanizing and elevating powers."[70] This was a common belief that influenced public perceptions of slave life. Many non-slaveholders in the North and throughout Europe also correlated the performing arts and happiness. Dance was a part of the calisthenics of daily life—used for exercises, free expression, and joviality in certain white Southern communities. Virginia planter and influential eighteenth-century writer William Byrd spoke daily on his evening dances. His reflection "I prayed and had tea. I danced" appeared in nearly every entry of Byrd's journal. The planter equated dancing with his desires for "good health, good thought and good humor."[71] English visitor Isabella Lucy Bird assessed that the "dancing, singing, and other amusements" are "actively promoted" to increase the "health and cheerfulness" of the slaves.[72]

The performing arts distracted from the atrocities of the peculiar institution while comforting many Southern whites into a false sense of black complacency. Either whites portrayed music and dance as a mechanism to make slaves happy or they averred that blacks were innately happy and that music and dance were simply public signs of their mirth. Daughter of a Virginia planter, Letitia M. Burwell believed that all of the slaves on her father's plantation "were merry-hearted, and among them I never saw a discontented face. Their amusements were dancing to the music of the banjo . . . and sometimes wedding and parties."[73] Simplifying blacks into laborers and entertainers allowed for the dismissal of emotions and mental capacities. Many Southerners initiated and distributed the opinion that "Negroes are naturally prone to gaiety"; however, it remains doubtful that many of them completely believed this façade.[74]

The use of the whip to force happiness purposely went unmentioned by most planters and overseers. In 1851, one Georgia planter, Nathan Bass, won an award for his "Essay on the Treatment and Management of Slaves," in which he specifically detailed the Southern slavery system from the perspective of white planters: "Negroes thus treated and managed are prolific, cheerful, industrious and happy. They need not the driver's lash to stimulate them to do their duty, but with alacrity and cheerfulness they perform the daily duty assigned them; and when labor of the day is past they . . . partake of the . . . wholesome repast . . . which may have been prepared for them." Bass either believed or wanted the readers of the *Southern Central Agricultural Society of Georgia* to believe that slaves were generally happy, and if they were "chanting some favorite ditty" or allowed to dance, which "most of them have quite a taste" for, then slaves remained happy, willingly docile creatures.[75] Bass's assessment typified the perception of planters throughout the South. Onstage music and dance fostered these ideals and allowed for this false veneer to cover the Southern landscape.

In their attempts to control slaves and construct the mythology of slave cheerfulness, slaveholders even sought to control song lyrics. The British actress-journalist Frances Anne Kemble, in her journal on the plantation society, noted that she "heard that many of the masters and overseers . . . prohibit melancholy tunes or words, and encourage nothing but cheerful music." She believed that most "Negro melodies" contained either "senseless words" or expressed "extemporaneous chants" in the planter's "honor." Due to the secretive culture within the black community, many white onlookers were unaware of the complex nature of the songs. The enslaved community performed a variety of songs throughout their daily lives: work songs, spirituals, harvest songs, secular songs, and plantation songs all held significance for the black population. However, many blacks tailored their onstage performances to amuse and appease white onlookers. Slaveholders' instrumental participation in black music allowed many whites to live under a veil.[76] Kemble offered an example of the songs she heard, which she believed to be "astonishingly primitive" and lacking meaning.

> Jenny shake her toe at me,
> Jenny gone away;
> Jenny shake her toe at me,
> Jenny gone away.
> Hurrah! Miss Susy, oh!
> Jenny gone away;
> Hurrah! Miss Susy, oh!
> Jenny gone away.

Kemble explained, "What the obnoxious Jenny meant by shaking her toe, whether defiance or mere departure, I never could ascertain."[77] Kemble's observation misses the underlying meaning of flirtation that Jenny was exhibiting by shaking her toe.[78] However, this may have been an intentional consequence, designed within the black community.

The interpretation of slave songs was shrouded in ambiguity due both to slaves' not wanting whites to fully understand their private world and to whites' deluding themselves into believing slaves were docile and happy. Many whites purposely and publicly asserted the nonsensical nature of black songs in order to demote the intellectual and cultural achievements of blacks. Part of the role that whites played in the onstage performances included inscribing upon blacks a childlike ignorance by downgrading their song lyrics. But slaves had their own intentions and meaning, and their views of performing arts challenged white plans.

Many slave songs held meanings unbeknownst to whites, while other songs were tailored to reflect the Southern façade. Take, for example, the following lyrics: "Me sing all day, me sleep all night; Me hab no care; my heart is light; Me tink not what to-morrow bring; Me happy, so me sing."[79] Songs praising slavery and the slave master could be heard throughout the South and were well known. For many outside of the South, happy lyrics, dancing bodies, and the sounds of music playing all revealed the positive nature of slavery. For many white Southerners, it was a purposeful façade that they continually enforced. By influencing the song lyrics, constructing stages, and casting blacks as innate performers, whites were not only defining blackness but also attempting to construct their own identity.

Onstage performances helped white Southerners construct a unique cultural identity by positioning blacks as subordinate and, by doing so, classifying themselves as superior.[80] Slavery exerted a profound effect on the development of political, social, and religious facets of Southern white society. Because many white Southerners claimed that music and dance were innate, those slaveholders could define themselves as generous in allowing its continuance within the enslaved community. Many would openly state that they "conceive it a duty" to the planter and enslaved community not to "change this inclination in [the slaves] but rather promote it," contending their own benevolence was an aspect of their whiteness.[81] To defend slavery and their role in the institution, many white slaveholders and overseers asserted their paternalistic duty to the black bondsmen and bondswomen. One South Carolina planter, bragging about his benevolence as a master, made this especially evident: "What can exalt the character and standing of a man to promote and spread widely happiness, not only amongst his own dependents but also, by his good example, through his neighborhood?"[82] He continued by stating that it was each planter's "duty" to promote the "welfare and happiness of many of his fellow creatures," which slaveholders believed they accomplished by continually coercing music and dance.[83] Ignoring their influence on black music and dance, the planters reasserted the erroneous belief that the performance arts were innate to enslaved blacks, a fable that served as evidence of the intellectual and emotional inferiority of the race. The public presentation of black slaves reflected the character and status of whites. In a series of letters to his brother, Henry C. Knight wrote in 1824 on how to assess slavery: "Where they have kind masters, the slaves look cheerful and happy."[84] However, this method, once again, neglected the manner in which whites purposely orchestrated the "cheerful and happy" appearance of their slaves. In addition to slaveholders who coerced music and dance from their slaves, whites who attended as spectators also defined race, both black and white, through their role as audience and often choreographers.

Southerners contributed much to their region's folklore of plantation settings and happy bondsmen and bondswomen singing and dancing.[85] "Music hath charms to soothe the savage beast," explained Georgia planter and physician John Wilson. "The musical tastes and talents of negroes are well-known to all Southerners. Here in the South many of them seem to have a kind of sixth sense—that is, a musical taste." Believing himself to be an excellent planter and businessman, John Wilson, in 1860 in the Southern newsletter *American Cotton Planter and Soil of the South*, asserted the myth that slaves in the South were innate performers regardless of their condition: "Indeed, Southern negroes seem to have a natural gift for music, and such thing as a non-singing negroe is almost unknown." In response to general knowledge about blacks in the South, Dr. Wilson addressed whether blacks' musical inclinations were natural or caused by the positive influences of slavery. Speaking as an expert, the Southern planter declared that "we are not prepared" to accurately confirm those beliefs; however, "be this as it may, there can be no doubt that the musical proclivities of negroes add much of the charm of Southern life—that they greatly increase the happiness of the negro by cheering him in his labors, and consequently" are "highly conducive" to promoting their health.[86] Dr. Wilson revealed in his advice to planters a major element of the Southern folklore. The "charm of Southern life" that Dr. Wilson described was part of a ruse, the construction of which began in the seventeenth century and which was firmly established by the antebellum period. The stereotypes of the enslaved community held a dual burden on bondswomen, being labeled due to their race as innately happy performers and due to their gender as naturally lascivious.

One constant throughout all early American societies, North and South, was the subordination of women, and this was doubly true for

Illustration of happy, dancing slaves being watched by white spectators in an effort to display a public image of contented blacks in
North American slavery. In the caption the elderly male slave says,
"God Bless you massa! You feed and clothe us. When we are sick
you nurse us, and when too old to work, you provide for us!" The
master responds, "These poor creatures are a sacred legacy from my
ancestors and while a dollar is left me, nothing shall be spared to
increase their comfort and happiness." This illustration was created
by Edward Williams Clay and published in 1841 to illustrate the
conditions of blacks in America as positive. (Cartoon Prints, American Collection, Prints & Photographs Division, Library of Congress,
LC-USZ62–89745.) Courtesy of Library of Congress.

African American women. Many whites invariably interpreted the physical movements and musical style of black females as lustful, seductive behavior that justified the subsequent actions of many white males. As the development of race was being performed on plantations and for white spectators, so was sex. Possessing both a racialized and gendered identity resulted in the assignation of additional societal expectations and attributes to black women. Black females were in a vulnerable position throughout the slave era, and the forced displays of music, song, and dance contributed to their condition. As ex-slave Harriet Jacobs wrote in her memoir of slavery, "Slavery is terrible for men; but it is far more terrible for women. Superadded to the burden common to all, they have wrongs, and suffering, and mortifications peculiarly their own."[87] Black women had the burden of entertainment and labor, similar to their male counterparts, but also upheld the horrendous role of providing sexual pleasure to their white masters, which often resulted in children. Therefore, appeasing white men's sexual and economic interests dovetailed. The displays of black females dancing entailed an erotic voyeurism for many white male spectators. Slave musician Old Dick recalled that his master often requested that he play in order to encourage such erotic spectatorship. On "moonlight night(s) he would set me to play, and the wenches to dance," recalled Old Dick. According to Old Dick's testimony, his master was "mighty ficious [*sic*] when he got among the negur [*sic*] wenches. He used to say that a likely negur wench was fit to be a queen: and I forget how many queens he had among the girls on the two plantations."[88] Ironically, this particular master's sexual interest in the dancing ladies resulted in his engaging in sexual relations with several of the women, which in turn led to his murder by the husband of one of the performing slave women.[89] The coercion of blacks to frolic contributed to a system of rape that was no less pervasive and structured than the slave system itself. Former slave Ellen Campbell remembered that during frolics on Saturday nights, the young white men of the area would attend and "push de nigger bucks aside and dance wid de wenches."[90] White men dancing with black women was a part of the sexual abuse prevalent throughout the institution.

The presumed promiscuous dances of black women proliferated into negative images of oversexualized black women that affected the experiences of slave women beginning in the West Indies and continuing in North America. Jamaican planter Edward Long commented in 1774 on the "languishing and easy" motions of the black women's dances he witnessed on his plantation. As a spectator of female dancing, he assessed that if black women were "that lascivious," then "a man could scarcely be blamed for succumbing against overwhelming odds."[91] Long's correlation between black women's dance and wantonness contributed to the planter's excuse for any sexual assaults against these females. Similar to Long's eighteenth-century account, Henry Krehbiel used comparable language in his description of black women dancing in the Deep South in the nineteenth century: "As for the dance—in which the women do not take their feet off the ground—it is as lascivious as is possible."[92] Such views contributed to dominating stereotypes that proliferated in early America. Black women danced in West Africa and throughout slavery as a form of cultural expression, but white spectators claimed that these performances represented overt sexuality, which was solidified in the racial and gender identity of black women. For the dancers, dancing held many and varied meanings. For whites committed to racial slavery, perceptions of those dances became a mechanism for defiling and denigrating black women and building a powerful racial order.

Black women being sexually abused and forced to perform sexual acts contributed to the trauma of slavery. This practice was so well entrenched that ex-slave William Thomas believed that music and dance were elements of the prostitution of enslaved black women. He remembered that "Some masters . . . make their female slaves prostitute themselves for hire. . . . hundreds of these women are found on Sundays . . . where there is plenty of singing and dancing to draw the people to come there."[93] Slave masters forced black women to seduce white men, using music and dance as sexual invitations; through this distortion, white slave masters contributed to the misconception of black females as lascivious. The prostitution of black women on the Sabbath underlined the black women's purported lack of morality. Women and girls were compelled to sing and dance in a fashion designed to invite sexual activity and to confirm whites' image of the black woman as seductress. Whites then concluded that black women displayed their lascivious nature through music, song, and dance in order to seduce white men. Onlookers often ignored the cultural significance of West African cultural trends in bondswomen's dance style, interpreting their movements instead as overtly sexual. One nineteenth-century observer stated in New Orleans that the "female dancer is all languishing, and easy in her motions . . . particularly in the motion of her hips . . . the execution of this wriggle."[94] Black women's use of the lower portions of their bodies in particular dance movements was used as evidence of their lascivious nature. White men (and, presumably, their wives) used this myth to convince themselves that sexual intercourse with slaves was not rape after all, but an answer to a black woman's shameless invitation.

The forced performance of black slaves, specifically women, confirmed many whites' beliefs that black women were innately oversexualized and therefore not able to be raped. Laws supported this; the rape of slave women was seldom considered a crime.

Enslaved female children also were forced into performances that often were sexualized. In 1861, Lavinia Bell was interviewed in Canada concerning her illegal kidnapping and enslavement in Texas. Although born free in Washington, Bell lived the majority of her youth on the plantation of William and Polly Whirl. There as a young teen "she was brought up as a 'show girl,' taught to dance, sing, cackle like a hen, or crow like a rooster," often for a crowd that the Mistress would attract from throughout the region.[95] After these performances, the young Bell would be forced back to the cotton field. Ironically, during these performances, she often was scantily dressed, sometimes wearing "no clothes" and often "exposed to the glare of the southern sun." Slaves' dance movements may have been sexualized, that being contingent on the type of dancing the slaveholder desired; however, the lack of clothing and the persistent reputation of the Jezebel black female caused these forced performances to be sexual and maybe even inviting for many white males, and females, present.

Southern slaveholders purposely created these images of black inferiority, sexual aggressiveness, and contentedness in bondage to garner acceptance and curb criticism from the North and Europe. The music and dance of slaves, which whites depicted as clear evidence of all three of these stereotypes, became an advertisement for the South. Slavery was constructed on public perceptions of race, sex, and power. The Southern system was built upon fictional ideals that needed to be reinforced by the enslaved population's performing music and dance. In order for the fragile master-slave, dominant-subjugate dichotomy to survive, Southern planters needed the public performances of music and dance not only for personal assurance but to gain general acceptance from the external communities.

Throughout the South whites always played roles beyond that of spectator and choreographer, for they also acted as performers. An aspect of the performance was their portrayal as benevolent masters. Performances were meant to pacify the slave populace as well as satisfy the non-slaveholding public, who regularly criticized and condemned the peculiar institution. English journalist William Howard Russell traveled extensively throughout the United States in the mid-nineteenth century to report firsthand the conflict between the North and South, which would eventually lead to secession and war. From April through June 1861, Russell traveled throughout the South to observe Southern whites and slaves in an attempt to fully understand the controversial institution. During his travels, he observed, "There were abundant evidences, that [the slaves] were well treated."[96] The majority of planters whom Russell encountered during his travels tried to display to Russell their slaves' happiness by having them perform music and dance for him, particularly because he was an Englishman and, more important, a journalist. On May 10, 1861, while traveling on a steamer through Mississippi, "a dance of Negroes was arranged by an enthusiast, who desired to show how 'happy they were.'" This foreign visitor realized that these onstage performances were a "favourite theme of Southerners." Such exhibitions of happy slaves and benevolent masters occurred throughout Russell's excursions. He continually referred to the public assertion throughout the South that "our Negroes are the happiest, most contented, and most comfortable people on the face of the earth." At St. Andrew's Parish in North Carolina, the mistress, Mary Crafts, brought the journalist to the slave quarters and coerced the children to sing for them. "The elder children were dressed into line; they then began to shuffle their flat feet, to clap their hands, and to drawl out in a monotonous sort of chant," performances which were later rewarded with "lumps of sugar." In almost every region Russell visited throughout the South, white slaveholders pointed to their allowance of music and dance as evidence of their kindness. Although he did encounter some planters who did not "grant" the slaves the "indulgence of a dance," the journalist soon began to evaluate the plantations he visited according to many of these performance scenes.[97]

Yet the English observer was not completely convinced of these planters' goodwill. Throughout his journeys Russell noticed that the performing blacks often were "ragged, dirty, shoeless."[98] Such observations contradicted the image that slaveholders attempted so diligently to portray. Another English visitor, John Davis, recognized that in the "opulent families" throughout the South, "there is always a negro placed on the lookout to announce the coming of any visitant; and the moment a carriage or horsemen is descried, each negro changes his every-day garb" of "ragged" clothing to a "magnificent suit of livery."[99] Similar to Russell, Davis and several other astute visitors recognized that Southern planters presented a guise to foreign visitors. Russell also noticed that the young children brought before him to sing and dance on the Crafts plantation "came shyly . . . oftentimes running away in spite of the orders of their haggard mammies, till they were chased, captured, and brought back by their elder brethren."[100]

The journalist glimpsed a private world, where the complex relationships between slaveholders and their slaves often were masked beneath the veneer of music, dance, and contentment. Many slaves recognized that music and dance were amusements and deceptive displays for whites; however, the slave children Russell watched had yet to learn their role as laborers and entertainers. Slave children had to practice these roles through onstage performances, such as those that Russell witnessed during his journey throughout the South. The journalist was not the only Southern visitor who noticed this ruse, and criticism grew throughout the late antebellum era.[101] In response, slaveholders redoubled their efforts to present happy slaves singing and dancing for whites, their proud parents.

The intentional Southern ruse was advertised propaganda that contributed to segments of the American and European populations' accepting the onstage performances as a part of Southern culture, black culture, and slavery. German trader J. G. Flugel contributed several journal accounts of slaves dancing in New Orleans. Believing that these dances had "postures and movements" that "somewhat resembled those of monkeys," Flugel excused their behavior due to their "ignorance of anything like civilization." This European tourist believed that white slave masters purposely "withhold everything from them that in the least might add to the cultivation of their minds" in an effort to keep them in their positions as slaves. However, while concluding that the fault of ignorance lay with the slave owner, he also believed that one "must not be surprised" at the slave dancing because this was "at least natural and they are free" to follow their passions. The strategies of Southern planters were effective; Flugel and several other foreign and Northern visitors accepted these performers as justifying the subjugated status of blacks while it also validating the racialized premises of the institution of slavery.

By the nineteenth century, black music and dance attracted tourists from all over to witness these well-known festivities. As a form of propaganda for the North and England, black music and dance performances were publicly displayed as a defense of slavery, as was made evident through the events on Major Ranny's plantation. Ranny was well known throughout New Orleans for hosting many "gay gatherings" for black slaves that were intended for white spectators and often covered by the local newspapers.[102] For example, the planter appeared in an article in the *Daily Picayune* for hosting the wedding of his cook to another slave. The "Uncolored Account of a Colored Wedding" detailed the music of a fiddle, dances such as the Virginia break-down, and a large supper that Major Ranny hosted for his black and white guests. The newspaper emphasized the open dance and music that "rose with its voluptuous swell, and all went merry as a marriage bell." Almost a year after this black marriage celebration on the New Orleans plantation, Ranny's antics were highlighted again during his popular holiday festivities. At twelve o'clock on Circus Street, friends, family, and slaves gathered at the request of the major to celebrate the New Year. Welcoming the onset of 1851, "this gentleman gave his negroes, some forty or fifty in number, what is called in fashionable parlance, 'A dejeuner a la fourchette,'" the *Daily Delta* reported.[103] It started with a feast of a "haunch of venison, a large roast turkey, a round of beef, etc.," and an assortment of liquors, including "brandy, whiskey and claret decanters." After the invited white guests partook of the planter's hospitality, the slave community commenced enjoying the plentiful meal. "The negroes entered in squads, one party relieving the other," while Ranny, the guests, and the invited local media watched. The event was an entertaining spectacle for the white guests, especially when the enslaved community "drank many toasts" for their master. The newspaper reported the exclamations of one slave who attempted to curry his master's favor by toasting, "Der New Canal Company-May de run on de banks of der canal increase." His optimism for the financial future of his master was followed by Ranny's "patriarchal advice" to the "comfortable and contented" slaves, as the *Daily Delta* reported. The spectacle on Major Ranny's plantation was only highlighted by the festivity of music and dance that the slaves provided. Although the enslaved population offered their well wishes, most likely they did so mockingly; these performances placated white fears of potential rebellion while amusing the white onlookers. For Ranny, the slaves acted as entertainment, labor, potential wealth, and a conduit to status. Ranny carefully choreographed the entire scene while also enacting his role as the benevolent paternalist for not only his friends and family but for the wider reading public. Wisely inviting the *Daily Delta* to show the "comfort, happiness and contentment of our slaves" allowed for the orchestrated amusements to positively advertise the overall institution of slavery while conveniently veiling Ranny's fears of the current political and social turmoil concerning the major debate on the continuance of slavery between the North and South.

The events on Ranny's plantation contributed to more than simply an entertaining story about activities in New Orleans. The *Daily Delta* was intentionally reacting to the social climate of antebellum America, responding to the "erroneous opinions" circulating in the North and within the growing abolitionist movement. In fact, the newspaper reporter directly proclaimed that he "wish[es] Thompson, or Garitt [*sic*] Smith," two well-known Northern abolitionists, "had seen it," for they surely would have not only been entertained but would also have understood that the Southern slavery system had "good masters" and happy slaves. This event ushered in the New Year and also celebrated a society that was built on a façade of paternalism and elated subjugation. In other words, it was a performance. The slaves' apparent elation during the holiday represented more than a simple New Year's jubilation; the article insisted that the slaves drank to the health of their master but also "wished" their "colored bredden at the North has as good masters."[104] The *Daily Delta* attempted to insert the cheerful demeanor and pleasantries of the enslaved community, for this event was used to veil the reality of these performances and the atrocities of the institution of slavery.

While major holidays such as Christmas, New Year's, and the Fourth of July were a time of celebration for both races, slaveholders also used those events to choreograph their power over and supposed benevolence toward their slaves. Respite from work, visits from loved ones, the exchanging of gifts, feasts, libations, and plenty of music and dance were often aspects of holiday festivities. As one Alabama planter explained, "Frequent holidays are given and as much interest as possible . . . to make them look forward to them with pleasure as seasons of enjoyment, where they can revel in the fun and frolic."[105] Many planters and overseers made as many provisions for their slaves as they did for their own families during the holiday season. They used the festivities of the holiday season to protect their own interests in portraying themselves as good masters, thereby defending slavery against increasing criticism from outsiders. One former bondsman recognized that the "holidays serve the purpose of keeping the minds of the slaves occupied with prospective pleasure, within the limits of slavery."[106] Former rice planter Elizabeth W. A. Pringle reminisced of the holiday season off the coast of South Carolina: "Every negro on the plantation came soon after daylight Christmas morning, to give good wishes and to receive substantial gifts themselves." She explained that the holiday festivities lasted for three days, during which time the slaves "always ended the day by two hours dancing on the piazza of the 'big house' to the music of fiddle, tambourine, bones, drum, and sticks."[107] With much nostalgia, this slave mistress spoke of the Christmas holiday as positive for both blacks and whites on the plantation. In many depictions of the Southern landscape, the holiday season with happy slaves and benevolent slave masters was a common image.

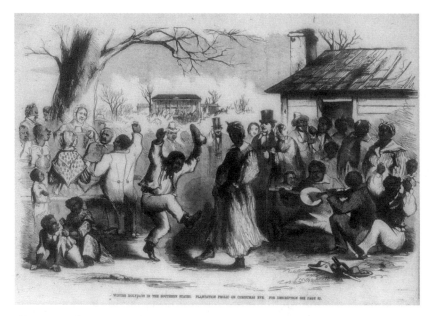

Illustration first appeared in *Frank Leslie's Illustrated Newspaper* on December 26, 1857, as a part of the false image of slavery, depicting a plantation frolic on Christmas Eve that has black slaves singing and dancing for a black and white audience. (Miscellaneous Items in High Demand Collection, Prints & Photographs Division, Library of Congress, LC-USZ62–49657.) Courtesy of the Library of Congress.

Liquor was used as a part of the music and dance festivities to coax the enslaved community to perform their role in the Southern ruse. Ex-slave Frederick Douglass asserted that whites used the holiday season to keep "down the spirit of insurrection among slaves."[108] Ex-slave Henry Wright, who was born on Mr. Phil House's plantation outside of Atlanta, similarly recalled that beyond "presents given at Christmas," some slaveholders also "gave each family half a gallon of whiskey."[109] Similar to building stages, providing musical instruments, and using the whip for coercion, liquor was a secretive part of the onstage displays. "New Years Day was no different from other days, except that Marse John gave the grown folks whiskey to drink that day like he did on Christmas morning," recalled Mose Davis, a former slave from Georgia. Another bondsman, Green Willbanks, recalled, "They always had something like brandy, cider, or whiskey to stimulate the slaves on Christmas Day. All we knowed bout Christmas was eating and drinking."[110] Bondsmen and bondswomen often remembered their masters offering liquor to the slaves to induce their participation in the Southern façade.

The holiday season was also a potentially perilous time for white slaveholders due to opportunities for the enslaved community to rebel and run away. It could be a depressing time for many blacks facing the rigors of bondage. Christmas and the New Year were often a time of rest during which the enslaved community might receive several days' repose from labor. This period was an optimal time to run away, plan rebellions, or revolt; therefore, liquor was used as a distraction through intoxication. "These holidays are conductors or safety valves to carry off the explosive elements inseparable from the human mind, when reduced to the condition of slavery," proclaimed Douglass. "We were induced to drink, I among the rest, and when the holidays were over, we all staggered . . . to our various fields of work."[111] As Mr. Wright noted, liquor given by slave masters made "the parties more lively"; however, Willbanks recognized that whites "had to be mighty careful about things like that in order to keep down uprising."[112] Ironically, despite the references to liquor at holiday celebrations, many white slave masters asserted their protest against slaves drinking. In 1851, a Mississippi planter stated in an article in *DeBow's Review* that he did not permit "spirits to be brought on the plantation, or used by any negro."[113] A few years later in Georgia, S. D. Wagg advised his fellow overseers, "Negroes should never be allowed the use of spirituous liquors, only when given to them by their master, or by his discretion . . . they are almost naturally fond of it."[114] The overseer's assessment of black slaves' affinity for liquor did not take into account the pressure placed on them by whites to drink, especially during the holiday season. The conflicting messages that slaves should not be allowed "ardent spirits" and that liquor should be allowed "for the pleasure it gives them" were prevalent throughout the South. Regardless of whites' proclamations concerning blacks and liquor, numerous slave testimonies provided evidence that alcoholic beverages were a common aspect of holiday celebrations, even if this element was hidden in onstage performances. The provision of intoxicating drinks by white slaveholders, drivers, and overseers to their slaves was a significant part of the "gross fraud" present throughout the Southern slavery system, as it was labeled in Douglass's autobiography.[115]

The Southern ruse was such an active element of the institution of slavery that many abolitionists attempted to remove the shroud of Southern paternalism and black innate joviality. In 1838, abolitionist Angelina Grimke, at the Antislavery Convention of American Women held at Pennsylvania Hall, the popular antislavery meeting place, addressed the

Southern mythical image of slavery while revealing the backstage nature of music and dance: "As a Southerner . . . I witnessed for many years its demoralizing influences and its destructiveness to human happiness. I have never seen a happy slave. I have seen him dance in his chains, it is true, but he was not happy. There is a wide difference between happiness and mirth. Man can not enjoy happiness while his manhood is destroyed. Slaves, however, may be, and sometimes are mirthful."[116] Grimke's testimony about the injustices of the Southern slave system revealed the erroneous images planters attempted to project. The forced displays of music, dance, and song attempted to display "mirth" through an exhibit of laughing, smiling, and jumping black bodies. Grimke recognized these scenes as staged performances created to justify the subjugation of blacks in the United States. The occasional "mirthful" disposition of blacks represented an exterior view intentionally created by the white master class that distorted the turmoil experienced among the slave population. As a child of a planter, Grimke disclosed the private life, or backstage, of many of these plantation performances.[117] She was forced to permanently flee her home as a result of her betrayal of white mythology. Many abolitionists throughout the North and England likewise attempted to expose the false belief that "singing among slaves" was "evidence of their contentment and happiness." Other abolitionists seemed determined to accept the Southern ruse.

Life onstage in the plantation South presented a false reality; it was constructed on a public image meant to support plantation society. Whites needed to believe their slaves were happy and contented in order to justify slavery while validating their role in the system. Although whites continually coerced music and dance from their enslaved population, such performances often were incongruous aspects of order in the slave society. The performing arts never simply represented the complacency of blacks, though whites continually enforced this ideology. The desire to construct this association derived from whites' interest in defining blackness and then enforcing their definition upon slaves. Southern planters purposefully constructed and asserted myths of blackness, whiteness, and the plantation community, but this façade proved quite fragile. Blacks were aware of this façade and used ingenuity to negotiate power through music and dance. Many whites, too, knew that music and dance, especially the onstage performances, were part of this false reality that only veiled their fears of black rebellion.

4 Backstage

"White folks do as they please, and the darkies do as they can"

It was a typical Sunday on that September 9, 1739, in South Carolina. The enslaved communities throughout a burgeoning North America customarily gathered on this day for the upkeep of their homes, to enhance family solidarity, and to exchange the collective cultural expressions of music, song, and dance. These gatherings allowed for a "temporary relaxation, the brief deliverance from fear and from the lash, producing a metamorphosis in their appearance and demeanor."[1] The black community relished the times they were able to come together for these music and dance gatherings, affectionately known among blacks as frolics, so when dozens of slaves began to gather, they did not initially garner attention from the white community as out of the ordinary. But then the insurrection began with several slave conspirators killing a local storekeeper before ransacking the store to steal firearms, ammunition, and other weapons.[2] Led by a bondsman named Jemmy, twenty slaves marched through town killing any white person and burning down every plantation they came across. The rebels marched, "calling out Liberty," and beat "two drums" while pursuing "all the white people they met with, and killing Man Woman and Child," according to one witness, General Oglethorpe. During their march, the rebels "set to dancing, Singing and beating Drums to draw more Negroes to them." One of the few witnesses recalled that the music and dance inspired other enslaved blacks to join the rebellion. "They increased every minute by new Negroes coming to them, so that they were above Sixty, some say a hundred."[3] With the sound of music encouraging the rebels and spurring more to revolt, these bondsmen and bondswomen, "acting boldly," battled the militia before eventually being dispersed and some defeated. Later, however, several slaves formed another group and proceeded toward the maroon city of St. Augustine in the free Spanish colony of Florida. About ten of them were caught fleeing the next day. The insurrection was still not over, however. A week later, a small group of slaves fought the militia about thirty miles from the original rebellion site.

Stono's Rebellion, named in honor of the Stono Bridge where the insurrection began, within twenty miles of Charleston, represented the complicated nature of music and dance within the emerging Southern plantation society in the early eighteenth century. Although whites used music and dance to assert and legitimize their dominance, the performing arts always held a concealed power for the enslaved populations. Their dances and drums were used as tools of encouragement for the rebels. Throughout West Africa, continued in the Middle Passage and brought to the New World, the South Carolina enslaved population carried with them their homelands' culture of music and dance. Drums in this insurrection could have represented two roles, first as a means of communication, for throughout West Africa the "talking drum" was an aspect of many societies, and second as a means of encouragement similar to "war drums" that were used during battles through their homeland region. Also, dancing was a political, cultural, and social expression that held long traditions throughout many areas of West Africa and parts of Central Africa as building martial acrobatic skills. Dancing to prepare for war, to express hand-to-hand combat, to train, and to establish stability, reflexes, and parrying skills was common in many West African cultures. Specifically, the war dances of the Central African kingdom of Kongo were well known at this time, and many African slaves in South Carolina originated in that region.[4] In some of the cultures that West and Central Africans brought to North America, dancing was a tool for sedition.

South Carolina experienced a continuous influx of African slaves entering the region to tend the growing rice fields. In the early eighteenth century, South Carolina was estimated to have three times as many blacks as whites.[5] South Carolina planters preferred slaves from Gambia, the Gold Coast, and Angola because rice was grown in these regions and so these slaves would have had previous experience with rice cultivation. Bondspeople from these areas accounted for 70 percent of the thirty-nine thousand blacks in South Carolina, more than half of whom had been there fewer than ten years by the 1730s.[6] The insurgents also illustrated the influence of a developing North American culture through their language. As they marched through the region declaring "liberty" through a sign and chant, these bondsmen and bondswomen were asserting an English term and ideology in their uprising. Also, they were well aware of the political climate of the region. With the impending war between England and Spain and South Carolina's close proximity to Spanish Florida some 150 miles south, the large, mainly African-born enslaved population picked the precise time of political and social unrest and the precise location, near free territory, to stage a rebellion. Instead of running away, these particular rebels protested publicly to the political and social system they were forced to endure through an often-sanctioned day—Sunday—when they were allowed to express their refashioned homeland cultures, while at the same time, displaying new traditions. As scholar Paul Gilroy declared, "[A]ll blacks in the West stand between (at least) two great cultural assemblages, both of which have mutated through the course of the modern world that formed them and assumed new configurations."[7] From the language used, protest style and performing arts exerted these South Carolina bondsmen and bondswomen expressed a polyethnic developing culture that infused West African, West Central African, West Indian, English, and North American customs in their protest.

The day chosen by the South Carolina rebels to stage an insurrection represented a developing culture among the enslaved black community. Bondsmen and bondswomen in South Carolina were able to gain momentum early in their insurrection due to the element of surprise. Sunday gatherings of music, song, and dance among the enslaved black community were commonly practiced early on throughout the colonies, so the dancing and drums did not garner attention, initially. This particular Sunday began typically for the white community until the lingering fear of slave uprising manifested. In colonial America Sunday gatherings were controversial due to religious sentiment; however, that was not the only trepidation whites had of black congregations. As one eighteenth-century Louisiana planter remarked, "No thing is more to be dreaded than to see the Negroes assemble together . . . under the pretence of . . . the dance. . . . for it is in those tumultuous meetings that they . . . plot their rebellions."[8] As early as the late seventeenth century, lawmakers began attempting to restrict black gatherings. In 1692, New York Common Council began passing laws to restrict black activities on Sunday. Eight years later, New York lawmakers attempted to control Sunday gatherings by reducing to three the number of slaves allowed to congregate and by reminding masters to control their slaves on Sunday.[9] This fear was apparent in the slave code of 1740, institutionalized in South

Carolina following the rebellion, which specifically stated that "due care be taken to restrain the wanderings and meeting of Negroes and other slaves . . . more especially on Saturday nights, Sundays and other holidays, and their using . . . or keeping of drums, horns, or other loud instruments."[10] The paranoia continued into the early national era, especially in the well-established slave society of South Carolina; however, most other regions initiated laws to prohibit black Sunday gatherings due to fear of rebellion. For example, a 1794 law made it illegal for persons to allow slaves to congregate, dance, and drink on their premises without the written permission of their owners.[11] Whites often masked their fear of rebellion, but it protruded through their continuous attempts to restrict blacks from congregating without supervision. The 1794 law built on an earlier piece of legislation adopted in Charleston, South Carolina, in 1740, which stated, "[I]t is absolutely necessary to the safety of this province that all due care be taken to restrain the wandering and meeting of negroes . . . or use or keeping of drums, horns, or other loud instruments, which may call together or give sign or notice to one another of their wicked designs."[12]

Regardless of the continual regulation against black Sunday gatherings, the enslaved community continued to play music, sing, and dance on Sundays throughout North America from the colonial era until the Civil War. English Traveler Nicholas Cresswell noticed in 1774 during his travels through Virginia that Sundays were the "only days . . . [they] have to themselves, they generally meet together and muse themselves with dancing," music, and song.[13] For decades regulation against Sunday gatherings existed in New Orleans; under Spanish rule in 1786 the army attempted to outlaw the "dances of the colored people." Regardless, the widespread dancing of blacks, free and enslaved, in New Orleans continued. A visitor in 1799 noted that "vast numbers of negro slaves, men, women and children assembled together on the levee, drumming, fifing and dancing in large rings." The use of drums in New Orleans can be seen throughout eighteenth and nineteenth centuries, even after the numerous laws attempted to regulate the potentially dangerous instrument. Slaves commonly used instruments to revel in early sixteenth- and seventeenth-century colonial slavery in the West Indies, with Jamaica specifically forbidding the use of drums and horns, since these were means of communication that might be used to help to resist, rebel, and run away. Drum prohibitions, like many other elements of colonial slave codes, proved difficult to enforce. In the West Indies and from New York to New Orleans, enslaved blacks openly violated these types of laws. The mid-nineteenth-century comment by former slave Rosa Sallins from Georgia Sea Islands illustrates this violation as well: "Duh folks heah beat the drum tuh let em know about [the frolics] in uddah settlements."[14] Despite more than a century of prohibitions, slaves still used drums for communication, recreation, and resistance, and they continued to congregate on Sundays.

Bondsman and bondswomen resisted white intrusion on Sunday gatherings while continually refashioning their homeland music and dance cultures and adapting American and European traditions throughout North America. Music and dance during Sunday gatherings or at any other time they chose to assemble often represented a manner of resistance against the subjugation of slavery; ironically, such expression was also an aspect of white's defense of slavery. However, music and dance were always more complicated than mere public signs of black innate happiness, as propagated by whites. Such pursuits benefited the daily lives of blacks while contrastingly subjugating, humiliating, and stereotyping the racial group. For the enslaved community, the performing arts strategically bestrode agency and subjugation. Music and dance symbolized a complicated dynamic within the slave community. The performing arts contributed to the development of a dual world that blacks continually straddled, one side representing entertainment and subjugation, the other symbolizing resistance and an emerging culture. It occupied a sacred position in the private, backstage world that the enslaved community created. Backstage performances allowed for the expression of aspects of music and dance that were often invisible to the whites. In the enslaved community, frolics or frolicking was a social time that allowed for an exchange of music and dance and provided autonomous freedoms. Music and dance existed among the few personal expressions allowed among the bondsmen and bondswomen. "Even with all the hardships that slaves had to suffer, they still had time to have fun and to enjoy themselves," remembered ex-slave Henry Wright.[15] These pursuits also held a complex and conflicting role in the white community: music and dance were forms of support and propaganda for proslavery advocates; simultaneously, such activities were also a cultural expression that illustrated blacks' continual assault on subjugation and demeaning characteristics. Whites both promoted music and dance while also prohibiting the same expression; it was an inherent contradiction of the American slavery system. Ironically, blacks were strategic in their manipulation and adaptation of music and dance to benefit their community.

Illustration of "The Old Plantation" shows a late-eighteenth-century portrayal of slaves on a South Carolina plantation expressing their culture in music and dance. Courtesy of Abby Aldrich Rockefeller Folk Art Museum, Colonial Williamsburg Foundation Gift of Abby Aldrich Rockefeller.

As early as the colonial period, bondsman and bondswomen developed a distinct folklife. Historian William Pierson's research regarding blacks in eighteenth-century New England (mainly Massachusetts, Connecticut, and Rhode Island) illustrates that the culture of music and dance was a continuance of the homeland traditions and "Yankee ways to create a truly Afro-American folk culture."[16] Evident in their parades and festivals—especially Negro Election Day, when the enslaved community elected their own governors and kings annually—black New Englanders were able to develop a distinct community, regardless of their small numbers compared to the white population and notwithstanding their farm rather than planation culture. Similarly in New York and New Jersey, the enslaved and free black colonial communities' refashioning of the Dutch Anglican holiday of Pinkster Day illuminates the early cultural development that could vary by region.[17] In the South, as a slave society solidified with large numbers of African-born and West Indian blacks entering the region, there were often stronger concentrations of African-based cultures that infused with European and North American traditions.[18] In the mid- to late eighteenth century the mainly American-born enslaved community developed a variety of holidays that varied according to region, crop, and ancestral background. Some common festivities remembered by former slave Mose Davis were "cornshuckings, cotton pickings, and quilting" festivities.[19] These specific events allowed the enslaved community to work together while creating unique customs. Born in Jackson County, Alabama, John Finnely remembered that, as a slave on Martin Finnely's planation, when it was time for "corn huskin' everybody come to one place . . . while we huskin' us sing lots."[20] This was a common aspect of slave life throughout the South.[21] Former bonds-man Green Willbanks of Georgia mentioned that "once a year they had big cornshuckings," which would "lead off in all the singing; that was done to whoops up the work."[22] As Willbanks illustrates, these events incorporated entertainment within slaves' daily work. They often used music and dance to keep pace within the field. Corn-shucking songs in-corporated fast-paced tempos that could be heard for miles during harvest season. As one song stated, "Come to shuck that corn to-night; come to shuck with all your might; come to shuck all in sight, come to shuck that corn to-night."[23] This song may have served as a public announce-ment to invite blacks from neighboring plantations to the festival and also provided a rhythmic cadence to increase productivity in the fields. Estella Jones remembered that on the plantation on which she was born, a "moonlight cotton pickin' party" began whenever any slave did not meet their daily quota. These parties, similar to "pea shellin'" parties, were common on Jones's plantation and functioned as an inventive way to alleviate the daily struggles of hard labor and to foster community.[24] These holidays sometimes functioned as both onstage and backstage events. White slaveholders greatly benefited from these work-related fes-tivals, which increased productivity and entertained whites, who were often present; however, the gatherings also contributed to the cohesive-ness of black communities. Backstage, neighboring bondsmen and bonds-women were able to congregate, exchange information, and possibly plan rebellions, while such encoutners also provided psychological uplift through encouragement in communal merriment. One former Georgia slave fondly remembered that during corn-shucking festivities, "slaves from other plantations would come over and help 'em," wearing their "good clothes" and challenging each other to see who could perform "de huskin'" the fastest.[25] Although corn-shucking, pea-shelling, and cotton-picking parties often served both the enslaved and white communities, some of these work-related festivities were meant only for the benefit and solidarity of the black community, especially quilting parties.

Music and dance became particularly important to the bond among black women within the slave community.[26] The dual burden of being both a female and a slave distinctly affected the daily experiences of black women. Succumbing to their expected gendered role, black women continually came together for the maintenance of their black communities. This was made evident through quilting parties, during which "four folks wuz to put at every quilt, one at every corner."[27] As Sallie Paul recalled, "Colored people would have quiltings to one of dey own houses, up in de quarter, heap of de nights en dey would frolic en play en dance dere till late up in de night."[28] Black women provided for the basic needs of their communities by participating in these productive festivals during the hours when they were not expected to work for their masters. Women also were expected to maintain the paltry clothing supply for their communities and took advantage of these opportunities to frolic. In 1850 on St. Helena Island in South Carolina, a female slave, Pamela, organized a quilting party to conceal the frolic she hosted for her daughter, Ellen. One witness stated that "Ellen's mammy Pamela, the laundress, had the quilting party for Ellen & the young ones dance." This guise was necessary because of slave master Colonel Williams's continual attempt to "discourage the slaves from socializing."[29] Work-related holidays varied according to region; however, there were other holidays that were celebrated by both the white and black communities throughout North America from the colonial era to the antebellum era.

The holiday seasons of Christmas, New Year's, and (by the early nineteenth century) the Fourth of July were often a special time for the black community because of the freedoms and privileges afforded them that otherwise were not available within the Southern plantation system. It was a time when "husbands is comin' home an' families is gettin' nunited [sic] again. Husbands hurry on home to see dey new babies," affectionately recalled a former slave in Virginia.[30] She further states that many of these reunions incorporated dancing and singing. Abroad, family members who were hired out and sometimes sold within the domestic trade were occasionally allowed to reunite with their families during the holiday seasons, especially Christmas. "We would have dances every Christmas; on different plantations. . . . We had a good time."[31] Bondsmen and bondswomen received allowances to visit other plantations, have a free day from work, experience lavish dinners, and enjoy a frolic with friends and family during the holiday season; these were some of the few joys of slavery. Throughout the rest of the year, the enslaved community work tirelessly. In Estella Jones's vivid recollections of slaves' experiences at the Powers Pond Place in Georgia, she adamantly explained how blacks worked night and day: "Slaves . . . had a hard time. . . . Marster had slaves all over de field to put lights on so dey could see

THE CHRISTMAS WEEK.

Illustration of an enslaved black couple dancing during the Christmas holidays in a series titled "The Slave in 1863." Frolics fostered the growth and stability of the black community. (Miscellaneous Items in High Demand Collection, Prints & Photographs Division, Library of Congress, LC-USZC4-2827.) Courtesy of the Library of Congress.

how to work atter dark."[32] Frederick Douglass explained that the "days between Christmas day and New Year's . . . allowed the slaves a holiday."[33] Throughout the South, the holiday season supported whiteness through the routines expected of the slaves to present themselves to the big house to accept gifts or liquor or simply to recognize their master's grace as an aspect of the onstage performance. Former slave Pearl Randolph remembered every Christmas on the Pamell plantation: "The slave children all trouped to de big house and stood outside crying 'Christmas gift' to their master and mistress."[34] However, Davis acknowledged that during these holidays, whites needed to be "mighty careful . . . in order to keep down uprising," as the holiday season offered an optimal time for revolts. The onstage expectations of the holiday season contributed to Estella Jones's comment that many blacks enjoyed the holidays of their own creation "better den dey did Christmas, or at least just as much."[35]

The continuance of West African and Caribbean cultures may be seen in how the enslaved community recreated the Christmas holiday season in North Carolina with the emergence of Junkanoo in the antebellum era.[36] Former bondswoman Harriet Jacobs noted in her personal narrative, "Every child rises early on Christmas morning to see the Johnkannaus."[37]

Although there were various spellings of the holiday and conflicting explanations of its origins, "John Conny" was believed to be a celebration
of an eighteenth-century African leader of Ghana's Gold Coast that was
continued in the Caribbean (mainly in Jamaica) and by the mid-nineteenth
century in North America. Scholar Janet DeCosmo argues that the holiday represents a polyethnic amalgamation of "ritual arts traditions of
the Mandingo, Fulani, Hausa, Ibo, Yoruba, Ashanti, and Congo peoples,
and their descendants who were brought to the islands from Africa and
the British colonies between seventeenth and nineteenth centuries."[38]
This holiday was often celebrated during the Christmas season (mainly
recorded on December 26) in which the enslaved community dressed in
colorful costumes and decorative masks while they perform music and
dance within the festivities. The presence of this holiday in North Carolina, and possibly other regions in North America, illustrates the preservation of African and West Indian Cultures in nineteenth-century African
Americans. For one month prior to the celebration, enslaved community
prepared costumes, songs, and musical instruments for these festivities,
according to Harriet Jacobs in her 1861 published autobiography. She re-
calls that there were "companies of slaves from the plantations . . . covered with all manner of bright-colored stripes. Cow's tails are fastened to
their backs, and their heads are decorated with horns." Jacobs continues,
describing the instruments created and used with the enslaved community: a "box, covered with sheep skin, is called the gumbo box. A dozen
beat on this, while the others strike triangles and jawbones, to which
bands of dancers keep time."[39] The ingenuity of musical instruments and
distinct lyrics for the festivities illustrated an African and West Indian
influence, a creolization of cultures that manifested this holiday. Jacobs
continues by relating that hundreds of the enslaved community would
go from door to door, aggressively requesting "Christmas donations" that
whites rarely refused because if he would, "they regale his ears" with the
following song:

> Poor massa, so dey say;
> Down in de heel, so dey say;
> Got no money, so dey say;
> Not one shillin, so dey say;
> God A'might bress you, so dey say.[40]

The satirical lyrics of this song of the masked Junkanooers creatively belittled whites who did not financially contribute to their festivities. Jacobs
notes that some within the enslaved community received donations that
"frequently amount to twenty or thirty dollars," which allowed many of

them to "spend . . . for good eating" and contribute to their families' well-being. There is power in the continuance of this holiday and within the lyrics of their songs, the autonomy needed to prepare and execute the festivities while at the same time creatively demeaning or ridiculing whites into participating illustrates the continual control blacks exercised in their cultural expressions. Although the African American community throughout North Carolina did not wholly celebrate this cultural holiday, it was an aspect of that region by the antebellum era and an active aspect of the colonial society in the Caribbean. According to scholar Michael Gomez, by the mid-nineteenth century, slaves made up 33 percent of North Carolina's population, which may have contributed to strong cultural ties to homeland traditions.[41] This Christmas Day celebration was "both with white and colored people" and was an aspect of the amalgamation of African, West Indian, European, and American cultures.

The fraternization of blacks and whites in music and dance contributed to a distinct Southern culture. This experience gave whites an opportunity to experience aspects of the backstage and interact with the black community, though with bondsmen and bondswomen always cognizant of their presence. Meanwhile, these encounters allowed blacks to openly mock whites and whiteness. Former slave Benjamin Rush recalled that as a "pastime" they would imitate whites in their dancing, "sometimes with the white folks" present. Rush was referring to such dances as the cakewalk, which was quite popular in the mid-nineteenth century within the black community.[42] Tom Felcher remembered his grandfather's description of the cakewalk: "There was no prancing, just a straight walk on a path made by turns and so forth," which couples performed often with "a pail of water on their heads" and strutted with perfect posture.[43] Balancing water on top of the head while dancing was a relic from West African dance culture.[44] Other aspects of the cakewalk reflected a parody of European waltzes and minuets that blacks witnessed at the white community balls and cotillions, especially highlighted in the often extravagant attire they wore.[45] As former slave Estella Jones recalled, "De womens wore long, ruffled dresses wid hoops in 'em and de mens had on high hats, long split-tailed coats, and some of 'em used walkin' sticks."[46] Mocking whiteness became an aspect of white entertainment, with numerous accounts from the antebellum era of the "master and mistress" often present at "dese parties . . . and dey 'cided who danced de best."[47] The cakewalk, similar to fraternization, bestrode onstage subjugation and backstage agency for the black community.

One group that frequently traversed the black and white communities was composed of black, typically male musicians who performed at festivities. Possessing musical skill afforded individual slaves mobility within both communities. Musicians were able to temporarily leave the station as chattel and enter other spheres. As the "community's secular ministers," they often found relief and opportunity in their special talents.[48] The term "musician" specifically refers to instrumentalists, those individuals who brought their communities together in a frolic, rather than to preachers or vocalists. Black musicians earned a special position of "folk elite" in the black (and white) communities.[49] Slaves who held the position of skilled musician often received the opportunity to perform at the "Big House." Solomon Northup's testimony represented the type of advantages a slave might earn as a result of his musical talent. He was met with "good fortune" because of his skills as a violinist. The instrument, according to the musician, was his "constant companion, the source of profit, and soother of my sorrows during years of servitude." For this violinist, music provided a mental escape from the rigors of daily slave life. "I was employed to play . . . so well pleased were the merry makers with my performance, that a contribution was taken for my benefit, which amounted to seventeen dollars. With the sum, I was looked upon by my fellows as a millionaire."[50] Many black musicians were extremely proud of their role and worked diligently to hone those skills. Northup's story mirrored those of dozens of blacks who received recognition for their performing arts abilities. One ex-slave reminisced about the advantages, stating, "I used to dance in the stores for men and women, they could give me pennies and three cent pieces, all of which . . . bought me shoes and clothes with the money collected."[51] Talents in the performing arts provided some slaves monetary compensation that allowed them to purchase necessities typically withheld from them; as well, slaves possessing performance skills recognized by whites also could be rewarded with other commodities, including alcohol. One ex-slave, John Adams, stated, "I always like to play for them white boys cause they would make this old Negro plenty toddys, or in other words, give me plenty whiskey to drink."[52]

Musicians determined the pace of the dance, influenced the songs sung, and acquired several liberties unavailable to the rest of their community. For their roles in black music and dance festivities, many musicians earned the title of "captain," as one former slave from Georgia remembered.[53] This title afforded special attention from young women while bestowing respect that other slaves did not receive.[54] Musicians were able to loosen the chains of enslavement and earn recognition outside of their slave status, to eschew elements of slavery while never achieving true freedom, thus epitomizing the duality of blackness in the slave community. The image of the musician truly exemplifies the duality of possessing freedom while remaining in bondage. It is difficult to imagine the experiences of these black musicians, having the independence to gain some income through their recognized talents while also being forced by the whip to sing and dance. The instrument they loved and the talents they cultivated became, at the hands of violent whites, tools of subjugation. Solomon Northup experienced the multiplicity of music and dance, having to play his violin for the violently coerced "merry-making" that was orchestrated to "gratify the whim of an unreasonable master" while at the same time recognizing that if "it had not been for my beloved violin, I scarcely can conceive how I could have endured the long years of bondage."[55] The true reverence for these instruments came not from the planter class but rather from relatives' roles as musicians and dancers in private black frolics. Former slave Fannie Fulcher remembered that the fiddler on Dr. Miller's plantation in Burke County, Georgia, was her "cousin who played fer frolics, and fer de white folks, too."[56] Similarly, Green Willbanks remembered that his father, Ison, was a respected musician in Jefferson County, Georgia. He positively beamed that his "pa was one of them fiddlers in his young days." Willbanks recalled that Ison sometimes was "marched" on his fellow slaves' shoulders "to the big house" as one of the "generals" of the corn-shucking festivals.[57] Interestingly, in numerous other accounts of corn-shucking festivals, the white slaveholders or overseers often were carried on the shoulders of the slaves, but Willbanks remembered that honor being bestowed upon his father due to his role as a slave musician. Fulcher and Willbanks remembered their family members as instrumental to one of the most enjoyable experiences on the plantation, the frolic. Musicians were temporarily able to progress beyond their state of bondage and offer amusement to their communities while simultaneously fostering cultural continuance and proving a melodic backdrop to personal expressions. Beyond musicians, many slaves spoke of their relatives' roles as talented dancers and singers on the plantation. Melinda Mitchell was boasting when she mentioned that her mother "wus de bes' dancer on de plantation. . . . [She] could dance so sturdy she could balance a glass of water on her head an never spill a drop."[58] Her dancing style was appreciated by those in "the big house as well as in the quarters." This dancer's skill in balancing water on her head signifies her ties to African culture.

The folktale of "Uncle Dick" sheds light on the significance of the slave musician among blacks. According to tales exchanged within the black community, Uncle Dick was a popular fiddler who played for "weddings, husking parties and dances" and whose "presence was essential." During one of his journeys to a wedding for the "colored gentry" in the area, Uncle Dick was traveling through the woods dressed in "carefully polished . . . glittering gilt buttons" and raised "shirt collar . . . and fiddle in hand." He journeyed with "all the weight of his dignity upon him" due to his role as the musician and "officiate or master of ceremonies" for the wedding. As he made his way through the forest, Uncle Dick encountered wolves ready to attack. "Instinctively he (Uncle Dick) thrusts out his fiddle at them. . . . Instantly the wolves sprang back as if he had fired a gun among them . . . never before had he played to an audience so fond of music."[59] Passed down as a trickster tale within the black community, Uncle Dick was an enslaved black man who had the freedom to voyage through the region and the power to subdue enemies through his talents as a musician. Instrumentalist skills offered enslaved blacks opportunities not afforded to other bondsmen and bondswomen, thereby earning them special recognition by their peers. That status also likely derived from the West African professional musician known as *griot*.[60] Similar to their West African predecessors, slave musicians often constructed their own instruments, which created another source of pride and respect. Former slave musician Henry Wright remembered that while some slaves bought their instruments, he proudly made his own fiddle form "a large sized gourd—a long wooden handle was uses as a neck, and the hair from a horse's tail was used fort the bow."[61] The manner in which slaves developed these tools represented a direct link with their ancestral homeland. Ex-slave John Cole recalled some of these methods: "Stretch cow-hides over cheese-boxes and you had tambourines. Saw bones from off a cow, knock them together, and call it a drum. Or use broom-straws on fiddle-strings, and you had your entire orchestra."[62] Using natural materials to construct instruments was a custom the blacks brought from West Africa to North America.[63] Cole's statement makes evident the slave population's ingenuity but also displays the continuance of West African culture. Slaves were ingenious as well in using local natural resources as raw materials to create their musical instruments. Ex-slave Aunty Jane recounted the innovative, creative manner in which the enslaved community made drums: "Yuh kill a coon an yuh skin um an yuh tack duh skin up side duh house tuh dry and yuh stretch um good till um tight an smooth. Den yuh stretch um obuh duh en ub a holler tree trunk."[64] Several other accounts refer specifically to a particular type of tree trunk, such as an oak, preferred over cedar tree trunks. Slaves used similar styles to create these musical instruments throughout the South.

The types of dances that Mitchell's mother was known for, the fable of "Uncle Dick," and the types of instruments chosen for these frolics reveal the powerful influences of West African cultures within the Southern slave communities. The African-derived banjo, for example, was a popular instrument among slaves in the United States, who commonly would dance "to the music of a banjo" under the direction of a black musician.[65] The banjo originated in the native land of the Africans captured within the slave trade. Although the musical instrument was altered over time and location, its importance within the black community was directly related to its culture significance.[66] In North America, the banjo was the second most popular instrument used on the plantation and was always heard at the cotillions, balls, and festivities of the whites. In several instances whites taught blacks how to play musical instruments, and it was not uncommon for whites to play musical instruments at black events. Furthermore, blacks continually played at white dances; such interactions illustrate a continual merger of black and white elements in musical sound.

Whites' interest in the world of slaves caused an interesting dynamic of fraternization and amalgamation that became an important aspect of Southern culture, especially among the white youth. In a variety of recreational settings, blacks and whites throughout the South mixed openly. George Clark Rankin spent his youth venturing between the slave quarters and the "big house," where his grandmother, the mistress of the plantation, resided.[67] "As the only white child" on the plantation, he had access to all the "good things"; he enjoyed the "pleasure to go down" and hear slave stories or to play with the "pickaninnies" while engaging in the music and dance of the enslaved community. On his grandmother's plantation, "the negroes were allowed to attend and to participate" with the white community in church services. During these religious meetings, the invited slaves were expected to lead the music, and both blacks and whites "joined in the singing."[68] The lyrical content and song themes, rhythmic style, and use of particular musical instruments, such as the banjo, were continually influenced by the black and white community, often resulting in an amalgamated musical style that manifested in both societies. Fraternization in the recreations of music and dance contributed to cultural exchanges that influenced the racial construction of blacks and whites in the South. As Wilbur J. Cash asserts, the "Negro entered into the white man as profoundly as white man entered the Negro—subtly influencing every gesture, every word, every emotion and idea, every attitude."[69] Southern slaveholders connected intimately with their slave communities. White youths on plantations throughout the South experienced minimal scrutiny for their social interactions with slaves.

The creolization of cultures continually manifested in the black and white communities throughout the South, as well as the North. Like musical instruments, dance had African roots and strong European and white American influences. "Instrumental music was . . . almost universally . . . discussed in the context of dancing," according to scholar Robert Winans.[70] European-influenced dances such as the waltz, quadrille, or square dances were referenced by many within the slave community. Dances among the enslaved population were influenced by West African cultural continuances and white dance style, as one former bondswoman noted: "Some of the men clogged and pidgeoned, but when we had dances they were real cotillions, like the white folks had."[71] While among members of their own community, many enslaved blacks performed more an African-influenced music and dance style. The most popular dances mentioned by blacks were the buck and wing, pigeon wing, and buzzard lope, dances that greatly resembled the West African cultural practice of imitating animals and inanimate objects.[72] In the pigeon wing, for example, "the performer would ape the manner of courting pigeon or cockerel, strutting around, holding his arms bent close to his side like wings."[73] In their homeland's ancestral tradition, many of the slaves' dances imitated their environment and daily activities.[74] The dances of the enslaved population were often named and choreographed after the movements of animals. An ex-slave from the Sunbury region of Georgia reminisced about the dance movements of the slaves, stating, "We does duh Snake Hip and duh Buzzard Lope . . . we did duh Fish Tail an duh fish bone an duh Camel Walk."[75] According to dance scholar Doris Green, dances also "commemorate everyday activities," so the cutting of wheat or corn shucking may have resembled the "Ziglibiti," a dance on the Ivory Coast that resembled the pounding of corn, a common task for women in the region.[76] The dance styles varied according to region and ancestral linkage. Dance scholar Katrina Hazzard-Gordon has asserted that a cultural heritage existed, that the enslaved population "brought to the Americas in the motor-muscle memory of the various West African ethnic groups."[77]

One example of West African dance persisting in the slave South was the ring dance. Ex-slave Hettie Campbell described, "We does plenty uh dances in those days. Dance roun' in a ring. We had a big time long bout wen crops come in an everybody bring sumpm . . . we gives praise fuh the good crop and then we shouts and sings all night."[78] This type of performance, also known as the "ring-shout" or just "shout" among blacks, was a religious/sacred dance that survived the Middle Passage and continued in North America.[79] The ring dance on plantations throughout the United States looked quite similar to the dances performed throughout various regions on Africa's West Coast.[80] In the regions of Ghana, the Ivory Coast, Togo, Burkina Faso, Benin, and Nigeria, where the majority of the Africans brought to North America originated, the circle or ring was a common aspect of the dance culture. Historian Sterling Stuckey deduced that the ring was an aspect of ceremonies that honored the ancestors. The Ekoi in southern Nigeria have a dance during funerals for great chiefs in which "seven men dance in the centre of an immense circle made by other performers," and these men sing songs that are "so old that their meaning has long since been forgotten."[81] P. Amaury Talbot estimated that many people throughout southern Nigeria often danced in a movement that "consists of slowly moving round in a circle," illustrating the ring-style dance that was quite common within the North American enslaved community. Depicting the widespread importance of the ring in West African dance, scholar E. E. Evans-Prithcard observed that the Azande have a dance in which "male dancers form a complete circle" and women also form a larger circle outside of the men while performing to the sound of a drum.[82] These types of dances were preserved in the minds of the captives through the Middle Passage, and though some elements changed over time, West African cultural relics remained in the dance movements of blacks in America while also being influential in the dance culture of many within the white community.[83] Early in the nineteenth century, one slave musician recalled that his "master himself could shake a desperate foot at the fiddle. There was nobody that could face him at a Congo minuet."[84] Blacks shaped white dances and music through these interactions. European and white American dance cultures were continually infused in their ancestors' homeland cultures, contributing to a distinct African American culture.[85]

In 1862, a white woman, Laura Towne, witnessed and misinterpreted a slave ceremony: "Tonight I have been to a shout, which seems to me certainly the remains of some old idol worship. The negroes sing a kind of chorus—three standing apart to lead and clap—and then all the others go shuffling round in a circle following one another. . . . and bending the knees and stamping so that the whole floor swings. . . . They call it a religious ceremony."[86] This ceremony varied according to geographical region and title, but it was seen throughout North America during the entire slave era. These ceremonies represented self-expression and continued the African tradition of using the performing arts during rituals. Whites who witnessed blacks' ceremonies often were unaware of their cultural

Illustration caption states, "Religious dancing of the Blacks, termed 'shouting.'" (Charles Stearns, *The Black Man of the South and the Rebels; or, The Characteristics of the Former, and the Recent Outrages of the Latter* [New York: American News, 1872]).

significance. On the Collins plantation in North Carolina around 1800, there were several "negroes just from Africa" who gathered in the slave quarters one night to "sing their native songs" and dance. After beginning this frolic, they, "setting their faces towards Africa, would march down into the water singing as they marched." After several of them drowned, their "owners" interrupted this ceremony so as not to lose any more slaves. This story was later relayed to an early-nineteenth-century historian, John Spencer Bassett, as evidence of West African ceremonies that whites did not fully understand. However, using music and dance, the enslaved populations were able to continue and adjust customs from their homeland.[87]

Beyond the continuance of dance styles, both the music's sound and lyrics transmitted native African cultures to North America. Many songs created by blacks in America used an assortment of West African words and musical techniques, such as call and response. In this song style, someone "takes the lead and breaks out with a song, to which there is always a chorus. In this they all join, and the union of such a number of voices produces a very animated and pleasing effect."[88] The call-and-response style came directly from West Africa and was prevalent not only on plantations in the American slavery system but also throughout the West Indies.[89] Slaves also performed for comparable ritual purposes, such as naming ceremonies, marriages, births, corn shucking, and harvest festivals.[90] The survival of West African styles of music, song, and dance formed the foundation of a distinctly African American tradition. Simultaneously, West African cultures were infused into the burgeoning overall American culture.

Backstage, then, the sounds of the banjo and the sights of the slave ring-shout revealed that the correlation of music and dance with negative stereotypes of contented, cheerful slaves conflicted with the benefits these performing arts provided to slaves. Furthermore, the labels many whites placed on black music and dance were often strategically restructured to facilitate powerful tools to rebel and resist their subjugated condition. Former bondsman Tom Wilson was held in slavery in New Orleans; after several attempts, he finally was able to run away during the Christmas holiday in the 1850s. During his escape, Wilson came across "men who were out watching for me, with guns and dogs." In order to elude capture, he began to "whistle and sing" while walking past them undisturbed. Wilson, who successfully escaped on a cotton ship bound to Liverpool, England, exposed an ironic aspect of slave life: because whites maintained that singing and dancing slaves were happily subservient, a singing slave must pose no threat. Wilson used the onstage façade and the romanticized idea of blacks' nature against the perpetuators of the myth.[91] However, backstage, Wilson was rebelling against his bondage, the overall institution, and the stereotype of blackness through the simple act of singing in the midst of his escape. Blacks continually expressed such ingenuity within the plantation system under the guise of the performing arts. The trickster tactics were an aspect of many West African cultures brought and continued within the black community. Blacks within the institution of slavery were able to transform the trickster into music and dance and incorporate them into their backstage performances.[92]

The simple act of singing may have appeased Southern sensibilities and contributed to the folklore of the South, but when examined further, it became evident that music was an active element of the opposition of slavery. Slaves sang songs onstage to "flatter the pride of the owner, and possibly, draw a favorable glance from him."[93] Frederick Douglass recounted the lyrics of a popular song sung for these performances: "I am going away to the great house farm, O yea! O yea! O yea! My old master is a good master, Oh yea! Oh yea! Oh yea!"[94] Onstage, these lyrics supported whites' ideas of benevolent paternalism, while for the enslaved community, the song was "full of meaning" and "every tone was a testimony against slavery."[95] Young children often found these lessons vexing—and the consequences of failing to learn them brutal. As a child, Susan Snow, like many slave children, spent a good amount of time in the big house. One day, she began singing a song that she often heard within the slave quarters:

> Ol' Gen'l Pope, he had a short gun,
> Fit it full of bum
> Kill 'em as de come,
> Call a Union band,
> Make de rebels understand,
> To leave our land,
> Submit to Abraham

These lyrics clearly express pro-Northern sentiment during the early stages of the Civil War. Snow describes her mistress as having "grabbed up de bresh broom an' she laid it on me" in response to hearing the lyrics.[96] Susan was unaware that the song lyrics she had recited constituted a part of the secret culture within the slave community. She heard her fellow bondsmen and bondswomen sing the song but was unaware that these lyrics were not meant to be repeated in the presence of whites. As a child, she had yet to recognize that the slaves lived within a dual world of subjugation and agency. This double consciousness was well concealed through the music and dance culture that developed shrewdly in the presence of whites, who often remained unaware of the multiplicity of music, song, and dance among the enslaved black population.[97] The ability to maneuver between the onstage and backstage worlds often was taught to children during their rearing; however, contingent upon their proximity to the slave community, some enslaved blacks may have undergone a longer process in obtaining the trickster elements of music and dance. As a Northerner kidnapped into slavery, it took Solomon Northup several years to acquire skills to perform subjugation. During his illegal ten-year enslavement, Northup learned how to address whites with "down-cast eyes and uncovered head—in the attitude and language of a slave."[98] Subservience was not innate, but it could be taught. Within the enslaved community, a false pretense of subservience was part of the private education of slaves, and music and dance were the tools needed to survive.

Adults had to teach these complicated rituals to younger generations of slaves. While slave children also were expected to perform onstage to entertain whites, backstage, older slaves taught them how to use the same tools to gain power and to cope within horrific conditions. In Tennessee, as soon as former slave Thomas Rutling "was large enough," his mistress brought him to the house daily to "sing and dance for her own amusement."[99] In the evening, the young Thomas returned to the slave quarters, entering the private community of his fellow slaves. At this time in 1862, the Civil War was in its early stages, and the enslaved black community was fully aware that this conflict regarded their freedom. In order to acquire knowledge, Thomas became a mole for the black community. Knowing that the mistress enjoyed his music and dance, the slave preacher gave Thomas specific instructions: "Now Tom, you mustn't repeat a word of this." He went on to tell the youth to "look mighty obedient" while performing for the mistress, all the while listening and reporting back to the enslaved any information about the war. In the evenings, after Thomas returned from the big house, within a "half an hour . . . every slave on the plantation would know what had been said up at massa's house." As the war continued, the "rebels kept getting beaten, and then it was sing, sing all through the quarters." "Old missus asked what they were singing for, but they would say, because we feel so happy," in an effort to reaffirm the Southern ruse and placate whites' fears.[100] They diligently affected onstage performances, yet all the while, Thomas Rutling and those on the Tennessee plantation were backstage, rebelling and obtaining covert information pertinent to their survival.

Other aspects of slave artistic performances, however, lay further from the eyes and influences of whites. The privacy of the frolics within the slave quarters was a major aspect of blacks' cultural development. Ex-slave Fannie Fulcher remembered that they "used to have big parties sometime" on the Miller plantation in Burke County, Georgia, and these were treasured in the black community because there were "no white folks" present. Though the overseer occasionally monitored these performances in the slave quarters, Fulcher believed that frolics were best held away from the watchful eyes of the white community.[101] Whites allowed slaves to sing and dance within certain parameters over which they had control, but slaves often found ways to frolic without whites' authoritative gaze. Secret meetings in the slave quarters or in the forest were known as "stealing away" by the slaves.[102] Ex-slave Chris Franklin explained that he "never heared of stealing niggers, 'cept" in the manner in which they would attend frolics away from the plantation without obtaining a pass or permission.[103]

Slaves relished these frolics in the slave quarters without the supervising eyes of whites as one of the most humanizing aspects of their lives in bondage. Blacks were "stealing" or reclaiming control, power, and culture through their covert gatherings. Ex-slave Albert Hill reminisced about slaves "stealing away" in Walton County, Georgia, stating, "Massa . . . don't 'low de parties. . . . We dances near all night Saturday night, but we has to stay way in de back where de white folks can't hear us. Sometimes we has de fiddle and de banjo and does we cut dat chicken wing and de shuffle!"[104] Whites wanted to control the entire black body, both physically and mentally. Private frolics away from the white gaze allowed slaves to "do as we pleased."[105] Many blacks recognized that they gained an outlet and a form of independence from these sacred, private frolics. Mark Gaffney, an ex-slave from Mississippi, commented on these covert assemblies: "That was the happiest time of the slaves because the rest of the time it was like being a convict, we had to do just like Maser told us. We would get together and dance, talk and have our fun, Maser he would not be there to holler instructions at us."[106] These events allowed blacks to gain authority over their own bodies and contributed to the clandestine tradition that developed in the black society. One ex-slave reminisced on their secret events: "Sadday nights we'd slip out de quarters an' go to de woods. Was a ole cabin bout five miles 'way from de house, an' us would raise all de ruckus dere we wanted."[107] Slave preferred to be as far away from the plantation house as possible. "We used to git back in de end cabin an' sing an' dance by de fiddle."[108] Another ex-slave likewise remembered, "When they wanted to sing and pray, they would steal off into the woods."[109]

Away from the gaze of whites, slaves often used frolics in order to socialize and strategize. During their frolics, enslaved blacks enjoyed each other's company and conversed freely within their quarters. Allen Dozier in Edgefield County, South Carolina, remembered that "the field hands and house servants forgot cares in merriment and dancing after the day's work was over."[110] These two groups coming together also allowed some exchanges to take place under the guise of a frolic. Former slave Benjamin Russell from Chester, South Carolina, reported on the manner by which slaves received news: "Many plantations were strict about this, but the greater the precaution, the alerter became the slaves, the wider they opened their ears, and the more eager they became for outside information." Often the "girls that waited on the table, the ladies' maids and the drivers, they would pick up everything they heard and pass it on to the other slaves" during these frolics in which field and house slaves were able to come together.[111]

Enslaved men and women often used frolics as a time to gossip. Former slave Elizabeth Rose Hite commented on the frolics, stating, "De slaves had a good time in dere quarters . . . Dey talked about de master's business in dere quarters too."[112] The sexual liaisons, domestic abuse, financial hardships, and insecurities present in the white society were likely topics during these frolics. The economic conditions of the planter class could have severely affected the slave community; therefore, it was tactical for blacks to stay abreast of the inner workings of white households. Former slave George Womble was raised on a plantation in Clinton, Georgia, during the antebellum era; he remembered that the enslaved community continually plotted how to get rid of their overseers. Every time the planter, Mr. Womble, would hire a new overseer, "he always told the prospect that if he couldn't handle the slaves his services would not be needed." Upon hearing this, the cook would inform the slaves, with frolics being one of the most opportune times to discuss these matters, causing the slaves to take advantage of the "prospective overseer" by slowing production and sometimes even threatening the new hire. As a result, the "overseer either found himself trying to explain to his employer or else looking for another job."[113] On plantations throughout the South, blacks exchanged ideas about how to manipulate whites; these conversations were concealed under the guise of music and dance. However, the slave quarters did not always provide a completely private space for the black community.

These private frolics not only served as personal expressions of independence, they also allowed for spiritual development without the infringement of the white community. W. L. Bost, born on Jonas Bost's plantation in Newton, North Carolina, remembered that they would "sneak off" to have "prayer meeting" and that his mother would "sing and pray to the Lord to deliver us out o' slavery."[114] During these private frolics, slaves used religious expressions to cope with their enslaved state. On plantations, whites attempted to assert control through biblical teachings, and they defended and justified slavery through religion. The September 1850 issue of *DeBow's Review*, one of the most popular antebellum journals in the South, contained an article that specifically illustrated a biblical defense of slavery. Offering evidence from the book of Genesis—namely, Abraham's possession of slaves—the anonymous writer emphasized that the Bible "teaches clearly and conclusively that the holding of slaves is right."[115] Ministers and slaveholders throughout the South regularly defended the institution of slavery through religious teachings. Former slave Hannah Lowery recalled that the slave community "didn't have a church," and to offer religious teachings, a "white man would go around through the quarters preaching to de slaves telling dem to obey dey marsters and missus."[116] Many slaveholders either forced blacks to attend the local white church, which provided sermons to their slaves,

or supervised religious meetings among blacks; this was done in an effort
to support the bondage system through Christianity. Green Willbanks
remembered that on his plantation, "slaves went to the same church as
their white folks and sat in the back"; however, due to his father's secret
ability to read, those blacks on the Jefferson County plantation "ran off
to the woods" to hear the literate slave read the bible. According to Willbanks, they usually found a "Negro to preach to them" and exchanged
music and dance to have their own religious experience, external to the
propaganda of whites.[117] Local and state laws betrayed whites' desperation
to prohibit these private exchanges. In Georgia's Richmond County, no
"colored preacher" residing outside of the region could preach, exhort, or
teach in that area. In a nearby county, "meetings of slaves or free persons
of color for religious purposes" were illegal, and if blacks were allowed
to meet, they had to be supervised by a white citizen and return to their
plantations by "10:30 at night."[118] These types of laws demonstrated a
purposeful effort by whites to limit blacks from stealing away to engage
in autonomous cultural exchanges of music and dance.

Stealing away to sing, dance, or play instruments in religious expressions and exchanges was an element of the rebellion of backstage performances, as is evident in song lyrics. Bose remembered the song his mother
sang in the concealment of the woods and at a distance from whites.

> We camp awhile in the wilderness, in the wilderness, in the
> wilderness
> We camp awhile in the wilderness, where the Lord makes me
> happy,
> And then I'm a-goin' home.

This song's emphasis on camping in the wilderness and then going home
represents the many metaphors that enslaved blacks used within their
song lyrics. These lyrics expressed the venturing of the enslaved blacks
into the woods to privately and happily frolic before returning to the
plantation. These lyrics also may have represented their lives as slaves
on the plantation and the freedom that they could realize in death.

Because stealing away represented a form of rebellion, it could result
in physical danger. On Trinity Plantation, ex-slave Elizabeth Rose Hite
commented on the danger slaves faced when stealing away: "If caught in
the act, slaves were whipped, and they must not look tired the next day,
for de first thing de driver said was you was out las' night."[119] However,
"whippings did not stop them from having meetings."[120] There was a
danger in appearing tired the next morning after these private gatherings,
which contributed to slaves' false energetic presentations in the fields

the next day. These private gatherings may account for Thomas Jefferson's assessment that the enslaved blacks preferred to express themselves through music, song, and dance at night rather than rest.[121] Jefferson, similar to many Southern planters, never fully understood the freedoms that music, dance, and gatherings offered to the enslaved community. Slaves cherished stealing away, or simply having free time, for as former slave Willbanks explained, "slaves worked all day . . . but . . . night was their free time, they went where they pleased."[122]

The non-slaveholding whites who patrolled the wooded areas throughout the South, often referred to by slaves as pattyrollers, also presented a danger to slaves who stole away. One former Virginia slave described these patrollers as "a club of men who'd go around and catch slaves on strange plantations and break up frolics, and whip 'em sometimes."[123] These patrollers were often poor whites in the community who did not own slaves but who viewed the institution as their only means of gaining status. The presence of patrollers throughout the South illustrates the white population's fear and awareness that blacks were neither innately happy nor docile. Roan Barnes, an ex-slave, remembered that slaves caught stealing away were "severely whipped" after being hunted by "bull dogs or blood hounds." "Sometimes slaves would be so badly lacerated by the dogs that they would bleed to death"; those "Paddle Rollers (as Barnes called them) . . . watched the plantation at night," waiting to beat any slaves stealing away.[124] They were a constant threat to the black community. One former slave stated that they "sho was devils in sheeps' clothing; that what we thought of them paterollers."[125] Slaves, who had little to look forward to save these covert gatherings, would enjoy music and dance as long as "de Patterolas didn't interfere." One ex-slave known as Old Tim recalled that they "used to run mighty fast to git home after the frolics" in order to avoid the wrath of the non-slaveholding whites. Condescendingly, blacks responded to the threat of the patrollers through their musical expressions. As one slave song states repetitively, "Whip or wop, whip or wop, you-ee; We gonna sing and dance an' sing; Whip or wop, whip or wop, you-ee!"[126]

In response to patrollers, the black community instituted novel ways to conceal their frolics. Mose Wright recalled that they sometimes slipped away to the woods to indulge in a frolic, and as a "means of protection they tied ropes across the paths where they would be less likely to be seen." Wright explained that these ropes were strategically placed to "knock a man from his horse if he came riding up at a great speed."[127] Bondsmen also had creative ways to limit the sounds of their frolicking. Throughout the South, an overturned vessel, normally a large pot turned upside down and placed outside the door, was believed to catch sound and help prevent the sounds of dancing, singing, and music from traveling to white ears. Ex-slave Ann Matthews reminisced about these occasions, stating that they "would turn a pot down en meet at de pot in de nite en sing en pray en de white folks wouldn't 'yer dem."[128] Although music and dance were activities permitted by whites, blacks preferred to meet in anonymity to express their emotions, even with the risk of physical harm.[129] On a plantation in Louisiana, Mrs. Channel remembered that the 150 slaves would steal away to hold religious services in the woods. "They would form a circle on their knees around the speaker who would also be on his knees . . . and speak into or over a vessel of water to drown the sound." The slaves on this plantation also would "quickly stop the noise" of any overly spirited attendants by "placing their hands over the offender's mouth."[130]

The covertness of stealing away continued in the slaves' songs, which allowed them to express many feelings, such as sorrow, rebelliousness, distrust, and anger. Former slave Jake Green detailed the defiant songs present in the plantation South that specifically mentioned the patrollers:

> O some tell me that a nigger won't steal,
> But I've seen a nigger in my corn field;
> O run, nigger, run for the patrol will catch you,
> O run, nigger, run for 'tis almost day.
> I fooled Old Master seven years,
> Fooled the overseer three,
> Hand me down my banjo,
> And I'll tickle your bel-lee.[131]

With smiles on their faces, the slave community sang this song, which illustrated their continual disobedience.

The simple act of slaves singing may have appeased Southern sensibilities and contributed to the folklore of the South, but when examined further, it becomes evident that music was an active element of the opposition of slavery. The boldness of many slave songs and the correlation of blacks, music, and happiness illustrate the continual conflicting nature of the overall institution. Of course whites tried to use other songs to keep their slaves in line. Former slave Anthony Dawson provided an example of a common song with lyrics controlled and directed by whites:

> Run nigger, run
> De Patteroll get you!

Run nigger, run,
De Patteroll come!
Watch nigger, watch,
De Patteroll trick you!
Watch nigger, watch,
He got a big gun!

After citing these lyrics to the interviewer, Dawson noted that this was one of the "songs de slaves all knowed," but he believed that the "white folks . . . make dat song up so us niggers would keep in line." [132] Dawson understood that the white slaveholding community and patrollers purposely influenced slave music. But he also demonstrated that many within the slave community could discern between onstage and backstage performances. When necessary, the black community projected images that suited whites' purposes. They knew how to appear docile and happy in the public onstage arena, causing these lyrics to appear to show a fear held within the enslaved community of patrollers. However, backstage they knew they were performing. In this backstage world, they were derisive toward whites, slaveholders, overseers, drivers, and patrollers.

The contemptuous nature of music within the enslaved community caused many of their songs to advocate open rebellion against the institution of slavery. A former slave, Antony, remembered a Sunday night on a plantation in the Isle of Cuba in Louisiana during which the enslaved community stole away. During their gathering, a "negro preacher" believed the "lawd put words" to this song and started singing these lyrics:

Slavery chain,
Broke at last,
Broke at last,
Broke at last
Slavery chain
Done broke at last.

The "congregation" began to sing along "louder and louder," waking those in the big house and the overseers. The slaveholder and overseers went "running" to this private gathering with "whips in their hands." "Then they commenced whipping the slaves for singing the song that the preacher gave them from the lawd. They whipped everybody but they whipped the preacher most of all," recalled Antony. [133] This story was said to date just before the Civil War at a time when the issue of slavery was being openly debated in the public forum, and through the internal network, many within the enslaved community were aware of this impending conflict.

"White folks do as they pleases, and the darkies do as they can."[134] This slave aphorism illustrates that blacks consistently created covert ways to rebel against or survive their servitude.[135] This pattern was quite apparent in their song lyrics. While some songs blatantly contained specific rebellious lyrics, others relied on a secretive language only decipherable by fellow bondsmen and bondswomen.[136] Many slave spirituals held a dual meaning for the slave population. Disguised as a religious spiritual, the song lyrics also relayed information for escape and potential freedom.[137] Slaves also commonly mocked their white masters through music and dance. Some songs referred to potential freedom (either on earth or in an afterlife), while others spoke of the abuses and hardships they suffered at the hands of whites. The hymns "Swing Low Sweet Chariot," "Go Down, Moses," and "Wade in the Water," just to name a few, were all spirituals that held multiple veiled meanings for the enslaved community. Harriet Tubman was a former slave who ran away to freedom and assisted in the escape of dozens of slaves for over a decade. Tubman, along with other abolitionists who assisted slaves escaping from the South to freedom (such those who were part of as the Underground Railroad), used spirituals to notify the enslaved community of opportunities to escape. When guiding escaped slaves, Tubman used spirituals to indicate places to hide and when it was safe to come out of hiding, as well as to warn of potential danger.

With the numerous subversive rebellions that slaves engaged in through ingenious uses of music and dance, the events of August 21, 1831, in Virginia should not have completely surprised the antebellum South. A century earlier, bondsmen and bondswomen joined together under the guise of Sunday gatherings and, with the impetus of music and dance, staged one of the most violent slave insurrections in colonial America. The spirit of that rebellion was apparent in Nat Turner, a slave born on October 2, 1800, in Southampton County, Virginia. After experiencing a religious revelation, Turner became a minister and decided to violently fight the institution of slavery. After months of stealing away mainly on Sundays to plot the rebellion, Turner and his conspirators decided to strike a blow to slavery on August 21. Similar to those in the Stono Rebellion, they traveled from farms to plantations killing every white person—men, women, and children—they met along the way. As the slave rebels marched through the region, they enlisted sixty to seventy insurgents. This was considered one of the most violent slave insurrections in American history, with more than fifty whites being killed—the largest number of white Americans killed in a slave rebellion. Although the story of Nat Turner's rebellion is a combination of witness accounts and folklore, a part of the memory prevalent in African American culture is the music they used during the insurrection. In cultural memory, Nat Turner and his conspirators sang, "Steal away, steal away home; I ain't got long to stay here," as a summoning code for the secret meetings to plot the rebellion. These song lyrics may have held multiple roles within the enslaved community: as a signal to meet in the woods, as a signal to run away or that the Underground Railroad was in the vicinity, or as a spiritual song that represented the Christian beliefs of freedom in death. However, within African American folklore, Nat Turner and his conspirators, similar to his Stono predecessors, used music as a strategic device for violent insurrection.[138]

Throughout backstage exchanges, blacks continually defined themselves through the dances they performed and the songs they sang. Some blacks stole away for religious exchange and growth, developing their own ideals of Christianity while incorporating West African cultures with American religious ideals to develop their distinct African American culture. Others sang songs that denigrated the dominant class. For still others, these backstage expressions provided a space in which to plan and coordinate open rebellion against slavery, their subordinate state, and whiteness. Lydia Parrish, a white woman, commented on the concealment of blacks' true culture from whites: "The secretiveness of the Negro is . . . the fundamental reason for our ignorance of the race and its background."[139] Slave secrecy allowed for agency and the attainment of some pleasures while simultaneously keeping many whites ignorant of black culture. Parrish's comment sheds light on the clandestine world of blacks that was hidden from whites. Some whites were unaware of the distinctive African American culture that developed under the veil of servitude. However, many other Southerners understood—and feared—the discontent and ingenuity of the enslaved populations.

Former slave Charley Williams from Tulsa, Oklahoma, remembered the last slave performance on the plantation of his birth. When the Yankees came, "four mens in blue clothes . . . told us to come up to de Big House," Williams remembered. The soldiers directed the "old Master" to dance. Williams stated, "Den dey asked him could he dance and he said no, and dey told him to dance or make us dance." The performing arts were well known as an aspect of Southern culture. Slaveholders were known for entertaining their white guests through the music and dance of their slaves, and the request of the Union soldiers for this performance came directly from what they had heard of the South and as a way to demean the white rebel. The tension of this standoff between the Union soldiers and the slaveholder who merely "stood inside a big ring of dem mens in blue clothes . . . and he jest stood and said nothing," was only somewhat relieved when the soon-to-be-freed men and women began to perform. "So some of us young bucks jest step up and say we was good dancers, and we start shuffling while de rest of de niggers pat." After gathering more instruments, they performed music and dance for the Yankees.[140] This dynamic during the Civil War reveals more than simply the reputation of blacks as entertainment and music and dance as demeaning; it illustrates a change that was taking place. White Southerners and their dancing and laughing slaves had become an aspect of American amusement that entered the North through stories, popular literature, through the theater of the day, blackface minstrelsy, and the public nature of the domestic slave trade.

The conflicting dynamic of the rebellious nature of private frolics and the benefits received through the performing arts provided an avenue for achieving power in the black community. It was evident within the black community that "the only weapon of self defense [one] could use successfully was that of deception."[141] Within the performing arts, blacks were able to gain agency in several ways, such as through clandestine cultural practices, continuation of West African culture, trickster activities, and communal and familial development. However, the positive aspects of music and dance for blacks were veiled, and the onstage performances had the strongest influence on the development of racial stereotypes within American culture. The negative stereotypes of the musical, minstrel black and the rationalization of the persistent rape and sexual abuse of black women were interlocked within the performing arts throughout every aspect of slavery.

5 *Advertisement*

"Dancing through the Streets and act lively"

"A singular spectacle, the most striking one of the kind I have ever witnessed," stated English traveler George William Featherston-haugh upon seeing the coffle in 1834.[1] There were "about three hundred slaves with them, who had bivouacked the preceding night in *chains* in the woods," being marched by land and by boat for hundreds of miles from Virginia to the Louisiana auction block. "In double files, about two hundred males manacled and chained to each other," while enslaved females and children were often unfettered. For this foreign traveler the scene was "revolting." They were chained together to "prevent their escape; and sometimes, when greater precaution is judged necessary, they are attached to a long chain passing between them. Their guards and conductors are, of course, well armed." This public scene was carefully organized by the slave traders who vigilantly observed their human cargo because the enslaved "often show a disposition to mutiny, knowing that if one or two could wrench their manacles off, they could soon free the rest, and either disperse themselves or overpower . . . and fly to the Free States." This custom of driving droves of slaves throughout the country to the southern and western markets was one aspect of the domestic slave trade that entailed a traumatic journey. These manacled droves were one phase of the big business of interstate trade that often began on the plantation, then to holding pens, and then to the auction block, with the coffle being the most visible component, and within each phase of this often public commerce, music and dance were a complicated aspect of the spectacle.

"The slave drivers, aware of this disposition in the unfortunate negroes, endeavor to mitigate their discontent by feeding them well on the march, and by encouraging them to sing 'Old Virginia Never Tire,' to the banjo," Featherstonhaugh believed.[2] Throughout the South, these lyrics could be heard, sung by the traveling human chattel:

> In Virginia's land, where corn-stalks grow,
> where the darkies are so gay,
> With spade and hoe, and away they go to work till the close of day.
> When work is done and night is come, 'tis the darkies jubilee;
> The girls so sweet, they look: so neat and merry as can be.
>
> Chorus
>
> The fiddle sing, the banjo ding, Virginia never tire:
> To laugh and sing is just the thing we darkies admire.
> Oh, happy is the darkey's life, when, hunting for the coon,
> He has the fun with the dog and gun to catch him very soon.[3]

"Old Virginia Never Tire" seemed to be a favorite of slave traders, with those in coffles throughout the South often singing that tune. The lyrics were a powerful device for deceiving onlookers, downplaying the grief of the enslaved and supporting the overall slavery system. Similar to the ruse of the plantation, the deceptive performance of music and sometimes dance within the domestic slave trade served as an attempt to mitigate the suffering of the slaves and justify the horrific trade while comforting the white spectators. Their strategy seemed to work for many witnesses, as Featherstonhaugh, who openly condemned the speculators and the overall institution of slavery as "atrocious practices" that should be "extinguished in every part of the world," believed that slaves in the coffle were cheerful because of the music they performed. Upon viewing the coffle performance, he deemed that the "poor negro slave is naturally a cheerful, laughing animal, and even when driving through the wilderness in chains, if he is well fed and kindly treated, is seldom melancholy . . . he is singularly docile."[4]

The spectacle that this Englishman witnessed was a major aspect of the landscape of slavery, "gangs" of enslaved black women, men, and children being forcibly marched by land and by sea. The slave coffle was a public event in which blacks were forced to travel, often by foot, throughout many towns and states in the United States to the auction block. This exhibition was witnessed by whites and blacks who would watch with fascination, curiosity, and disgust. For slaves, the coffle meant the loss of a family member or friend to a distant and feared destination. For many slave owners, it represented a strategic economic decision on commodities, but it also enhanced their feelings of control and domination in the social system; for slave traders it was a highly profitable business.

This scene in 1834 resembled for Featherstonhaugh "one of those coffles of slaves spoken of by Mungo Park," the Scottish explorer who wrote a travel journals in the eighteenth century depicting the collection of West Africans for the Atlantic journey. However this was southwestern Virginia, and the scene this English traveler witnessed was a part of an internal slave trade in which thousands of enslaved blacks were forced to leave their families to be sold on the auction block. "Black men in fetters, torn from the lands where they were born, from the ties they had formed . . . driven by white men." Featherstonhaugh's correlation between the coffles witnessed by Park in West Africa in the late eighteenth century and the coffle in antebellum Virginia was quite accurate. The international slave trade deposited West Africans from throughout the region into the New World colonies to be sold, bartered, and rented into a chattel slavery system. Influenced by the well-known performances of music and dance intentionally incorporated on plantations, farms, and in urban communities throughout the South (and several areas in the North) as evidence of white benevolence and black inferiority, slave traders incorporated music and dance in the new economic system of internal slave trading after the institution of slavery became an organized system in the beginning years of the nineteenth century.

UNITED STATES SLAVE TRADE.
1830.

Illustration depicting the internal slave trade in 1830 United States. (Cartoon Prints, American, Prints & Photographs Division, Library of Congress, LC-USZ62–89701.) Courtesy of the Library of Congress.

The commercial practice of internal slave trading began after several significant economic and social changes. Beginning in the seventeenth century, the plantation system became a central part of the economy of colonial North America. With the tobacco-producing colonies expanding in the Chesapeake region and the first British settlers arriving in South Carolina to cultivate rice in the 1670s, a plantation slavery system similar to that in the West Indies developed firmly.[5] As cash crops flourished and England dominated the African slave trade with the establishment of the Royal African Company in 1672, West Africans entered the region in droves. By the mid-eighteenth century, England was transporting an average of forty thousand to fifty thousand African captives into North America.[6] Britain's dominance in the trade had been a major topic of debate in Parliament since 1713 because abolitionists and several political figures viewed the method of transport to be inhumane and uncivilized. After internal and legislative debates, the African slave trade was abolished in England by 1807, and the newly independent United States imposed a tax or duty on the importation of African slaves in international trade in its constitution soon after.[7] With the continual population growth of black laborers and flourishing crop production, by the mid-eighteenth century a new occupation was developing within a growing domestic trade. In 1787, slave trader Moses Austin advertised in a Richmond, Virginia, newspaper that "one hundred Negroes . . . for which a good price will be given. . . . are to be sent out of state" to be sold.[8] Although there was always internal trading of slaves in North America, a formal, organized business of slave trading did not develop until the second decade of the nineteenth century.

Early on, the domestic trade was a minor aspect of the American slavery system, but with the changes in national law and agricultural development, it would take center stage. This new domestic slave trade prospered with changes in the landscape of the United States. The cotton gin invented by Eli Whitney in 1793 offered a simple and quick way to remove the seeds from cotton and instigated a major new enterprise of cotton crop production throughout the southern and western United States. By 1818 cotton had reinvigorated the slave-labor system, and it also marked the federal end of the international trade. With cotton and the end of the triangular trade, it became commonplace to see chained droves of enslaved blacks being marched by the sound of music to the slave market further south and west to work the fertile cotton and sugar plantations.[9]

By the early nineteenth century, slaves no longer required the seasoning that was such an integral element of the Atlantic slave trade. Instead, enslaved blacks were native born alongside white men, thus perfecting the major enterprise of human commodities. The controversial status of the international slave trade that led to its demise may also be seen in the negative review of the internal trade. Virginia Legislator Thomas Jefferson Randolph opined that the internal trade was "much worse" than the international trade.[10] To help quiet the controversy surrounding the interstate trade, which "put millions into the pockets of the people living between Roanoke and Mason and Dixon's line," according to the *New Orleans Courier*, music and dance were advantageously incorporated into every aspect.[11]

The internal slave trade as big business developed rather swiftly in the nineteenth century. There is not a formal date of initiation since planters had always bought and sold their slaves either within their communities or in an interstate/intrastate trade. However, by the 1830s, slave trading as an organized enterprise was evident. A formal process, as depicted in this chapter, was not a generic experience for every bondsman and bondswoman. But with rising competition and the lucrative nature of slave trading, there was a formula that many professional slave traders used that entailed the process from the farm, plantation, or urban community to the coffle, slave pen, and auction block that often incorporated the performing arts. Music, song, and dance seemed to increase in the trade, becoming almost a staple characteristic for many slave-trading businesses in the thirty years leading up to the Civil War.

The first step in the slave-trade business, gathering human chattel, usually occurred during the summer and autumn months.[12] During this time, speculators visited plantations, mainly in the upper Southern states, to gather any slaves that planters and overseers were willing to sell. Former slave Sella Martin remembered that the trader forced those headed to the market to sing in order to "prevent among the crowd of negroes who usually gather on such occasions, any expression of sorrow for those who are being torn away from them." However, those with "very little hope of ever seeing those again who are dearer to them than life, and who are weeping and wailing over separation, often turn the song thus demanded of them into a farewell dirge," revealed the former slave.[13] For the black community, the arrival of speculators often meant the loss of family and friends to a feared and unknown destination. Slave narratives repeatedly reference the terrible days when speculators arrived on the plantation. Sam T. Stewart never again saw his father after the speculators entered their plantation in Wake County, North Carolina.[14] Likewise, traders took Mary Gaines's "grandma, mother and her three brothers," and ex-slave Sophia Word of Kentucky remembered that when the "old slave trader" came to the plantation, he took "my mother's brother and sister" to the auction block to be sold like a "cow."[15] Many within the enslaved community considered slave traders "soul drivers," the most terrifying sight on the plantation. Fannie Moore, a former slave, recalled, "When de speculator come all de slaves start a-shakin'. No one know who is a goin'."[16]

The greatest fear for slaves was to be sold. Mrs. Betty Guwn and many of the slaves on the tobacco plantation near Canton, Kentucky, "heard awful tales of the slave auction block." Their fear led them to take preventive measures, such as making their masters "solemnly promise them that they should not be sold" whenever it was time for their to-bacco crop to be sold in the New Orleans market.[17] When the specula-tors arrived, "all de darkies know what dis mean . . . oh dem was awful times," remembered Sarah Gudger on the Hemphill plantation.[18] The threat of being sold spurred the courage of some slaves to run away. Julia King recalled a telling song that her formerly enslaved mother, Matilda Ward, had sung after successfully escaping to the North.

> Don't you remember the promise that you made,
> To my old dying mother's request?
> That I never should be sold,
> Not for silver or for gold
> While the sun rose from the East to the West?
>
> And it hadn't been a year
> The grass has not grown over her grave.
> I was advertised for sale.
> And I would have been in jail,
> If I had not crossed the deep, dancing waves.
>
> I'm upon the Northern banks
> And beneath the Lion's paw,
> And he'll growl if you come near the shore.[19]

These lyrics expressed the sentiment of many bondsmen and bonds-women who chose to escape their bondage after learning that they or their children were to be sold. The song illustrates not only the slaves' abhorrence of the auction block but also the contradictions inherent within the plantation community. Planters who sold their slaves were betraying a false responsibility that they continually asserted in their writings, speeches, and rhetoric. Slaves recognized that their planters were not paternal, as they attempted to portray; rather, they were deceit-ful when making the economic decision to sell their slaves. Although King refers only to those masters who sold their slaves as "mean and cranky," many slaves regarded masters who sent their slaves to the auc-tion block as the worst sort.

Planters sold their slaves in the interstate trade for several reasons. The domestic slave trade was constructed under the premise that humans could be "sold, transferred, or pawned as goods, or personal estate," according to William Goodell in his antebellum review of the American slave code.[20] Sometimes, slaves were brought to the auction block only as a necessity to settle an estate, which normally occurred after the death of the previous master. However, planters sold their slaves for a number of other reasons as well. From direly needing money to repay debt or attempting to dispose of a rebellious slave, planters freely used the auction block whenever it suited their personal or financial needs. In one of the most detailed slave narratives of the nineteenth century, former slave Charles Ball recalled that his father was sold to "prevent the perpetration of this suspected crime of *running away from slavery*."[21] Planters and overseers often used the auction block as an open threat to the enslaved community to coerce increased productivity and submission.

Speculators, planters, and overseers utilized subversive tactics to collect their human cargo because of the continual rebellions and tumultuous nature of slavery. The rebellious reactions of some slaves heading to the auction block spurred planters and slave traders to strategize on the manner in which they removed slaves from the plantation. Frederick Douglass spoke of a house slave, William, who, after expressing disapproval of his master, was informed by the overseer that he "was now to be sold to a Georgia trader. He was immediately chained and handcuffed . . . without a moment's warning he was snatched away . . . from . . . family and friends."[22] In the 1840s, Isaac Johnson, a former slave, witnessed the removal of numerous slaves by traders whose plans were "kept secret from the slaves." At about "ten o'clock the night before, twelve men were sent into the cabins" to handcuff the chosen bondsmen. The next day, these manacled men, together with the often-unshackled women and children, joined the coffle of slaves being marched to an auction block in Nashville.[23] This experience was extremely emotional and traumatic, which caused slavers to incorporate music to divert attention from these scenes.

Music that the slavers forced to distract the enslaved or even to cheer them, as was expected during the Middle Passage, instead often expressed the emotional trauma of being torn from family and friends. One of the farewell dirges heard throughout the slave states expresses such poignant sorrow:

> Oh! Fare ye well, my bonny love,
> I'm gwine away to leave you,

A long farewell for every love,
Don't let our parting grieve you.

[Chorus]
Oh! Fare ye well, my bonny, &c.
The way is long before me, love,
And all my love's behind;
You'll seek me down by the old gum-tree,
But none of you will find me.

I'll think of you in the cotton fields;
I'll pray for you when resting;
I'll look for you in every gang,
Like the bird that's lost her nesting.

I'll send you my love by the whoop-o-will;
The dove shall bring my sorrow;
I leave you a drop of my heart's own blood,
For I won't be back to-morrow.[24]

Slaves "loved their families" and fought to keep them together. The enslaved communities were singing to say their goodbyes and to express pain in the allowable art form of music. This song expressed the hypocrisy of the planters and proslavery propaganda that asserted that enslaved blacks showed "insensibility to ties of the kindred," an opinion endorsed by Chancellor William Harper of South Carolina.[25] Slave masters who traded their slaves were seen as cruel by their slaves and inferior by many within the white community. Former slaves evaluated their masters according to two major criteria: if they fed their slaves properly and if they continually sold slaves on the auction block. The "slave may forget his hunger, bad food, hard work, lashes, but he finds no relief from the ever-threatening evil of separation," said former slaves Tabb Gross and Lewis Smith.[26] Sophia Word determined that her master was "better . . . than most of them" because he "didn't auction off his slaves."[27] William Wells Brown told the story of Dr. Gaines, who, due to his economic mishaps, was unable to keep all of his slaves. Dr. Gaines, the "high-bred planter, through mismanagement, or other causes was compelled to sell his slaves, or some of them at auction, or as those within the enslaved community would say to let the 'soul buyer' have them."[28] The slaves often discussed their masters' status concerning economic standing, gambling problems, familial issues, or any situations that would have an effect on their daily lives and may result in being sold or rented out within the domestic trade.

Aside from what slaves thought, many masters viewed fellow planters who continually sold their slaves as weak and economically unstable. In 1792 Thomas Jefferson (who was at the time Secretary of State) wrote several letters to his attorney, Bowling Clarke, giving instructions for selling eleven slaves. After specifically mentioning which slaves he wanted to sell, Jefferson stated that he did "not (while in public life) like to have my name annexed in the public papers to the sale of property."[29] He continued in future letters to ask that the sale of those chosen slaves occur away from his home estate, Monticello. As a public figure, Jefferson did not want to appear economically deficient or lacking in the business skills needed to properly care for his slave community. As the domestic slave trade became more established as an element of the overall slavery system with the growth of the cotton industry, selling slaves became more acceptable. Nonetheless, many supporters of the proslavery movement campaigned against the slave trade due to ideals of paternalism and religion.

Beyond appearing deficient economically, planters who sold their slaves also were viewed as lacking the paternal, Christian characteristics that many proslavery advocates proclaimed formed the basis of the institution of slavery. In 1851, a Southern planter stated that the obligations of the planters "stop not with starting in good time and working industriously through the day." The good time mainly applied to music and dance and other rewards deemed appropriate by the white slave owner. He continued further by asserting that planters should be compelled to provide for the "moral government of the negroes on the farm" and he questioned, "Who then should care for and provide for their wants, if not the master?"[30] This planter asserted that all white slave holders had a duty to religiously instruct and nurture their bondsmen and bondswomen. In 1837, one Virginia planter stated that the "master should ever bear in mind that he is the guardian and protector of his slaves, who if well treated are the happiest laboring class in the world."[31] Therefore, if blacks were innately cheerful laborers requiring nothing more than "proper control," then the planter selling his slaves due to their rebelliousness was not successful in his role. One South Carolina overseer asserted in 1836 that slaves' "proper management constitutes the chief success of the planter."[32] Many people viewed the slave trade as contradicting the proslavery ideology of propagated paternalistic planters and docile, child-like slaves. Born within the planter class, Nathaniel S. Shaler reasserted the paternalistic notion that because their slaves were "well cared for," they were "mostly pretty decent and fairly industrious people." Many masters openly purported that they did not sell their slaves; however, due to the nature of slavery and the profitability of the trade, many planters were involved in some aspects of an internal trade by the mid-nineteenth century. Also, strategically throughout the slave society, it was a "common threat" that "if you don't behave, you will be sold South."[33] Whites constantly warned of the consequences of slaves' falling out of line, and the enslaved were always aware of the precarious position in their respective communities. The masters and overseers often publicly asserted that those chosen for the auction block were at fault for their condition, rather than that responsibility falling upon the personal deficiency of the master. However, although white slaveholders publicly proclaimed this propaganda, some actually believing this paternal relationship, the actions they took to maintain a lucrative slave trade contradicted their rhetoric. For more than half a century, many slaveholders participated as sellers or buyers in the domestic slave trade, even with its duplicitous nature and contradiction of proslavery philosophy. The hypocrisy of the institution was evident in the often-coerced music performed by slaves with the domestic trade. While being interviewed, Eliza Washington remembered that just before the speculators took the bondsmen and bondswomen from the plantation, the enslaved community began to sing. The former slave noted that "some of the songs were pitiful and sad," with one song in particular lamenting, "The speculator bought my wife and child; And carried her clear away!"[34] These types of songs could be heard on farms and plantations, and in some urban communities throughout slave societies, starkly contrasting the false cheerfulness expected from the coerced music of the coffle, which was the next stage of the domestic trade.

Music was a fundamental feature of the slave coffle, which represented the most visible stage of the interstate trade. After slave traders ventured to several plantations and farms to garner "a large drove. . . . then the slaves were fastened together with chains. . . . lined up like soldiers in double file," and publicly transported to auction blocks that were often further south," said former bondsman Sam T. Stewart from Wake County, North Carolina.[35] In 1822, Reverend James H. Dickey was "drove hastily to the side of the road" by "the sound of music." Initially believing it was a "military parade," Dickey soon discovered that "about forty black men" chained and "thirty women, in double rank" were being marched in "solemn sadness" to the "sounds of two violins" being played by fettered musicians.[36] The slave coffle was a public event in which blacks were forced to travel, often by foot, throughout many towns and states in the United States to the auction block. Born in Hartford, Connecticut, Frederick Law Olmstead traveled through the "cotton kingdom" in the 1850s after witnessing numerous aspects of the internal trade, including a coffle on a railroad freight car with "about

Illustration depicting a common scene of a slave coffle in the internal trade of slaves that used music during their route to the auction block. (Prints & Photographs Division, Library of Congress, LC-USZ62–30798.) Courtesy of the Library of Congress.

forty negroes" being transported to the Deep South; he believed that the "slave trade . . . is to be seen every day" in some form.[37] This "spectacle" elicited a variety of emotions from those who witnessed the scene.

Slave traders used music and dance in coffles as tactical tools to disguise the manacled bondage, the heavily armed guards, and their own degraded status from curious onlookers. Such exhibitions were witnessed by whites and blacks, who watched with fascination, curiosity, and disgust. In 1816, politician and historian George Tucker witnessed a coffle while visiting Portsmouth, Virginia. Those bound to the auction block marched while "singing a little wild hymn of sweet and mournful melody; flying, by a divine instinct of the heart, to the consolation of religion, the last refuge of the unhappy."[38] For Tucker, the crack of the whip by drivers who wanted only "good prices" and masters who "wanted money" was an atrocity against Christianity and humanity, and no person should have to "tolerate an abuse of this horrible character." He viewed the music as the only solace for the tortured lot. Music influenced the perspectives of the coffle onlookers, who often "gathered around the captives, from motives of curiosity or compassion."[39] British abolitionist Wilson Armistead believed that "few persons who visited the Slave States have not, on their return, told of the gangs of Slaves they had seen on their way to the southern market."[40] For this abolitionist, such scenes were not only "revolting and atrocious" but also the most visible aspect of the slavery system. "There is not a neighborhood . . . village or road that does not behold the sad procession," asserted a member of the Presbyterian Synod of Kentucky.[41] The visible chains and handcuffs caused one witness to ask, "What is their crime?" Another white observer asked, "Why do they chain you?" Many whites who witnessed these scenes wanted to believe that these slaves were being treated harshly and sold due to their own wrongdoing. Assuming that slaves in the coffle had perpetrated some crime allowed whites to view the unfortunate situations of the slaves as the slaves' own responsibility. This estimation deflected criticism away from the slave trade and the speculators, allowing them to be perceived as a "species of social workers who redeemed the dregs of society," as proclaimed by Maryland Congressman John C. Weems in a speech on the floor of the House of Representatives in January 1829, rather than as perpetrators of infractions against humanity.[42]

For Featherstonhaugh, it was not simply the manacled slaves who made "this spectacle still more disgusting and hideous," but the "principal white slave drivers, who were tolerably well dressed . . . standing near, laughing, and smoking cigars." The visiting Englishman considered these slave drivers as representing the hypocrisy of "the language of the American Declaration of Independence." For Featherstonhaugh and many who witnessed the atrocities of the coffle, the white slave traders were the true deviants in the slavery system. "I could not but be struck with the monstrous absurdity of such fellows; so wishing them in my heart all manner of evil to endure": such was the disgust vehemently expressed by the Englishman toward those "engaged in the exercise of such a horrid trade." He was not the only spectator to evaluate the coffle with such rhetoric.[43]

For some, slave trading was considered one of the most despicable professions. Many speculators were "miserable anti-human critters, walking on two legs," commented Philo Tower after his three-year journey in the 1850s through the Southern states.[44] Similar to poor whites, slave traders were viewed by many within the enslaved community to occupy the lowest rung of the white race. A former slave described Walker, a St. Louis slave trader, as an "uncouth, ill-bred, hard hearted man, with no education."[45] A traveling Englishman reiterated this perspective, deducing that those who participated in "the revolting traffic" were the "sordid, illiterate, and vulgar . . . men who can have nothing whatever in common with the gentlemen of the Southern States."[46] Many European visitors, Northerners and Southerners, and free and enslaved blacks alike viewed white slave traders as the lowest class.

The social status of speculators seems to have been a continual topic of discussion and debate, which contributed to the recurrent incorporation of music in the public spectacle of the internal trade. "Negro Brokers, Negro Speculators, Negro Auctioneers, and Negro Breeders, &c., are by that class universally despised and avoided," assessed Thomas Dwight Weld in his 1839 review on the institution of slavery. However, he concluded that it was not their work in human trafficking but instead their status as "working men" that contributed to their position in society. In antebellum plantation society, duplicity existed between planters and slave traders (and overseers) within the hierarchy of the South. Weld believed that those who entered the slave-trading business with "property and good standing" or from a privileged background could embark in "negro speculation" without losing social status, as long as this slave trader held the role of supervisor who "employs a dozen 'soul drivers' to traverse the country, and drive to the south coffles of slaves." According to Weld, the physical labor and "vulgar drudgery" involved in slave trading were the factors that lowered a trader's status. If a wealthy trader employed others to do the dirty work for him, his status was immune. However, poor whites attempting to move up in Southern society faced a harder trudge.[47] Although Weld's assessment, in fact, was, ironically, likely rejected and resented by many white Southerners, traders (initially) were often Northern entrepreneurs or landless Southern whites attempting to enter into the planter class. However, Nathan Shaler believed that a gentleman "should not run any risk of appearing as a 'negro-trader,'" for "the last word of opprobrium to be slung at a man" was a reference to him as a slave trader. He further asserted that "social ostracism was likely to be visited on any one who was fairly suspected of buying or selling slaves for profit." This social rule was the opinion held by the "better class of slave-owners," according to Shaler.[48] Both Weld and Shaler regarded slave trading as despicable; however, while Shaler believed that to be the case no matter what, Weld thought that the extent to which the act was despicable was prescribed by situational factors. Regardless, speculators, drivers, and traders were well aware of their degraded status, and in order to alter the public's perception, they incorporated clever ways to manipulate music and sometimes dance to reconstruct the public's opinion of the coffle, slavery, and those within the occupation of slave trading.

Witnesses of the coffle often held conflicting perspectives of these traveling spectacles. For many spectators, the scene affirmed or contributed to their advocacy against the overall slavery system. Many white observers, regardless of their antislavery or proslavery ideology, held expectations of black behavior imposed by the prevailing racial attitudes of

Illustration of a slave coffle traveling in the Capital while white spectators watch the public display. (Miscellaneous Items in High Demand Collection, Prints & Photographs Division, Library of Congress, LC-USZ62–2574.) Courtesy of the Library of Congress.

the era; these notions tailored their perceptions of the coffle performance. At age seven, Levi Coffin witnessed a drove of slaves headed to the block, and his "childish sympathy and interest were aroused." After his father asked one of the slaves, "Why do they chain you?" the distraught slave replied, "They have taken us away from our wives and children, and they chain us lest we should make our escape and go back to them." Personalizing the experience, Coffin thought of how terrible he would feel if "father were taken away from us." Due to this first awakening, he became an ardent proponent for abolition, eventually becoming a leader within the Underground Railroad.[49] Coffin and several observers viewed music and dance as an aspect of the atrocity of the slave trade, while others believed, as did Virginia observer George Tucker, that the performing arts were the religious expressions of the enslaved community. However, for many who witnessed coffle performances, music and dance confirmed the racialized ideologies put forth by the proslavery community.

The association of music and dance with happiness was an acceptable ideology promoted within the slave trade. One South Carolina planter, N. Herbemont, advocated in the *Southern Agriculturalist* newsletter that speculators found it to their advantage to "produce gaiety in their miserable captives." Herbemont continued in the article to state that by "causing them [slaves] to listen to and dance at the sound of some instrument, there must be some virtue in the practice," therefore deducing that the performing arts added humanity to the trade. Because speculators appeared to invest in the general "comfort and pleasure" of their slaves, music and dance assisted in rescinding the vices of the slave trade, at least from the perspective of the white witnesses. The strategy of incorporating music, dance, and cheerfulness benefited the slave traders' economic needs and spectators' perceptions of the act. The slave trade and those who worked within it were made palatable by this farce. The conflicting language of gaiety and misery in reference to the "dependent captives" positioned the slave trade as a necessary evil, and the speculators were simply attempting to make the best of a bad situation.[50] Although the trade was abhorrent, the music and dance distracted from the visible restraints and sadness of the performers, thus comforting the spectators and enhancing the reputation of the drivers.

Coffles were walking advertisements announcing to potential customers that they could buy not only labor but docile, happy, submissive bodies. Slave traders forced slaves to portray a happy disposition, and music was their favored tool. Milly Edmondson recalled that when she was sold by the trading company Bruin and Hill, as soon as the coffle began, "they that carried us away captive required of us a song, and they that wasted us required of us mirth"[51] The slaves performing music, dance, and false cheerfulness within the coffle shaped the public's perception of not only the slave trade but also the black race. The happy disposition confirmed societal stereotypes about blacks. In the 1830s, Irishman Tyrone Power witnessed a caravan of slaves; he determined that the "loud merriment" of music and dance fostered an overall "holiday spirit" that diminished the slaves' "great fatigue and . . . miserable appearance."[52] These public performances contributed to a shroud being placed over the hardships of bondsmen and bondswomen and allowed for the public perception of blackness to be flawed by stereotypes of innate jollity and musicality.

Slave traders used not only music and dance strategically in the trade; to advertise their human commodities and defend the institution of slavery and their role within it, they also fostered this façade through intoxicating liquids and false promises. Former slave Rosa Barnwell remembered the stories of her mother's experience of being sent from her only home to the cotton fields of Georgia. During the "despairing journey," the slave trader continually tried to console Barnwell's mother through the "promise of tender treatment" and "the pledge that he would try to get her a kind master."[53] Many slave traders attempted to subdue their human chattel with such promises, while others used liquor as the inducement. After a coffle was assembled in Rowan County, North Carolina, Reverend Jethro Rumple witnessed that at their departure, the trader coordinated a "grand jollification. A band or at least a drum and fife would be called into requisition, and perhaps a little rum be judiciously distributed to heighten the spirits of his sable property."[54] This festive exit from the holding pen to begin a journey to the auction block was an intentional display orchestrated by the slave traders to advertise their commodities while also publicly illustrating the humanity of the slave trade. These slave traders intentionally staged extravagant coffle scenes to entice the public to believe in the quality of their business and happiness of their slaves. Similar to a traveling circus that passes through the center of town to spur interest and attract potential customers, slave traders produced a carnivalesque atmosphere within the domestic slave trade. This spectacle involved the coffle and their guides "dancing and laughing, as if they were going on a holiday excursion," spurring a "curious crowd" to come out to "witness the scene." The liquor provided for the coffle induced bondsmen and bondswomen to perform while also distracting them from attempting to escape or rebel. In this most despicable aspect of slavery, the slave traders sought to distract from the breaking of families and friendships and from the contradictory ideals of paternalism; they did so by strategically using music and dance to garner acceptance for the horrendous business, with the additional exhilaration of liquor to assist in the festivities. Regardless of the promises and performances, it was evident that slave traders feared for their safety. Serving liquor to the slaves bound for the market allowed slave traders to assert more power over them and maintain not just their appearance of happiness but also their docility. In their attempt to bring their goods to market in a way that appealed to the public but that was also safe, many white speculators also incorporated black bondsmen into the trade.

Beyond forcing slaves to perform music and dance, speculators commonly forced enslaved blacks to perform as slave drivers in the trade.

As a slave, William Wells Brown was continually hired out. Within the institution of slavery, enslaved blacks commonly would be contracted to work on plantations for a fee that was paid to their owners. Although Brown was forced to work for many cruel masters, the worst torture of all was hearing that he had been hired out to a speculator, what he referred to as a "soul driver." Participating in the gruesome trade was a wretched experience for many of the coerced black slave traders. Brown, who was hired to the trader Mr. Walker for one year, described the experience as "the longest year I ever lived"; to him, the slave trade was an unjust system, and he would rather be sold to the feared South than work as a trader in the market. However, according to Brown, there were a few enslaved slave traders who enjoyed their authority within the trade. An external observer to the coffle scene witnessed that "negroes trained by the slave-dealers to drive the rest" were an interesting and entertaining aspect of the trade. Their presence may have validated the interstate trade for many white observers. These black slave traders were responsible for disciplining the human cargo, preparing them for market, and entertaining and comforting the slaves, witnesses, and white slave traders. Many black slave traders were expected to amuse the slaves bound for the market with "lively stories, boasting of the fine warm climate they are going to, and of the oranges and sugar which are there to be had for nothing."[55]

Beyond land, droves of slaves also traveled by waterway to the auction block, a method often referred to by slave traders as "down the river." As in the inland droves, music and dance were a part of the riverboat coffle. Slave traders and speculators often chartered riverboats or bought tickets on passenger ships to transport their slaves to the auction block. On these trips south, slave trader William A. Pullman of Lexington, Kentucky, put the bondsmen and bondswomen "on deck of the boat . . . they were chained together two by two until," after arriving "in the broad Mississippi River, there was little chance for the slaves to escape from the boat," so they were often unchained at that point.[56] Traders attempted to counter the rigidity of this passage by compelling slaves to sing and make music. European tourists, statesmen, and influential leaders witnessed these performing festivals of manacled slaves and constructed their ideals of slavery from these scenes. Prior to becoming one of the most influential presidents of the United States, Abraham Lincoln witnessed a drove of slaves bound for a Southern plantation on his steamboat trip from Lebanon, Kentucky, to St. Louis, Missouri. On September 27, 1841, Lincoln wrote a letter to his friend, Mary Speed, describing what he referred to as "the effect of condition upon human happiness." "A gentleman had purchased twelve negroes in different parts of Kentucky . . . taking them to a farm in the south. They were chained six and six together. A small iron clevis was around the left wrist of each." Lincoln recognized that within this "condition," families were being separated "forever from the scenes of their childhood, their friends, their fathers and mothers, and brothers and sisters. . . . going into perpetual slavery where the lash of the master is proverbially more ruthless and unrelenting than any other." However, Lincoln, similar to many witnesses of the coffle, assessed that those bondsmen and bondswomen headed to the southern farm were "the most cheerful and apparently happy creatures on board." This happiness appeared evident to the future president by their playing of the "fiddle almost continuously" while the "others danced, sang, cracked jokes, and played various games with cards from day to day."[57] The intentional distractions provided by the slave traders influenced onlookers, such as Lincoln, in their political ideologies and personal beliefs about race and slavery. Lincoln's conflicting opinion that slavery was atrocious but that enslaved blacks were happy was quite common among whites throughout the United States. The duality of his thought regarding the slave trade was made evident in the indecisive stance on slavery that he took during his presidency. Lincoln pondered the coffle scene, stating, "How true it is that 'God tempers the wind to the shorn lamb,' or in other words, that he renders the worst of human conditions tolerable, while he permits the best to be nothing better than tolerable."[58] Music and dance equated to cheerfulness for the Illinois politician in a way similar to many whites who witnessed the traveling performances and thought that these slaves were not only content, but also happy, which contributed to the overall justification of slavery. The public nature of slave coffles, either by land, train, or river, with slaves performing music, song, and dance repeatedly throughout the United States, had influential power in the development and perception of race that will never be fully understood or quantified. Coffles, unlike the slave pen and auction block, were not viewed by select audiences that intentionally ventured to a designated facility but instead were a central aspect of life in American society.

The next step after the public coffle was the entrance of thousands of manacled droves into slave pens throughout the South and in western towns. Either en route to the auction block or upon their arrival, many slaves were housed in slave pens, which often were referred to as jails, that existed throughout the South. According to former slave Isaac Johnson, slave pens "were divided into groups, women in one, men in another, girls and young boys by themselves." Here, planters examined the human commodities prior to the public bidding. Some slave pens were professionally run by outside contractors, while others were part of the slave trader's enterprise. Others were local jail facilities fitted "with bolts and bars," as was Hope H. Slatter's pen in Baltimore. The common term "slave jails" correlates to some of the white public's perception that slaves bound for the auction block had committed an infraction resulting in the punishment of being sold. These slave pens varied in appearance and extravagance with the average daily charge, which typically ranged from twenty-five to forty cents.[59] Larger facilities, such as one run by well-known slave trader Richard Lumpkin of Richmond, Virginia, "consisted of four buildings, which were of brick. One was used by the proprietor as his residence and office. Another . . . a boarding house for . . . those who came to sell their slaves or to buy. A third as a bar-room and kitchen," and the last building was the "old jail" that housed the men and women to be "disposed of at private or public sale."[60] For many slave traders, the slave pen not only housed their "merchandise" but also represented the respect they had for their craft. Lewis C. Robards was the leading slave trader in Lexington, Kentucky, by 1849; his success enabled him to purchase and transform the local theater into a slave pen.[61] Advertised as the "largest and best constructed building for a jail in the West," Robards was able to display his "choice stock" of female slaves in the so-called fancy trade, an offshoot of the domestic slave trade in which bondswomen were sold for sexual use. The auction experience for many female bondswomen was sexual. It was a customary aspect of the market experience to create rudimentary examinations to determine the price of a woman believed to be a "good breeder." Hattie Rogers recalled that in the North Carolina markets, "slave buyers would come around and jab" women "in the stomach" to determine if they could quickly produce children, which would only increase the prospective wealth of the buyer. The various slave pens scattered throughout the United States to house bondsmen and bondswomen only served to decrease the humanity shown to the slaves and provided white predators with easy access to vulnerable slave women.[62]

Upon arriving at the slave pen, speculators advertised the forthcoming sale in local newspapers and with fliers. A Lexington, Kentucky, slave-trading firm, Griffin & Pullman, advertised in a Mississippi paper, "Slaves! Slaves! Slaves! Fresh Arrivals Weekly. . . . a large and well-selected stock of Negroes, consisting of field hands, house servants, mechanics, cooks, seamstresses, washers, ironers, etc., which we can and will sell as low or lower than any other house here or in New Orleans."[63] Similar to advertisements specifically referring to "fancy ladies" or good breeders, enslaved musicians and recognized amusing dancers also were detailed in pamphlets and newspaper announcements. "FOR HIRE . . . the celebrated musician and fiddler, George Walker," advertised the trading firm of Toler & Cook in the *Richmond Daily Enquirer* on June 27, 1853.[64] The announcement continued by stating that the available musician was recognized to be the "best leader of a band in all eastern and middle Virginia."[65] Walker was not for sale but only available for temporary hire due to his master's desire to continue to gain revenue from such a popular musician. Several particular talents, especially in music and dance, appealed to potential masters. In Georgia, "Blind Tom" was considered a young musical prodigy, and his master continually gained money from hiring out this slave to perform in public concerts.[66] Beyond being hired out or sold as performers, there were numerous slaves within the enslaved community who were coerced to display specific musical or dancing performances within the slave pen, to illustrate to potential buyers that they were not only buying labor but also entertainment. Music and dance were integral to the institution of slavery, and slave trading was a highly competitive business. Throughout the year, especially in the Deep South, advertisements of human commodities regularly appeared in local newspapers. These announcements were often quite specific regarding the type of slaves either wanted by potential buyers or available for sale at the market. Northern traveler Olmstead noticed in Texas that "in the windows of shops, and on the doors and columns of the hotel, are many written advertisements."[67] Once the advertisements reached the papers and fliers, slave traders moved into the next phase of preparing slaves for the block.

The staging for the auction block began at the slave pen. Former slave Jennie Kendricks of Sherman, Georgia, remembered the story of her grandmother being sold off to Virginia as a young girl. "She used to tell me how the slave dealers brought her and a group of other children along much the same as they would a herd of cattle . . . when they reached a town all of them had to dance through the streets and act lively so that the chances for selling them would be greater."[68] Forcing slaves to perform upon their arrival at the holding pen served as a calculated move by slave traders. Beyond performance, speculators forced bondsmen and bondswomen in the pen "to wash thoroughly, and those with beards to shave." The male slaves were often "furnished with a new suit" and the women with "frocks of calico," contingent on the wealth of the trader. [69] In addition to these provisions, the human chattel were "better fed than slaves generally" to make them appear healthier in the hopes of garnering higher bids on the auction block.[70] As former slave John Brown acutely mentioned, "The slaves are bought from all parts, are of all sorts, sizes, and ages, and arrive at various states of fatigue and condition; but they soon improve in their looks" due to the preparative process they experience in the pens.[71] Such preparations occurred commonly within slave pens throughout the United States. One former slave who was employed as a slave trader, William Wells Brown, detailed the manner in which he was forced to prepare slaves for the market. He was ordered by the white speculators to either pluck grey hairs or dye them with a "blacking brush" to make the slaves look "ten or fifteen years younger." In addition to transforming their outer appearance, Brown, similar to many other slave traders, taught the slaves to lie about their age, present a willingness to work, and conceal past rebellions against their masters. This staging of human commodities in the pen involved "tricks of the trade" that slave traders practiced. One bondsman, Pompey, was told by his master, Walker, a slave trader, to always put "a little grease" on their faces so that they may "look black an' slick, an' make you look younger."[72] For as former bondsman W. L. Bost remembered, those that looked "'tween eighteen and thirty always bring the most money." This preparation was used intentionally to deceive potential buyers. Traders and auctioneers were salesmen who told detailed stories about the slaves, their past lives, and their potential futures in order to paint a picture of good and faithful laborers ready to contribute to a plentiful harvest. The speculators who became quite wealthy in the trade often invested greatly in making sure that they only brought "young and likely Negroes" who immediately would be able to turn a profit on a plantation, and they created lavish facilities to house those headed for the block. The potential buyers were investing in their future status in society and in their impending fortune in crop production. Economically, it was necessary that slave traders "should not show any signs of ill treatment," nor should any indication of insubordination among the bondsmen and bondswomen be publicly displayed lest it affect the sale.[73] In these pens, black bodies were displayed, inspected, and assigned a monetary value that traders believed was enhanced by coercing the human commodities to perform music, dance, and cheerfulness in the holding pen.

The slave pen was the dress rehearsal that invited potential buyers and other spectators into the fantasized world that slave traders intentionally created. A former bondswoman, Ms. Martin, stated that at the pen, the slaves were ordered to "strike up lively," which they understood to mean "begin a song."[74] The song's lyrics may have been sad with a melancholy tone, or spirited, such as "Old Virginia Never Tire"; regardless, those interested in purchasing slaves were led to believe that a spirited lot would soon be on the block. After arriving in New Orleans, a major city

Illustration of illegally enslaved Solomon Northup in a slave pen in Washington D.C., waiting to be sold on the auction block in the domestic slave trade. (Solomon Northup, *Twelve Years A Slave* [Baton Rouge: Louisiana State University, 1853, 1968], 24.)

Illustration of slaves on display in the streets of New Orleans before being placed on the auction block. Courtesy of the Library of Congress.

within the domestic trade, John Brown was placed in a slave pen facing the St. Charles Hotel. This prime location allowed slaves to be visible to buyers in town specifically for the auction as well as to the normal traffic in this major city center. John Brown was placed in a pen that could potentially hold five hundred men, women, and children; it was often full for the auctions.[75] Slave traders from Washington, D.C., Kentucky, Georgia, and Virginia brought their coffles by land and sea to this popular Southern market. While waiting for the sale to begin, the human commodities were "compelled to walk, and dance, and kick about the yard, for exercise" on a "nicely gravelled" lot purposely constructed for these public exercise routines. This slave pen also had in full-time attendance "a mulatto named Bob Freeman" who "had charge of the arrangements that concerned the slaves." To demonstrate the health of the slaves and appeal to potential customers, Bob acted not only as a full-time attendant but also as a musician. In the evenings, Bob played spirited "jigs" on the fiddle and coerced the slaves to dance. John Brown remembered that "if we did not dance to his fiddle, we used to have to do so to his whip, so no wonder we used our legs handsomely." These public performances occurred after the evening meal and during the intervals between auctions to both entertain and entice those at the auction block. In 1841, Joseph

Sturge visited a slave-trading establishment in Alexandria, Virginia, that was a "square court or yard, with very high walls, in which about fifty slaves" were being housed. In this pen, some of the slaves were "dancing to a fiddle" while others appeared in "silent dejection," according to Sturge.[76] Regardless of the fast, cheerful tempo of the music within the pen and on the auction block, the traders' alterations to the physical appearance of the slaves, or the order to "strike it up lively" in the marketplace, the entire episode was a horrific experience for the enslaved community.

These slave-pen performances induced whites to attend the auctions and to buy particular slaves who not only entertained them in music and dance but fulfilled their fantasies of hard labor and cheerful submission.[77] Similar to John Brown, William Wells Brown, while serving as an enslaved slave trader, spoke of the "negro pen," noting that after the slaves were "dressed and driven out into the yard," they then were "set to dancing, some to jumping, some to singing, and some to playing cards" as the potential buyers entered the facility.[78] Brown, well aware that "this was done to make them appear cheerful and happy," was responsible to "see that they were placed in those situations before the arrival of the purchasers." "I have often set them to dancing when their cheeks were set with tears," recalled William Wells Brown of this atrocious experience in which he acted as both bondsman and slave trader.[79] Whites bought human chattel not only for economic profit, but also to enforce the belief that they were benevolent, paternal masters providing a positive service in their purchase of black bodies. In many ways, exchanges between slaves and buyers were rehearsals for the plantation experience. The performances allowed whites to imagine their profits and status. The slave pen, similar to the entire slave trade experience, appeared quite different from the various perspectives of potential buyers, traders, and the enslaved community. As in the coffle, whites' use of blacks in the slave pen to coerce these façades allowed whites to uphold their fantasy that the enslaved population performed these roles naturally, without the coercion of whites. In a Richmond slave market in October 1853, Northerner Olmstead viewed the large rooms of the pens with "a few comfortably and neatly clad negroes, who appeared perfectly cheerful, each grinning obsequiously."[80] Whips were intentionally absent, especially from the hands of white men. However, hidden rooms existed in many slave pen facilities: John Brown's slave pen contained a "flogging-room" within which slave dealers used "instruments that will not cut the skin."[81] Tactically, slave traders understood that physical signs of whippings diminished the quality and therefore value of the slave on the market; therefore, torture instruments were intentionally used that left few to no marks. Men, women, and children were all "punished alike" into submission to perform these cheerful acts and behave accordingly in the pen and on the auction block. Such punishments were inflicted for various offences, especially the "unpardonable" ones, such as not responding to questions correctly or not "looking bright and smart" when the buyers were surveying the human chattel. In his personal narrative, John Brown described the importance of "looking bright" and its contribution to a slave's final price, which could be "impaired by a sour look, or a dull, vacant stare, or a general dullness of demeanour." The term "smart" did not refer to connate intellectual abilities but instead the ability to exert the public image of body agility and contented docility, which music and dance assisted in illuminating for the white customers. This was why Brown and the thousands to be sold at the market were told to "speak up and recommend themselves," sing and dance while putting on "a smiling, cheerful countenance . . . conceal any defects . . . and not tell their age."[82]

The deceit of the auction block was accomplished only by an often unspoken agreement between the trader and the slave. Within this arrangement, both parties had power. Part of this negotiation began early, with many traders questioning those bound for the auction block.[83] Slave trader Walker of St. Louis had a conversation with a bondsman, Sam, while also inspecting his body to see if he could garner a good price. The examination included checking the teeth, for Walker claimed that he could "judge a nigger's age by his teeth," and then asking if he ate properly to make sure he was healthy. Next, Walker asked Sam to "get out on the floor and dance; I want to see if you are supple," to which Sam replied, "I don't like to dance; I is got religion."[84] Sam was not only refusing to dance but also rejecting the racialized expectations that blacks were simply docile, cheerful performers. Sam used his Christianity to assert his personal choice and power within the trade and over his body.

Auction block facilities took on various forms and appearances from city to town. But all were stages of a sort for the ultimate performance of white power over black bodies. In Manchester, Kentucky, the auction block was made "from rough-made lumber" built as an open platform. In New Orleans, the auction block was often extravagant. Some facilities were large enough for hundreds of slaves to line the wall and be questioned by potential buyers, and they often contained a raised platform upon which slaves would stand and be sold to the highest bidder. With their painted walls and extravagant art, these facilities were common meeting places for wealthy men, poor overseers, and the curious. Upon stepping on the raised platform, the auctioneer would proclaim, "Now gentlemen and fellow citizens, here is a big black buck Negro. He's stout as a mule. Good for any kind o' work and he never gives any trouble. How much am I offered for him?" With these words, the sale began.[85] The auctioneers, similar to circus ringmasters, honed their craft in selling black men, women, and children. Auctioneers could be slave traders or white men who made a living from their ingenuity in entertaining and figuratively fulfilling the buyer's hopes and desires for these human commodities. Similar to magicians, auctioneers, especially those who were skilled, were able to distract from the atrocity of the scenes and divert attention through various entertaining antics to the amusement of the sale. Drawing attention through hyperbole, as scholar Walter Johnson extensively analyzed in *Soul by Soul*, auctioneers had the power to expel the humanity, or lack thereof, within the auction block and objectify and replace other ideals of wealth, sexual pleasure, and desires upon the enslaved community. After addressing the gentlemen in the crowd, the auctioneer typically would relate not only the age and working background of the human commodity but also comments regarding the slave's character. "He is an honest boy, can be trusted with any thing you wish," the auctioneer said of one slave, and for another, "Jenny," the auctioneer stated that she "can do good work" and was a "very pious old woman" that "will neither lie nor steal." Such assessments helped to increase profits on each sale.[86] Setting the price of those on the auction block was a negotiation constructed through the creative stories relayed by the auctioneers; however, it was not the only factor that contributed to the sale.

Even in this moment of most abject exploitation—the literal sale of humanity—slaves maintained some power. Their influence over their sale was well known among the black community. On the auction block and in the holding pens, several slaves openly asserted their unwillingness to be sold to a particular master. While on the auction block in Missouri, Delicia Patterson openly addressed the "wealthiest slave owners in the county, and the meanest one" by stating, "Old Judge Miller don't you bid for me, 'cause if you do, I would not live on your plantation. I will take a knife and cut my own throat from ear to ear before I would be owned by you."[87] Patterson had heard that Judge Miller was "so cruel and the slaves . . . hated him," so she openly rebelled on the auction block. Because many slaves were openly addressed on the auction block and in the pen, they used these exchanges to tactfully determine who they wanted to have bid on them and their families. When several family members were on the block together, it was quite common for them to appeal to those bidding to buy their wives, husbands, siblings, or children. Beyond

Illustration caption states, "Sale of Estates, Pictures and Slaves in the Rotunda, New Orleans." This image depicts the selling of slaves by auctioneer to the highest bidder in the domestic slave trade. (J. S. Buckingham, *The Slave States of America* [London, 1842].)

Illustration of the most dreaded experience within the American slavery system, the auction block, with black men, women, and children being sold to the highest bidder. (Miscellaneous Items in High Demand Collection, Prints & Photographs Division, Library of Congress, LC-USZ62–2582.) Courtesy of the Library of Congress.

overt appeals to potential buyers, many within the enslaved community used music and dance to influence the purchase. Almost 150 years after slavery ended, Ruth Galmon, at age 105, recalled the story of her enslaved grandmother's sale on the auction block. "They brought her down here and sold her you see they have them on a big block . . . and make them stand up and act a certain way . . . if they think you good they buy you . . . you didn't act right they wouldn't buy you."[88] Black women, men, and children often were aware that they could sway particular persons in their purchasing decisions.

Music and dance served as malleable tools that the enslaved community used to negotiate their sale. Sophia Word recalled that in the slave pen and on the auction block, they were expected to "jump around" to illustrate their dexterity, strength, and overall health. The pretense of cheerfulness, agility, and docility could be altered according to the manner in which blacks performed on the auction block. The style of dance and agility of feet of Fred, a bondsman, contributed to the high price he garnered. Jolly Old Uncle Buck, a slave in the same drove placed in the pen and on the block with Fred the day that they were to be sold, noted, "Dat nigger wid de banjo settin' on de bench waitin' to be sold, he plunk his banjo." Clearly, it was quite common to position an enslaved musician either in the pen or on the block to assist in the sale. While the music played and the traders coerced the potential buyers, Fred "'gin ter shuffle. . . . he slap his big feet on de banjo table" while the white men attending the auction watched with amusement and desire. The "white man laugh an' clap dey hans. Make him dance some mo'." Then Fred "dance de buck-an'-wing." The dancing was enforced by speculators, but Fred, like the others to be sold, determined the extent of his own effort in the performance. His dancing style was so influential that "de white man what bought Fred say he done paid hundert dollars mo' fo' dat nigger cause he could dance like dat," recalled Jolly Old Uncle Buck.[89] In maintaining power over his performance, Fred influenced his future destination. Ruth Galmon recalled that if a slave was good at performing and appearing happily submissive, then "they buy you," and if slaves decided to act sluggish or sickly through slow movements, sad through depressing song lyrics, or rebellious by refusing to perform, like Sam, then they risked being sold at a lower price or not at all. The repetitious mandate for slaves to perform and act cheerful caused a separation of black bodies from their humanity and constantly positioned them as commodities.

Music and dance may have been used to advertise and commodify black bodies; however, within the enslaved community it was also used to encourage, strategize rebellions, and relay information to assist in

survival. Historian Michael Tadman estimated that one in five marriages were prematurely terminated due to sales, and fully half of all
slave children younger than age fourteen were taken away from their
families; fellow bondsmen and bondswomen caught within the domestic
trade assisted with this emotional trauma. Former slave Peter Randolph
recalled a song used for encouragement among the black community
forced within the domestic trade:

> O fare you well, O fare you well,
> God bless you until we meet again;
> Hope to meet you in heaven, to part no more.
> [Chorus]
> Sisters fare you well; sisters, fare you well;
> God Almighty bless you, until we meet again.[90]

Leaving behind friends and family to travel to an unknown and likely
dangerous destination made the auction block experience dreadful and
traumatic for the enslaved community. Through ingenuity within musical lyrics, the black community used religious language to express
farewells and anguish from being separated from their families, with the
only chance of being reunited through death in an afterlife. The presence
of performances, both initiated by the trader's whip and autonomously
expressed by the enslaved, illustrates the duality of music, song, and
dance in the slavery system. For Randolph and many others, music and
dance were powerful tools of self-expression, spirituality, rebellion, and
autonomy that whites could not obstruct through their ruse of the performing arts.

The gathering of the enslaved community from various regions allowed for an exchange of stories, songs, and cultures. For example, the
distinct Creole, French, West African, and Haitian cultures that were
strong throughout New Orleans music and dance must have influenced
those hundreds of slaves entering the popular slave-trading hub. Slaves
from small rural farms came into contact with those from urban centers,
such as Lexington, St. Louis, Charleston, or Richmond, and exchanged
their distinct lyrical expressions and dance styles. In many ways the domestic slave trade had a stronger influence on the public image of slavery
than the plantation and small-holdings farm communities of the nineteenth century. These exhibitions of black subjugation and false joviality within the traveling coffle performances were seen throughout the
United States and had a major effect on the public. Beyond those caught
within the trade, the hundreds of onlookers, regardless of race, were culturally imprinted with different sounds and movements from the forced

amusements of coffles traveling through their towns and cities to the sounds of mirth coming from slave pens. For some the spectacle contributed to their abolitionist sentiment; for others the scene only confirmed their racial ideology of black subjugation. Regardless, the type of music performed, the lyrical expression, and dance movements of bondsmen and bondswomen from regions throughout the United States influenced white and blacks, North American and European visitors, and proslavery and antislavery spectators alike. The depths of these exchanges may never be completely comprehended. However, it must be recognized that the enslaved population entered the domestic trade with various music and dance customs, and the domestic trade as an enterprise has its own performing-arts culture, so this public stage within the institution of slavery influenced American culture, as a whole. The songs and themes of the domestic slave trade contributed to American popular culture with "carry-me back" songs that spoke of happy times on the plantation, similar to the one heard by George Featherstonhaugh, infiltrated the rising entertainment culture.[91] From the Middle Passage to the plantation and throughout the domestic slave trade, images and stories of happy black slaves singing and dancing throughout the South infiltrated the North and manifested in an emerging entertainment genre, blackface minstrelsy.

6   Same Script, Different Actors

"Eb'ry time I wheel about, I jump Jim Crow"

"Then turn next to Africa, wild, To view the sun-burnt negro Child; Has music charms for him? Ah! Yes; His Song to him is happiness," sang comedic British actor Charles Matthews on the theater stage.[1] On Thursday, March 25, 1824, the English Opera House introduced black characters who depicted the "American Negro" as inept, humorously entertaining, and musical.[2] Matthews performed those song lyrics to introduce the characters he encountered while visiting the United States During a nine-month trip to America from September 1822 to the following May, visiting Boston, New York, Philadelphia, and Baltimore, Matthews collected material on the "peculiarities, characters, and manners" of Americans for his one-man theatrical production, "A Trip to America." Renowned for his talents in mimicry, Matthews used incidents and people encountered during his travels in America to construct segments of his show. His portrayals of "authentic Americans" were incorporated into the 1824 performance, and Matthews openly admitted that his portrayal of "Negro characters" caused him to "be rich in black fun." To recreate the Black American and portray the black characters he presented to British audiences, Matthews exuberantly proclaimed in his memoirs that he "studied their broken English carefully." Periodically changing his attire, features, and linguistic styles, Matthews introduced in this highly popular theater production "a black tragedian," "fiddling negro," "Maximillian the Nigger" and "Agamemnon."[3]

From minor to major sketches on black characters, Matthews was, according to historian Robert Toll, the "first to build Negro stage characterizations" on purportedly "detailed observations" of blacks in America.[4]

Illustration of the characters that British comedian Charles Mathews performed in his famous "A Trip to America" theater production wherein he mocked North Americans. His character of Agamemnon, a poor runaway black slave, was one of many black characters he introduced to a London audience on March 25, 1824, and contributed to the beginning and popularity of the American blackface minstrel show. (TCS 44, Harvard Theatre Collection, Houghton Library, Harvard University.) Courtesy of the Houghton Library, Harvard Theatre Collection.

A lithograph drawing portraying the festivity of this final interaction represents the six characters within this last scene of "A Trip to America." Matthews enthusiastically accepted American folklore as real, believing that black Americans possessed innate musicality regardless of the circumstance. Following his musical theme, he introduced a "fiddling Negro" who offered "little amusement" while traveling through Providence, Rhode Island. Next, in a scene titled "All Well at Natchitoches," Matthews introduced "Agamemnon, a poor runaway Negro," who was an "unwieldy fellow" with many "bad qualities, and is not only very fat but addicted to laziness." Although Agamemnon was not described as a musician, his image illustrates a robust, smiling black man performing a shuffle dance with fiddle in hand. Another laughable character that Matthews claimed to have encountered during his venture through America was a waiter referred to as "Maximillian, a Nigger, or Negro." While serving dinner, Maximillian continually and intentionally drops a "tureen of soup" on the floor and down a "gentleman's back"; laughter is the only response offered by this seemingly incompetent yet innately happy waiter. Matthews seemed to have witnessed and recreated the naturally jolly, musical simplicity of American blacks. While many of these black characters were minor within the overall production, Matthews's depiction of a "black tragedian" illustrates one of the most controversial and extensive portrayals of blacks in America at the time.

The black tragedian was performed in "A Trip to America" as follows:

> Mr. Matthews next informs us that he went to a theater, called the Niggers' (or Negroes') theatre, where he beholds a black tragedian in the character of Hamlet; or just enters as he proceeding with the speech, "To be or not to be? That is the question; whether it is nobler in de mind to suffer, or tak' up arms against a sea of trouble, and by opossum end 'em." No sooner was the word opossum out of his mouth, than the audience burst forth in one general cry, "Opposum! Opossum! Opossum!" and the tragedian came forward and informed them that he would sing their favourite melody with greater pleasure; when, to please his audience, he gave them.
> Song.—"Opossum up a Gum-Tree.[5]

Within three months, James Hewlett, the "black tragedian" whom Matthews evidently had mimicked, responded publicly in the *National Advocate* to his distorted performance.[6] Hewlett was the leading actor at the first Black Shakespearean theater company in New York City, the African Grove Theater, which opened in 1821.[7] In a statement published on May 8, 1824, Hewlett responded to Matthews's "A Trip to America" performance that "ridiculed . . . and burlesqued . . . the negroe actors" from the New York theater. Hewlett further asserted that his performance of Hamlet was "perfect to a letter" and was unjustly caricatured in the British performance. Hewlett openly condemned Matthews for intentionally shaming the black actors due to their "complexions" by asking, "Now, when you were ridiculing the 'chief black tragedian,' and burlesquing the 'real negro melody,' was it my 'mind,' or my 'visage,' which should have made an impression upon you?" Politely accusing Matthews of mimicking the negative racial ideology of blackness more so than the performance he had witnessed, Hewlett told the British actor at the end of the letter to "remember when you next ridicule the 'tincture of the skin,' not to forget the texture of the mind."[8]

Charles Matthews's portrayal of the black tragedian has been discussed, disputed, and debated by other black actors in the African Grove Theater, scholars, and theater enthusiasts for more than a century, for his rendition of the original performance was an assault on not only black professional actors but also the reputation and public racial image of all blacks in America. Although Hewlett's letter in the *National Advocate* indicates that Matthews visited the theater and interacted with the "negro actors," theater scholar Marvin McAllister suggests that the British actor never even visited the African Grove Theater but instead invented a fictional, satirical skit.[9] Due to the black actor's preference for "English ballads" rather than "Negro airs," it is doubtful, according to McAllister, that Matthews either visited the theater or accurately depicted the performance. Also, musicologist scholar Sam Dennison, in *Scandalize My Name*, asserts that Matthews was far too "elitist" to interact with those associated with the African American theater.[10] Though these arguments center on delegitimizing Matthews's purported American experiences and encounters, it is also important to examine the manner in which this foreign visitor depicted black Americans to an English audience.

Although Matthews remained within the Northeastern states during his travels, the representations of blacks in "A Trip to America" focuses on characteristics often applied to Southern enslaved blacks, as is evident in the lyrics of the famously sung "Old Possum up a gum tree":

> Possum up a Gum-tree
> Up he go, up he go
> Raccoon in the hollow
> Down below, down below
> Him pull him by hims long tail
> Pully hawl, pully hawl
> Then how him whoop and hallow
> Scream and bawl, scream and bawl.
>
> Possum up a Gum-tree
> Raccoon in the hollow
> Him pull him by hims long tail Then how him whop and hallow.
>
> Massa send we Negro Boy
> Board a ship, board a ship
> There we work and cry "Ye hoy"

Cowskin whip, cowskin whip
Negro he work all day
Night get groggy, night get groggy
But if Negro he go play
Massa fog, Massa floggy.
Possum &c[11]

The images of the Southern slave performances that had long permeated American society, including black slaves happily performing music,
song, and dance throughout the Middle Passage, the domestic slave trade,
and on the plantation, contributed to Matthews's perception of blacks
in America. The entertainment that many Northern blacks provided
for white festivities contributed to Matthews's perspective of American
blacks, yet in his theatrical portrayal he focused on the erroneous image
of the Southern slave. In the song lyrics, to "go play" at night directly
refers to the frolics of blacks upon the plantation, either under the watchful eye of the master or in private. Also, discipline from the "cow skin
whip" and references to "massa" all invoke images and language present
on the Southern plantation. As revealed through the main characters in
two of Matthews's songs, the fiddling and dancing slave and the fiddling
stagecoach driver, Matthews accepted the racial ideals that blacks happily danced and sang. These images that Matthews brought to Britain
came from the intentional misrepresentation of blacks perpetuated by
white Americans. Matthews's black characters thus obscured the reality of black Americans' lives. Additionally, his performances revealed
the importance of music and dance within the American slavery system
and entertainment culture.

In America and abroad, distinctive images of blacks singing and dancing proliferated from the Southern slavery system either through travel
journals or fictional literature, the public spectacle of the domestic trade,
newspaper accounts of plantation festivities, or through oral stories. Blacks,
both free and enslaved, were stigmatized as slavery thrived in America,
and blackness was characterized as the antithesis of whiteness. The history of America, in fact, correlated with negative black stereotypes. The
South's slave system constantly constructed racial categories, presenting
erroneous, negative depictions of blacks while creating (by default) the
positive, dominant antithesis, whiteness. These images and their racial
hierarchical structure assisted in creating a normalcy of culture uniquely
related to the development of the Southern plantation system.

The dominant racial ideologies that were intentionally perpetuated in the South through the public display of bondsmen and bondswomen performing music, song, and dance infiltrated Northern culture

and associated the public image of blackness with façades of Southern slavery. The image of black slaves singing and dancing throughout the plantation economy was thus accepted by many Northerners, as well as foreign visitors such as Charles Matthews, regardless of whether or not they had visited the South and witnessed the performances. The South's plantation economy and the North's industrial society took different social and cultural paths. Matthews, like many Europeans and North-erners, may have never ventured to the Southern slave society, but both regions held similar negative perceptions of blacks, whether enslaved or free. In 1827, the biography of a former bondsman named "Aaron," was transcribed by a Northern abolitionist; the text specifically referred to the popular false concepts apparent in these common performances. The writer responded to the erroneous story that many Northerners and foreigners were "told that slaves showed by their actions that they are happy" and to the fallacious myths that slaves "sing, laugh, dance and make merry" as an "effort of the mind to throw trouble." Anecdotally, "Aaron" asks, "Why do prisoners sing in jails? We all have heard them. Does it prove solitary cells are a paradise?" In order to emphasize the point, the former slave mentions a "colored woman at work on a plan-tation, who was singing . . . whose general manners" made her appear to be the "happiest of the gang;" however, when asked if she was pleas-ant in her occupation, she responds, "No part pleasant. We forced to do it."[12] Ex-slave and abolitionist Frederick Douglass, in his autobiogra-phy, made the same point about the false perceptions held by Northern whites. After escaping to the North and becoming a spokesperson for the abolitionist movement, Douglass soon became aware of the false ideals of slavery and blacks that dominated there: "I have often been utterly astonished, since I came to the north," he wrote, "to find persons who could speak of the singing among slaves, as evidence of their content-ment and happiness." Although he condemned that line of thought as a great "mistake," Douglass recognized it as a prevalent cultural belief throughout the North. Blacks in the North were affected by the stories that poured into the North of the enslaved communities in the South supposedly singing and dancing happily. African Americans in the North may have escaped the brutal hardships of life in the legal bondage system of slavery, but the racial stereotypes that were perpetuated in slavery also entered Northern culture, regardless of the varying histories of the regions. Until the mid-nineteenth century, blacks were held in bondage throughout the United States. Large slave populations existed in states such as New Jersey and New York, and the institution of slavery was an active part of the legal and social organization of the North and the

South.[13] Certainly, differences emerged. Slavery in the North was usually marginal in the overall labor system. Northern slaves, while still subordinate in society, could sometimes achieve freedom. Even after slavery diminished in the North in the early nineteenth century, white Northerners generally accepted the dominant racist stereotypes that reinforced the system. Similar to the performances of Southern slaves, blacks throughout the North were also exploited as entertainment. The spectatorship of festivals, such as the Pinkster Festival or Negro Election Day, and the use of blacks as musicians for white community socials remained commonplace in Northern communities. In writings on his boyhood experiences in Massachusetts, Congressman Robert S. Rantoul recalled that he "never knew the whites and blacks to intermix in dancing, though the fiddler was a negro."[14] Also, in New York City, for example, there was a tradition beginning in the early nineteenth century of free and enslaved blacks performing music and dance for whites in order to earn "prizes of money or dried fish or eels" at Catherine Market.[15] Throughout the North, there was a public performance culture of blacks that existed prior to Matthews's arrival and may have contributed to his evaluation of Blacks in America. Similar to patterns in the South, the achievements of black performers in the North, as for African Americans generally, were categorized as natural, therefore denying the intellectual abilities and artistic achievements of musicians and dancers.

A racialized theater culture also existed in the Northeastern United States long before Matthews's visit. For almost two centuries, the black characters in Shakespearean theater had been performed in blackface or black shroud. The most enduring black masquerade character was Shakespeare's *Othello*, probably the longest-running blackface role in theater history.[16] The blackface aspect of Shakespearean theater, including Othello, acquired a distinctly American contribution through its incorporation of Southern plantation culture.

The prevalence of theater in the United States that emerged in the nineteenth century enjoyed a rich mixture of high, low, and folk culture. Shakespearean plays held a place in America's public sphere, and a distinct folk culture continued to develop within these plays, contributing new linguistic styles, dances, skits, gymnastics, and songs.[17] Nineteenth-century theater owners also introduced into Shakespearean plays intermission performances by blackface entertainers known as Ethiopian Delineators. These Ethiopian Delineators existed in North America prior to the American Revolution and usually portrayed black characters as either noble savages or comic buffoons.[18] Throughout the

1820s, traveling blackface entertainers continually grew in recognition and developed their performance style. Parades of whites masquerading as blacks quickly became widespread in the theatre of the United States.[19]

Increasingly, blackface theater performances came to reflect the racialized stereotypes of American blacks central in the Southern plantation regions. These shows attempted to mimic black dialect and mannerisms in their performances. The 1820s introduced to white Americans many blackface performers who often claimed to perform "legitimate Negro songs and dances" in circus-style performances.[20] These performances, often incorporated into intermissions between plays, derived primarily from the images and stories flowing from Southern plantations. For example, "Negro and Buckra Man," a comic intermission monologue performed by the Ethiopian Delineators after 1810, reflected American slavery ideals.

> Great way off at sea
> When at home I benee,
> Buckra man steal me,
> From the coast of Guinea;
> Christian masee pray,
> Call me hea[t]hen doggee
> Den I run away,
> Very much he floggee.
> Ri tol lol lol la.[21]

These song lyrics depict a black bondsman who, after being abducted from Africa and attempting to run away, is caught and whipped by his master. The traumatic experience of the Middle Passage, bondage, and physical abuse all are diminished by the happy ditty at the end of the song. The lyrics illustrate the belief that enslaved blacks could endure any degree of personal trauma and hardship by happily singing. The performance of these Ethiopian Delineators represented precisely the kind of exaggerated view of black life and culture that influenced Matthews's racial depictions in "A Trip to America." Although his performances focused on the black performers of the African Grove Theater, the popularity of Shakespeare and the Ethiopian Delineators in American productions certainly effected his perception of Americans. However, those elements were certainly not the only significant factors that influenced Matthews. In his months traveling the Northeastern regions of the United States, Matthews's perspective of American life was strongly influenced by the major innovations and transformations of the area.

The regions that Matthews visited in the early nineteenth century were experiencing major social and cultural transformations that influenced the British comedian's experiences, encounters, and theatrical performance. The beginning of the nineteenth century brought industrial development, a rise in immigration, and urban growth to the North. After the War of 1812, the United States witnessed rapid economic, social, and political change. An economy based on farms, artisans, and local markets became one marked by commercial farming and national markets.[22] This Jacksonian Era brought not only a new market revolution but also the rise of a metropolitan industrialization in the North, where dramatic improvements in transportation, communication, and other technological advancements were revolutionizing the country.[23] Innovations in transportation fostered the development of factory systems, and centralizing and expanding cities allowed for an upsurge in an urban working class and a decrease in artisan fields in this new industrial age.[24] Nineteenth-century capitalism reordered formal social relations by class.[25] Competition in resources, housing, and employment developed alongside growing hostility among native-born American whites, free blacks, and a surging immigrant population.

The early nineteenth-century industrial revolution brought an influx of European immigration to the United States.[26] Immigrants from Germany, Ireland, England, Scotland, and several other European countries traveled to America because of poor economic conditions in Europe and prospects for a better life in the developing nation. Many of the incoming immigrants were poor laborers in search of opportunity in the urbanizing North and burgeoning West.[27] Many migrated from countries that had previously experienced industrial revolutions, thereby avoiding further decline in economic status in their native countries. After two years of observing the United States, Frenchman Michael Chevalier stated in his travel narrative published in 1834, "The United States are certainly the land of promise for the labouring class."[28] The majority of immigrants who entered the United States were the Catholic Irish, who mainly migrated to the industrialized North. From 1821 to 1850, the number of Irish immigrants doubled, many of whom settled in New York.[29] Charles Matthews infused this new diversity of the North into his "A Trip to America" performance, equally mocking the new immigrants, native whites, and free blacks who were part of this developing amalgamation.

Matthews's comical exaggeration of the "distinct flavor" of America on the theatrical stage resulted in a negative backlash from many Americans, and not only within the black community.[30] "Yankee, Negro, Dutch, Irish, Scotch and French" caricatures were his stock in trade—to the amusement of "English ears" and the abhorrence of many Americans.[31] As one American critic stated about the British actor, "The scoundrel ought to be pelted from the American stage, after writing his book . . . Matthews's caricature of America. This insult upon Americans ought to be met with the contempt it deserves. . . . [D]rive the ungrateful slander from our stage forever."[32] This sentiment was especially representative of the working-class, native-born white men of the North, who received the most criticism throughout Matthews's performance. Matthews created a character in his show that represented "the home-bred American prototype, a country fellow, unpolished," who was named Mr. Jonathan W. Doubikin.[33] This "Yankee" character was depicted as unintelligent, often using terms such as "the doubtful—I guess, I reckon, I calculate."[34] Matthews openly criticized the working-class whites in the North and drew a satirical picture of the American scene at a time when the North was being transformed by industrial and economic changes. Visitors to North America from all over Europe, but especially English tourists, reviewed and criticized the burgeoning nation. The condemnation readily expressed by many English tourists of Americans contributed to native-born whites' direct onslaught against the free black and immigrant populations that grew out of a desire to assert their own whiteness.[35]

Racial identity and nativism rose to the forefront of American culture to counter an emerging society that was continually being categorized by class status, resulting in the development of laws and organizations that stripped away the political, economic, and social rights of free blacks in the North. The nineteenth century witnessed two seemingly contradictory trends: first, the rise in abolitionism that focused on blacks' equality and civil rights, resulting in an increased consciousness of the plight of blacks in America; and second, new laws that countered the social and political power of free blacks. In New York State, for example, the 1821 Constitution required free blacks to possess $250 worth of property to qualify for voting rights.[36] Either through intimidation or legislative change, native-born whites attempted to gain power against the emerging populations of free blacks and immigrants. Native white males wanted to defend their exclusive claim to whiteness and citizenship against the rise of the immigrant populations, the growing dependence on wage labor, and the progress of free blacks.[37] The lack of racial separation and the continual onslaught of negative descriptions of working Americans resulted in a desire for racial clarity. As Chevalier assessed American life in the 1830s, "[laborers] in the Southern States are slaves . . . In the Northern States, the labouring classes are white."[38] Blurring the distinction, however, was the European practice of referring to native whites working in the industrial sphere of the North as "wage slaves."[39] Native whites faced losing power in the developing industrial cities, and they wanted to assert some control in their leisure amusement. Therefore, in creating a "new sense of whiteness," whites donned blackface in order to recreate or reinforce a "new sense of blackness" in the North through entertainment—transforming intermission performances into a major cultural production of the minstrel show.[40]

Within the context of these social, racial, and economic changes, in the early 1830s white actor Thomas Dartmouth Rice limped on stage donning blackface makeup and, in tattered clothing, performed a jig dance while singing a song, drastically transforming American entertainment.

> Come listen all you galls and boys
> I's jist from Tuckyhoe,
> I'm going to sing a little song
> My name is Jim Crow
>
> [Chorus]
> Wheel about, an' turn about, an' do jis so;
> Eb'ry time I wheel about I jump Jim Crow.
>
> Oh, I'm a roarer on de Fiddle,
> And down in Old Virginny,
> They say I play de skyentific
> Like Massa Pagannini.[41]

Rice performed "Jim Crow" throughout the North and ignited a new phenomenon in American popular entertainment culture. Jim Crow became "one of the best-known and most-loved theatrical personalities of his day both in the United States and in Great Britain"[42] and was considered one of the "most popular characters in the world."[43] Mystery surrounds the creation of "Jim Crow" and its initial performance that caused Rice to rise to prominence in the theater. According to myth, Rice had witnessed an elderly black stable hand, slightly deformed due to rheumatism, wearing ill-fitting clothes and oversized shoes while singing a funny song and dancing. Initially working as a minor actor in a traveling troupe, Rice did not specifically state where he had witnessed this performance; however, the actor's extended period in Kentucky during the late 1820s may have offered the opportunity, if any such encounter had ever actually taken place at all.[44] More than thirty years after Rice's infamous performance, journalist Robert P. Nevins offered a rudimentary historical account of the manner in which "Jim Crow" was introduced to the blackface performer. In Boston's *Atlantic Monthly* Nevins stated that in 1830 as Rice "sauntered along one of the main thoroughfares of

Cincinnati . . . his attention was suddenly arrested by a voice ringing clear" that belonged to a "negro stage-driver, lolling lazily on the box of his vehicle," performing the famous "Jump Jim Crow" song.[45] According to the monthly publication, within the same year, Rice limped on a Pittsburgh stage and performed the character. Regardless of the date or location of his first performance or the number of times he performed this character before it became a popular figure, Rice's performance ignited a cultural phenomenon.[46]

Rice's "Jim Crow" was the first major blackface minstrel caricature.[47] Jim Crow represented a Southern slave who was fond of music and dance despite his social status and health deformity. Notwithstanding the popularity of the stereotypes, a rarely asked question remains: Why would a rheumatic black man be dancing and singing? To move in the manner Rice mimicked would have caused pain for the physically deformed, destitute, elderly man. The assumption behind the myth of the rheumatic dancing and singing slave is that he performed for no other reason than innate musicality and happiness. This explanation fit well among the prevailing racial myths emanating from the Southern regions.

The rise of Jim Crow started a national and international sensation of white men donning blackened makeup, exaggerating their dialect, and singing racialized ditties. Spearheaded by Rice's caricature Jim Crow, the American minstrel show peaked in the 1840s with the formation of numerous minstrel troupes that hoped for fame and fortune. The Virginia Minstrels—Billy Whitlock, Dick Pelham, Frank Brower, and Dan Emmett—formed in New York City and debuted in 1843.[48] The Virginia Minstrels was the first major group to establish the full theatrical enterprise of the minstrel show. They contributed to the diversity of musical entertainment, combining the violin, bone castanets, tambourine, banjo, and fiddle. They were advertised as "negro extravaganzas" that introduced the "oddities, peculiarities, eccentricities, and comicalities" of "humanity."[49] With unparalleled success, the Virginia Minstrels introduced to mass audiences the model for the American blackface minstrel show. Following in their success, E. P. Christy organized Christy's Minstrels, making their debut in New York City in 1846. Christy's Minstrels were "the first to harmonize negro melodies, and originators of popular type of Ethiopian entertainments, authors of all the most popular negro melodies that have been introduced in concerts of this character."[50] In this traveling group, the first major American songwriter, Stephen C. Foster, was introduced; his musical contribution to blackface entertainment contributed to his title as "father of American music." In 1852, Foster wrote: "I have done a great deal to build up a taste for the [minstrel] songs

JIM CROW,

Illustration of Thomas Dartmouth Rice in blackface and tattered clothing portraying the character of Jim Crow and introducing the popular entertainment of the blackface minstrel show. (MS Thr 556 [157], Harvard Theatre Collection, Houghton Library, Harvard University.) Courtesy of the Houghton Library, Harvard Theatre Collection.

among refined people by making the words suitable to their taste, instead of the trashy and really offensive words which belong to some songs of that order." Minstrel melodies became part of the American sound that extended beyond the theater stage and represented black Americans in the United States and aboard.

Minstrel performers continually purported that they had visited Southern plantations to gather material for their performances in an effort to portray authentic blackness.[51] T. D. Rice is considered the father of American minstrelsy due to his claims that after watching a singing and dancing slave, he simply mimicked this performance on a Northern stage. Scholar Eileen Southern claims that "to obtain material for their shows, the minstrels visited plantations, then attempted to recreate plantation scenes on the stage. They listened to the songs of the black folk as they sang at work in the cotton and sugar cane fields, on the steamboats and river docks. . . . [T]he melodies they heard served as bases for minstrel songs, and . . . the dances."[52] E. P. Christy, for example, lived in New Orleans in the 1820s and often witnessed bondsmen and women singing, dancing, and congregating throughout the area, later refashioning their cultural expressions into the distinct performance style of the Christy Minstrels.[53] Several minstrel performers were able to witness first hand black music and dance, specifically in the South, while others may have claimed authentic reenactments of Southern blacks without venturing to the region. Regardless, the onstage performances that were coerced either by the whip or by threats, or which were simply situated as a duty within slave society, influenced blackface minstrelsy. While backstage, cultural expressions of the black community, either witnessed or incorporated within the lore of the Southern region, also became an aspect of the staged minstrel performances. The popularity of the music and performance style offered a counterfeit blackness, or rather the blackface of enslaved blacks that catered to the assertion of whiteness in American society.

Blackface minstrelsy was not, therefore, a display of black culture but instead was mimicry of the façade of slavery that pervaded the United States. Set in the North amidst an active black population, blackface white actors usually focused their skits, songs, and caricatures on the racial images of blacks, often in a Southern plantation setting. The changing culture and demographics of the urban North could be ignored temporarily through the fictional world of happily singing and dancing slaves on a plantation. The sentimental admiration with which the slavery culture throughout the South was regarded often manifested in some of the most popular melodies from the minstrel stage. In 1851, "Old Folks at Home" was initially performed by Christy's Minstrels to a Northern audience consisting primarily of native, white, working-class men and immigrants.

> Way down upon de Swanee Ribber,
> Far, far away,
> Dere's wha my heart is turning ebber,
> Dere's wha de old folks stay.
> All up and down de whole creation
> Sadly I roam,
> Still longing for de old plantation,
> And for de old folks at home.

> [Chorus]
> All de world am sad and dreary,
> Eb-rywhere I roam;
> Oh, darkeys, how my heart grows weary,
> Far from de old folks at home!

> All round de little farm I wandered
> When I was young,
> Den many happy days I squandered,
> Many de songs I sung.
> When I was playing wid my brudder
> Happy was I;
> Oh, take me to my kind old mudder!
> Dere let me live and die.

> One little hut among de bushes,
> One dat I love
> Still sadly to my memory rushes,
> No matter where I rove.
> When will I see de bees a-humming
> All round de comb?
> When will I hear de banjo strumming,
> Down in my good old home?[54]

This song purported to convey the perspective of a black slave desiring to return to the plantation. These early minstrel performances reflected a developing nostalgia of the hierarchy within Southern plantation society. The romanticized Southern plantation became a place of happy blacks performing music and dance within a carefree life. This particular song evokes the belief that black men and women truly belonged on the plantation. The hardships of daily slave life are minimized and replaced by a longing for simple enslavement, introduced to an audience that may have never owned slaves. The continual references to the plantation society in minstrel shows were an aspect of the white working-class culture that used Southern slavery in references to their own labor conditions. Scholar David Roediger states that the working class "computed rates of exploitation that putatively showed that a much greater proportion of the value produced by a Black slave was returned to him or her than was returned to the white slave in the North." Therefore, in an effort to stress their dire conditions, many working-class whites illustrated Southern slavery as less oppressive and without the threat of "starvation, over-exertion, deprived children and uncomforted sickness" due to the "master interested" in preserving the slaves life.[55] Minstrel shows portrayed these perspectives through music, skits, and dancing of bondsmen and bondswomen living a relatively easy, happy life within the Southern slavery system. These lyrics equate music and dance to happiness, affirming the Southern propaganda of happy slaves singing and dancing. Such equation also contributes to the social and political plight of the white working-class audience members who were able to express their daily woes through this amusement, which was more representative of their plight than the Southern black experience. This song presents the sympathetic reflection of an older bondsman or recently freed black man who, for unknown reasons, is unable to return to the only home he knows and loves, the Southern plantation.

Advertisements sounded the same note. Minstrel show advertisements and playbills served as the template for antebellum entertainment, often illustrating caricatured black men playing various musical instruments, from the banjo to the tambourine and fiddle. Blackface performers likewise depicted their skits, songs, and dances on their playbills while reinforcing white stereotypes of blacks. Christy's Minstrels performing in New York included various skits and dances on their playbill, such as "The Jolly Darkies," "Let's Be Gay," and "Plantation Banjo Song," thus openly stating that the performers were "Portraying the Peculiar Characteristics of the Southern Plantation Negroes."[56] These playbills and programs emphasized the theme of happy, singing, and dancing slaves. For pre–Civil War Northern audiences, minstrels recreated the fantasy of plantations populated by blacks who were cheerful in their bondage, devoted to their masters, and content to frolic like children all day and night.[57] The preponderance of information disseminated about the South excluded or minimized the coercive power of the whip and essentially bequeathed a romanticized world of benevolent masters and "happy darkies." The forced performances throughout all of the stages of slavery were reconstructed and romanticized on the minstrel stage. As the father of American music, Stephen Foster wrote some of the most lingering minstrel songs that borrowed the onstage slave performances and

Illustration is of a Christy's Minstrel playbill for their November 16, 1857, in San Francisco. As depicted in the drawings, the minstrel show often mocked free blacks in the North and enslaved blacks in the South. As the playbill states, in "Part Third" their routine portrayed "Life among the Happy—Portraying the Peculiarities of the Southern or Plantation Negroes"; characters are drawn dancing, playing the banjo, and being entertainment. (MS Thr 556 [324], Harvard Theatre Collection, Houghton Library, Harvard University.) Courtesy of the Houghton Library, Harvard Theatre Collection.

interpreted them for a Northern audience.[58] In September 1853, Foster's composition, "My Old Kentucky Home, Good Night!" was performed by Christy's Minstrels; it reflected the common theme of Southern nostalgia within minstrel performances.

> The sun shines bright in the old Kentucky home,
> 'Tis summer, the darkies are gay,
> The corn top's ripe and the meadows in the bloom,
> While the birds make music all the day.
> The young folks roll on the little cabin floor,
> All merry, all happy and bright:
> By'n by Hard Times comes a knocking at the door,
> Then my old Kentucky Home, good night!
>
> [Chorus]
> Weep no more, my lady,
> Oh! weep no more today!
> We will sing one song for the old Kentucky Home,
> For the old Kentucky Home far away.[59]

This song, like many minstrel melodies, reflected with admiration upon a particular Southern region. References to Kentucky, Alabama, Louisiana, and several other areas in the Deep South were common in minstrel songs. These songs became regional anthems infused in the American identity. The distinctive cultural construction of the United States became intertwined in the popular theater productions that continually presented façades of black life as authentic.

The romanticized Southern plantation depicted in minstrel shows often illustrated the dual consciousness of many Northerners who accepted the stereotypes of happy slaves while shunning the institution of slavery.[60] References in many songs to slaves moving throughout the Deep South directly evoked the domestic slave trade, which many Northerners viewed as a deplorable aspect of American slavery. Historian Steven Deyle referenced the "carry me back" songs that expressed the point of view of slaves who missed their previous experiences on the "old plantations." Such songs as "Carry Me Back to Old Virginny," which was performed by actual slaves traveling in coffles within the domestic slave trade, illustrated the contradictions of slavery. As Deyle argues, these minstrel songs "exposed the delusional capacities of the slaveholders' paternalistic ideal" by exposing to the Northern audience the abuses of slavery that included separation from families.[61] However, these songs performed in minstrel shows presented an illusion that slaves, if treated fairly (which often entailed being stable on the "old plantation" and allowing the basic liberties of music and dance), would be immensely happy and submissive. In 1856, Englishwoman Isabella Lucy Bird unwittingly observed the exchanges between blacks in America and the entertainment of whites in blackface. "The slaves . . . are a thoughtless, happy set, spending their evenings in dancing or singing to the banjo." This being a common observation, Bird continues by stating, "'Oh, carry me back to Old Virginny,' or 'Susannah, don't you cry for me,' may be heard on summer evenings rising from the maize and tobacco grounds of Kentucky." [62] The forced performances of slaves throughout the South influenced the blackface minstrel show; simultaneously, the minstrel show influenced the culture of slaves in the South. The "carry me back" songs often were associated with the domestic slave trade, and while the "Susannah" ditty was written by Stephen Foster, both songs were interchangeably used in minstrel shows and on the plantation by actual blacks. Minstrel music became an active part of American popular culture and influenced slave music. Simultaneously, in a desire to accurately portray black culture, minstrel performers also popularized the music of bondsmen and bondswomen.

Some aspects of minstrel shows did accurately reflect African-based cultural traditions, particularly the staple use of certain instruments.[63] The banjo and drum were two such native instruments. The banjo was originally an African lute brought to North America by Africans and played almost exclusively by blacks until the 1830s.[64] The African-derived banjo was an active part of the slave performing arts throughout the plantation community. According to scholar Robert Winans, the banjo was the second most common instrument on the plantation utilized by slaves.[65] Although Rice did not use a banjo with his introduction of Jim Crow, the first major minstrel troupes, the Virginia Minstrels and Christy's Minstrels, both incorporated banjo players.[66] The banjo became the central instrument in minstrelsy, a staple of minstrel songs, advertisements, and skits.

Blackface performers routinely characterized the mannerisms of blacks in America, but at the same time, many of the dance and music styles represented a distinct African and African American culture. In the 1850s, minstrel performer Dave Reed "emerged with a dance he said he learned from Negroes when he was working on Mississippi riverboats."[67] Throughout the minstrel era, traditional African American dances, such as the buzzard loop, the buck and wing, the walk-around and the cakewalk, regularly appeared in the blackface displays.[68] Whites in blackface often mocked Southern whites and immigrants through ingenuity and strategic wordplay within their performances, similar to the dual

Illustration of the sheet music cover design of "Old Dan Emmit's Original Banjo Melodies," which contained a collection of minstrel songs performed by the Virginia Minstrels. The image illustrates the popular perception of happy Southern slaves playing the banjo, dancing, and singing while on the plantation. (MS Thr 556 [59], Harvard Theater Collection, Houghton Library, Harvard University.) Courtesy of the Houghton Library, Harvard Theatre Collection.

meaning of music and dance within the black community. The minstrel show's satirical style and the use of actual black dances and songs often resulted in the incorporation of African and African American culture into American culture. Therefore, the minstrel show allowed for various aspects of black culture to be depicted accurately in public society and also created a niche for blacks to enter American entertainment. However, the constant mixing of these culturally accurate depictions with grossly distorted images within the same staged performance fostered a complicated dialectic between black cultural forms and their appropriation by white blackface performers that influenced the development of a white racial identity, or whiteness.[69]

Part of the popularity of blackface minstrelsy in the North derived from native whites' desire to assert their whiteness and protest their social status. Minstrel troupes in antebellum America rarely ventured to the Deep South because Southern whites, with their access to and power over the enslaved community, could view onstage performances by actual bondsmen and bondswomen. The minstrel show intentionally distinguished whites from blacks and immigrants through mimicry and mockery of blacks. During the first years of their prominence, native, working-class white males dominated as actors in American minstrel shows. Although the European immigrant and free black populations eventually became the main blackface minstrel performers, native, working-class white males originated this entertainment genre. The first major minstrel actor, Thomas D. Rice, once apprenticed as a woodworker. Similarly, Dan Emmett, a member and founder of the Virginia Minstrels, once worked as a printer, and Billy Whitlock, another member of the Virginia Minstrels, worked as a typesetter before donning blackface on the minstrel stage.[70] Coming from working-class backgrounds allowed these performers to create blackface performances that identified the particular longings, fears, hopes, and prejudices of the Northern, Jacksonian, urban, working-class white male. [71] Therefore, the blackface minstrel shows that displayed negative, stereotypical images of blacks were actually more representative of whites. Native, working-class white men were able to reestablish the dominance and power that came from their whiteness through the continual degradation and representative subjugation of blackness in the minstrel show.

The challenges to blacks' political rights and the rise of racial violence illustrated native whites' resistance to the changing urban Northern society, which was evident early in the entertainment culture. The first black theater, the African Grove Theater that Charles Matthews mocked and distorted, followed within the American high-art tradition of Shakespearean theater but met with great hostility from the white population. The company was started by William Alexander Brown, a freeman and former ship steward, as an all-black social gathering place.[72] On August 3, 1821, the *National Advocate*, a newspaper in New York, announced the opening of the African Grove pleasure garden that offered a "modicum of pleasure" for the "black dandies and dandizetters" whose "number increased. . . . partly from high wages, high living, and the elective franchise."[73] Journalist Mordecai Noah's description of the progressive free black community in the North parodied the community as being pompous. His article introduced to the New York reading public the facility that would house theatrical Shakespearean performances beginning September 17, 1821. Similarly, the *National Advocate* also announced the initiation of the first black Shakespeare Company, about which one critic stated only four days after their first performance, "Negroes resolved to get up a play, and used the upper apartments of the African Grove for a performance of Richard III."[74] Initially an all-black theater, Brown later opened the performances to white audiences, resulting in periodic violence from primarily young white men who verbally and violently assaulted the black actors.[75] Believing that Shakespeare was "white cultural property," whites contributed to the continual harassment and arrest of several black actors and the eventual closing of the African Grove Theater on August 8, 1823.[76]

During the theater's brief existence, the black actors made futile attempts to appease white audiences, such as transitioning from Shakespearean productions to plays that portrayed the slave rebellion and revolution in Saint Domingue. However, many Northern whites, similar to their Southern counterparts, wanted to enforce their ideals of subordinate blackness upon the black population. African American performers tried to showcase their talents in theater companies controlled by blacks. However, in challenging white stereotypes and white control over theater and theater revenues—and a key basis for white power—they were met with resistance and even violence. The vehement aggression against this black theater and the insincere introduction by the *National Advocate* of the "black dandies and dandizetters" contributed to a new caricature in blackface minstrelsy, the Urban Dandy or Zip Coon.

Minstrel shows mocked and distorted free blacks in the North in a noticeably different way than their Southern slave caricatures. In 1843, Zip Coon was introduced through song and character to a theater audience. The song begins, "O ole Zip Coon he is a larned skoler," representing early on the major theme of ridicule toward free blacks in the North regarding their supposed intellectual inferiority and undeserved arrogance. The following verse emphasizes this point, mocking the free blacks' attempt at gaining political and social rights:

> And wen Zip Coon our President shall be,
> He make all de little Coons sing possum up a tree;
> O how de little Coons, will dance an sing,
> Wen he tie dar tails togeddder, cross de lim dey swing.[77]

Zip Coon represented the ineptitude of Northern free blacks. Although minstrelsy sympathized with the experiences of Southern blacks in slavery, many performers depicted that region as the best environment for blacks. Free blacks were lazy and incapable of grasping the English language, while Southern blacks under slavery were industrious. The antislavery movement and the end of artisan republicanism brought new fears about the status of native, working-class whites in Northern society. If blacks were intellectually and morally equivalent to whites and able to receive social and political rights, then how would that affect the status of whites and whiteness? Equating wage labor to slavery further blurred the demarcation between white and black.[78] For centuries, the foundation of whiteness in society was defined as the antithesis of blackness. Therefore, whites gained status through the degradation of blacks. Whites did not want to compete with blacks for political power, employment opportunities, or status in a society increasingly conscious of class. The Zip Coon character representing free blacks in minstrel performances continually emphasized their inability to truly compete in a free labor society. This Northern dandy became such a staple of the minstrel show that the Virginia Serenaders' theater productions were separated into two parts, "As Ethiopian Dandies of the Northern States" in "Part First" and in the final act, "As Southern Slaves."[79]

The Northern dandy, often referred to as Zip Coon, Dandy Jim, or the Urban Coon, soon became a standard aspect of minstrelsy.[80] Whites incorporated these "dandy darkies" to emphasize the ideas of blackness that they wanted to believe, representing Northern blacks as foolish and egocentric, formally over-dressed, and forever using complicated language improperly while demonstrating what not to do in the city.[81] Skits portrayed Northern dandies as frequently "tricked out of their money by con-men, run down by trollies, shocked by electric batteries, and jailed for violating laws that they did not understand."[82] Foolishly inept for freedom, the Northern dandy proved that blacks were best suited to serve as slaves under the protection of the Southern plantation system. Minstrel caricatures often were portrayed as having unattractive, distorted faces and bodies through the use of exaggerated "beef-steak lips," wooly hair, and robust buttocks.[83] The minstrel shows of the North intentionally perverted the superficial features of blackness while reinforcing the active stereotypes propagated by Southern plantation folklore. Although many blackface minstrel performers did not support slavery, as often reflected in their sympathetic songs and skits, these same blackface performers did not believe that blacks should reside or compete with whites. The hostility toward the free blacks of the North caused many minstrel shows to focus on the respectability of Southern slaves.

Assigning favorable characteristics to bondsmen contributed to the demeaning of free blacks. Famous minstrel performer Dan Emmett of the Virginia Minstrels composed several minstrel melodies that reflected Southern folklore. Performed in 1843, "The Fine Old Color'd Gentleman" looks with some degree of admiration towards the "Sambo" in the song lyrics.

> In Tennessee as I've heard say
> There once did used to dwell
> A fine old color'd gentleman
> And this nigger know'd him well;
>
> Dey used to call him Sambo
> Or somethin' near de same,
> And de reason why dey call'd him so
> Was because it was his name.
>
> O Sambo was a gentleman,
> One of de oldest kind.
>
> His temper was very mild
> When he was let alone,
> But when you get him dander up
> He spunk to de backbone;
>
> He wail de sugar off you
> By double rule of three
> And whip his weight in wildcats
> When he got on a spree.
>
> O Sambo was a gentleman,
> One of de oldest kind.
>
> He had a good old banjo
> So well he kept it strung,
> He used to sing de good old song
> Of go it while you're young;
>
> He sung so long and sung so loud
> It scared de pigs and goats,

Because he took a pint of yeast
To raise de highest notes.

O Sambo was a gentleman,
One of de oldest kind.

When dis nigger stood upright
And wasn't slantin' dicular
He measured 'bout eleven feet,
He wasn't very particular;

Or he could jump and run a race
And do a little hoppin,'
And when he got a goin' fast
De devil couldn't stop him.

O Sambo was a gentleman,
One of de oldest kind.

Old age come on, his teeth dropp'd out,
It made no odds to him;
He eat as many taters
And he drink as many gin;

He swallow'd two small railroads
Wid a spoonful of ice cream
And a locomotive bulgine
While dey blowin' off de steam.

O Sambo was a gentleman,
One of de oldest kind.

One very windy morning
Dis good ol' nigger died;
De niggers come from other states
And loud wid joy dey cried;

He layin' down upon a bench
As straight as any post;
De coons dey roar, de possums howl
When he guv up de ghost.

O Sambo was a gentleman,
One of de oldest kind.[84]

According to this song, black slaves were more respectable and possessed more enduring qualities than free blacks. This song reflected white Northern desires more so than the lack of enslaved "gentlemen," such as Sambo on the Southern plantation. The chorus seemed to compliment this elder slave who drank "gin," played the banjo, and sang "de good old song" in Tennessee, as being of better character than the Northern free men. The image of the "gentleman" Sambo represented a false reverence and nostalgia for a racial hierarchy that was clearer throughout the South yet problematic amidst the diversity and changing sociopolitical atmosphere of the North. Although slavery remained a contentious topic throughout Europe and the North, the South's public image was solidified through the established master-slave society. Whites, regardless of class, had power and status when compared with the enslaved blacks. The plantation South offered venues where whites practiced domination and believed in their "natural right to rule," therefore fulfilling their whiteness in society.[85]

The influence of blackface shows spread far beyond the theaters and their paying audiences. Adages and songs from minstrel performances found their way into American culture. For those who may have never attended a blackface show, the ditties, catch phrases, and caricatures became a part of the popular culture that spread throughout the United States and abroad. The racialized images permeating the minstrel stage also entered the popular medium of fictional literature.

Literature, especially from Southern writers, entered the public arena with a similar setting as the popular minstrel shows. Born in Baltimore, lawyer and writer John Pendleton Kennedy published *Swallow Barn* in 1832, the first major work of fiction that glamorized the Southern plantation community.[86] As a picture of "country life in Virginia," Pendleton's book is written somewhat as a travel account of Mark Littleton, who visits a Southern estate and records his interactions and impressions for his fellow Northerners: "Swallow Barn is an aristocratical old edifice. . . . the residence of the family of Hazards." Frank Merriwether, the proprietor of Swallow Barn, was described as a man of "great suavity of manners, and a genuine benevolence of disposition," a "kind master . . . for which reason, although he owns many slaves, they hold him in profound reverence, and are very happy under his dominion."[87] Early in the novel, the main character, Littleton, introduces the first "over-contented blacks" in Richmond, who were playing a "contumacious clarionet" and a "thorough-going violin" while dancing to "Virginia reel" on the public streets. Later, the Northern tourist is serenaded by the slaves on Swallow Barn. While engaged in conversation, Littleton's "attention was suddenly drawn to another quarter by the notes of a banjoe, played by Carey," who is described as "a minstrel of some respute, and, like the ancient jongeleurs, he sings." Explaining the scene as "really picturesque," Carey is described as "old, and the infirmities of age were conspicuous upon his person"; however, he was eager to engage in "running his fingers over his rude instrument" for almost an hour due to his desire to please the curious white guests. Interestingly, Carey appears quite similar to the elder minstrel character, "Jim Crow," that was simultaneously being performed throughout the North and England by blackfaced white men. The relationship between Southern fiction and the rise of blackface minstrelsy becomes quite apparent when Carey is asked to sing "Jim Crow" while performing several ditties on the plantation. Pendleton's Carey was a literary manifestation of the false images being presented in the popular blackface performances. Pendleton's novel was the first of many nostalgic plantation novels that created a picturesque plantation community complete with happily singing and dancing slaves and benevolent masters, the precise onstage performances purported by defenders of slavery. Southern literature entered popular culture, alongside minstrelsy, as entertainment and as an influential voice in the contentious debate on the institution of slavery and future of the United States.

South Carolina–born writer William Gilmore Simms was one of the most influential Southern writers of the antebellum era. His career included editing ten periodicals and authoring more than eighty works, several of which were nationally popular novels.[88] Simms began actively publishing novels in the 1830s, using slavery as a common setting throughout his work, with slaves happily singing and dancing as part of the landscape of the plantation.[89] Simms landscapes the South in the 1838 novel *Richard Hurdis*: "The negroes are particularly famous for the lightheartedness of their habit while journeying in this manner. You will sometimes see . . . listening to the rude harmony of some cracked violin in the hands of the driver, and dancing and sing as they keep time with his instrument. . . . The grin of their mouths, the white teeth shining through the glossy black of their faces, is absolutely irresistible." Simms recognizes the music and dance of bondsmen and bondswomen as entertainment: "Sometimes the whites hover nigh . . . partaking . . . in the pleasure and excitement which such an exhibition" offers. To trivialize the abilities of those bondsmen and bondswomen, Simms reminds the reader that "the verses" performed by the slaves "were full of rough humour which is a characteristic of all inferior people."[90] Simms, similar to Pendleton, expressed a sympathetic view of slavery and emphasized the innate happiness of slaves.

A third example of this trend can be found in *Recollections of a Southern Matron*, authored by proslavery advocate Carolina Gilman in 1852. Gilman repeated the popular slave performance scenes prevalent throughout the plantation South. In this book, slaves provided entertainment for white visitors during a Christmas celebration at a plantation. Gilman, similar to other slave-era writers, described a scene of slaves performing music, song, and dance on the planation: "All the musicians kept their own feet and bodies going as fast as the dancers themselves . . . Hector started up and began dancing."[91] In these and many other fictional stories, the musically inclined dancing slave(s) are central to the idealized plantation scenes. The Southern landscape in nineteenth-century literature often was described as abolitionist Harriet Beecher Stowe depicted it: "The old plantation; a great mansion; exquisitely gowned ladies and courtly gentlemen moving with easy grace upon the broad veranda behind stalwart columns; surrounding the yard an almost illimitable stretch of white cotton; darkies singingly at work in the field, Negro quarters, off on one side, around which little pickaninnies tumbled in gay frolic."[92] Interestingly, the image consistently appeared in works written from both sides of the slavery argument. The myth of the Southern plantation with "happy darkies" and paternalistic whites was continually reasserted in popular culture, regardless of whether the author was anti-slavery or pro-slavery. But of all the books that affected the development of race and entertainment culture in America, none compares to the book that was considered by President Abraham Lincoln as having initiated the Civil War.

Harriet Beecher Stowe's *Uncle Tom's Cabin* was one of the most influential and controversial books of the antebellum period. It was published in 1852 and sold over 3,000 copies on its first day of release. Within the first year, over 300,000 copies were in circulation. Stowe was one of the first authors to center her work on the life and emotions of black slaves on the plantation. This abolitionist work specifically appealed to Christian sympathies by emphasizing the horrors of slavery. In an attempt to draw attention to the anti-slavery movement, Stowe deliberately displayed blacks sympathetically as docile, innocent creatures forced into an unjust, immoral institution. One major flaw in her work was the acceptance of stereotypes; instead of countering the romanticized views, she incorporated them into the text. Although she contributed greatly to the abolitionist cause, the book also influenced the continuation of caricatures in the pro-slavery argument.

Although abolitionists embraced Stowe's book, the characters in *Uncle Tom's Cabin* were easily distorted by the defenders of slavery.[93] The scene of blacks exhibiting happiness in their singing and dancing was present in Stowe's work. The main character, Tom, was depicted in the novel as "capering and dancing" as a "matter of daily occurrence in the cabin, the declaration no white abated the merriment, till every one had roared and tumbled and danced themselves down to a state of composure."[94] The jollity attributed to Uncle Tom displayed the belief in blacks' innate merriment and dance that was evident in this scene and throughout the novel. Also, music and dance could (somehow) induce docility in blacks, as Uncle Tom was able to dance into a "state of composure." As described by Stowe, in the slave quarters, "After a while the singing commenced, to the evident delight of all present . . . naturally fine voices, in airs at once wild and spirited . . . for the negro-mind, impassioned and imaginative, always attaches itself to hymns."[95] The idea of blacks possessing "naturally fine voices" and displaying their "evident delight" contributed and gave credence to the misrepresentations of blacks. Although Stowe intended to fight the harsh world of slavery, she instead assisted in perpetuating romanticized ideals. According to Stowe, slavery was negative due to the horrible conditions in which it placed blacks, these Christian, child-like, happy, naïve creatures. Stowe and many abolitionists accepted the stereotypes of music and dance as positive aspects of blacks, whose performances contributed greatly to American society. In 1838, white female abolitionists Angelina Grimke attempted to rectify this false ideology to Northern, primarily abolitionist audience in a speech that openly stated that although music and dance prevailed throughout the Southern plantation system, such performances by no means equated to "happiness" among the slave community. Regardless, the acceptance of these ideals by many white abolitionists was evident in their writings, speeches, and treatment of black Americans, including in *Uncle Tom's Cabin*. Abolitionists like Stowe, even as they espoused sympathy towards the condition of enslaved blacks, were unable to overcome their assumptions and prejudices.

The supposed natural happiness of slaves insisted upon an innate relationship between performing arts and blacks' good-natured naivety. In antebellum America, whites' fixation with black amusement contributed to the construction of blackness on the minstrel stage in the North, while also influencing major political and social debates. Stowe's anti-slavery text was distorted, adapted, and performed thousands of times on the theatrical stage, according to Stowe's son, Charles E. Stowe.[96] Although minstrel caricatures existed prior to the novel's publication, this anti-slavery text contributed greatly to the diversity of black caricatures portrayed on the minstrel stage.[97] Uncle Tom may have been the most popular black caricature taken directly out of Beecher's novel and portrayed in minstrels throughout North America and Europe.[98] The songs performed by these portrayed caricatures within the popular rendition of *Uncle Tom's Cabin* reflect the infusion of black stereotypes and distortion of black cultures.

These songs performed in the popular theater were adaptations of Stowe's novel. Minstrel songs often reflected various aspects of the

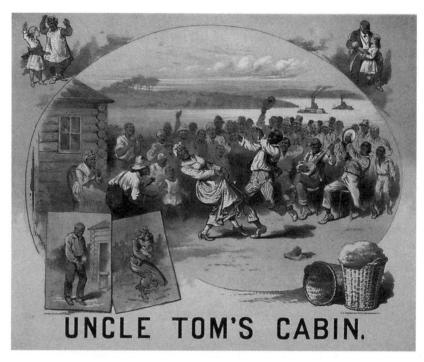

UNCLE TOM'S CABIN.

Illustration of Harriet Beecher Stowe's novel *Uncle Tom's Cabin*, depicting happy slaves dancing and singing on the Southern plantation. (Theatrical Poster Collection, Prints & Photographs Division, Library of Congress, LC-USZC4-11152.) Courtesy of the Library of Congress.

Southern slave experience and culture infused in public knowledge. Written in 1852, the song "Early in de Morning" portrays a typical day on a Southern plantation, as illustrated in minstrelsy. Stage adaptations of *Uncle Tom's Cabin* distorted the initial intentions of Harriet Beecher Stowe and soon became more popular than the novel, which was one of the most popular burlesqued novels in theater for almost a century.[99] As one of hundreds of adaptations of Stowe's literary work, this song illustrates that the daily lives of bondsmen and bondswomen centered on labor, music and dance.

> Early in de morning by de break of de day,
> We shoulder shubble an de hoe an to de fields away;
> We dig an hoe, we dig and hoe de taters and de corn,
> Tobacco and de hemp we weed from early in de morn.
>
> [Chorus]
> So we come so come make holiday,

So come make holiday,
The way we'll heel and toe it out
Will be a sight to see

Now Massy gib us holiday,
He giv us leave to play
So darkies all come dance a bit,
Now put our tools away;
Come lay it out you niggers,
Come hoe it down wid me,
The way we'll heel and toe it out
Will be a sight to see.[100]

This song was first presented at the Boston Museum in a production of *Uncle Tom's Cabin*. The language of the blackface minstrel show was active within the song lyrics. "Heel to toe" was a common phase that became popularized by Rice with Jim Crow and became infused in Vaudeville Theater. The song illustrates the confluence of abolitionist and proslavery ideology in the fictional literature and theater entertainment within American culture. Stowe's antislavery novel was easily transformed into language that supposed the institution of slavery due to the prevailing stereotypes that continued in it. Music and dance in this song inspired by the novel distracted from the hardships of slavery and simplified slave life. "Will be a sight to see" was in many ways an informal invitation for white guests to attend these "innocent amusements."

The antebellum era witnessed the rise of the most popular entertainment that broadly entered the Western world: minstrelsy in which American blacks' lives were perverted and distorted by whites in blackface on stages. The national and international image presented throughout fictional literature and on the theater stage contributed to the plight of actual African Americans. The social and psychological tensions surrounding the institutional of slavery in antebellum America intensified the racist sentiment throughout the region. Lincoln's statement to Harriet Beecher Stowe that her novel instigated the Civil War has been repeated in American history; however, its significance has yet to be fully understood. The most popular media of the nineteenth century, literature and theater, influenced public sentiment and affected the political and social climate of antebellum America and impressions of blackness abroad. Blackface minstrelsy enjoyed popularity throughout nineteenth-century Europe. In 1836, it was stated that people throughout Dublin "crowded with anxiety to see, and seemed to relish, the absurdities and grimaces of Rice."[101] Blackfaced white men gained wealth and popularity throughout their minstrel performances, and these performances had a profound impact on American popular culture and the lives and images of African Americans. Blacks, both free and enslaved, throughout the United States were directly affected by these representations on the antebellum American stage. And one of the first and most blatant examples of this backlash of minstrelsy involved the same group that was first caricatured by British actor Charles Matthews: the actors from the African Grove Theater.

The distortion of "A Trip to America" and subsequent rise of blackface minstrelsy directly affected the careers of the Shakespearean actors James Hewlett and Ira Aldridge. With the closing of the African Grove Theater in 1823, James Hewlett, the main actor at the theater who had been burlesqued by Matthews, ventured to London, hoping to personally confront his fellow actor and pursue his acting career abroad.[102] Hewlett found that he could neither confront Matthews nor secure permanent acting positions in England, resulting in his quick return to the United States. Audiences, it seemed, preferred whites in blackened face distorting African American culture and people to black performers themselves. Hewlett's acting career concluded with his final performances as an "aboriginal ecce homo," or rather a "museum oddity" at the New York Museum.[103] His colleague Ira Aldridge did gain greater success on European stages and was able to continue his Shakespearean performances. Interestingly, due to popularity of caricaturing American blacks, Aldridge incorporated into his theatrical performances mimicry of Matthews' skit. Openly stating that Matthews' performance was a "ludicrous scene" that "never occurred at all," Aldridge included the (now) popularized song "Opossum Up a Gum Tree" in his European performances. As Aldridge and Hewlett imitated, in order for black entertainers to succeed in their industry, they needed to impersonate the white mimicry of the façade of bondsmen and bondswomen by performing music, song, and dance choreographed by whites.[104] The hardships Aldridge and Hewlett faced illustrated how the blackface minstrel show sculpted American entertainment and drastically affected the plight of black entertainers and African Americans overall.

The blackface minstrel show was a manifestation of the American cultural tradition of perpetuating negative stereotypes of the black body for public consumption and entertainment. Blackface minstrelsy has often been viewed as the foundation of American entertainment culture. In many ways this assertion is quite accurate. Minstrelsy contributed greatly to the development and circulation of America's ideals of race, culture, and

Illustration of a poster advertisement for the Callender's Colored Minstrels, a postslavery minstrel troupe formed in 1872, displaying a plantation scene of happy slave children dancing while older, cheerful slaves watch their performance. Images showing the continuance of a false image of contented musical, dancing slaves were popular even after the end of the slavery system in the United States. (MS Thr 556 [25], Harvard Theatre Collection, Houghton Library, Harvard University.) Courtesy of the Houghton Library, Harvard Theatre Collection.

entertainment. However, minstrelsy was not the foundation of American entertainment culture; rather, the performances that were fictionally described in travel journals and forcibly expected from blacks on the plantation and in the horrid trade were the foundation. The blackface minstrel performance style continued through the development of various mass media, such as radio, film, and television.[105] And nearly 150 years after Appomattox, it continues still.

Epilogue

THE SHOW MUST GO ON

On *the Oprah Winfrey Show* on February 3, 2006, Dave Chappelle had his first national interview after walking away from a $50 million contract and his hit comedy series, *The Chappelle Show*. His show had debuted in 2003 on Comedy Central and was considered by audiences and critics alike to be one of the funniest shows on television. Chappelle, who created and wrote the show, is a professional comedian and African American actor whose trademark, politically incorrect humor, explored popular culture, race, sex, drugs, and fame. *The Chappelle Show* became one of the highest-rated programs on Comedy Central, earning three Emmy nominations. It went on to become the bestselling TV show in DVD history.

Then, in April 2005, a year after signing a two-year contract to continue the show, Chappelle abruptly walked off the set and traveled to Africa. In his first national broadcast after his disappearance, Chappelle explained why he had abandoned his hit television series. In a racial skit in which Chappelle played a blackface pixie, which he described as the "visual personification of the 'N-word,'" he had begun to question the social ramifications of these satirical performances. During the taping of this particular sketch, Chappelle noticed, "somebody on the set (who) was white laughed in such a way—I know the difference of people laughing with me and people laughing at me—and it was the first time I had ever gotten a laugh that I was uncomfortable with. . . . I don't want black people to be disappointed in me for putting that message out there. . . . It's a complete moral dilemma."[1] The "moral dilemma" with which Dave Chappelle grappled concerned the racial images he was propagating in the public sphere of mass media through his comedy show. The social responsibility of African Americans in the entertainment industry has always been a topic of great controversy due to the negative, stereotypical manner in which blacks continually have been portrayed.

Similar to so many black entertainers in American history, Dave Chappelle continuously balanced on the thin line between parody and racial stereotypes.[2] Furthermore, the racially charged rants directed toward black targets by famous white figures in the first decade of the twenty-first century, including Michael Richards and Don Imus, fueled discussion on the manner in which blacks are portrayed in popular culture. These controversial events also mobilized black activists to seek retribution against public displays of racism by mainstream media. Richards and Imus—who was fired (though rehired)—experienced social and professional repercussions for their racist displays.[3]

The Richards and Imus controversies, however, had a secondary effect: a negative backlash against blacks in the entertainment industry. Interestingly, in the aftermath of these controversies, the current generation of black entertainers has been left holding the blame for promoting negative stereotypes in popular culture. At the same time, these racially tinged media incidents have raised questions about differences in popular culture intended for white or black consumption. Today, a heated debate continues within the African American community centered on what responsibility black actors and actress have within the entertainment industry. With the 2012 success of black actresses Viola Davis and Octavia Spencer in the film *The Help* and the continual controversy regarding blacks within the music industry, black entertainers currently are bearing a heavier burden concerning race and gender within their public performances.[4]

African American entertainers often are blamed for the continuing racist ideology present in mass media. For instance, after making racist and sexist comments on a publicly televised radio show, Don Imus defended his comments by stating, "I may be a white man, but I know that . . . young black women all through society are demeaned and disparaged and disrespected by their own black men." Currently, the African American community is involved in an introspective debate on the racial responsibility of black entertainers. Conversations regarding the prevalence of racist ideology in mainstream entertainment have seriously neglected the historical significance of these events. The racist ideology prevalent in mass media has become inappropriately legitimized due to the pervasiveness of African Americans reenacting black stereotypes.

This phenomenon has deep historical roots, running all the way back to the beginning of the institution of American racial slavery. This work has revealed the foundation and infiltration of black stereotypes into the entertainment culture in the United States. Rejecting the notion that African Americans should be used as scapegoats for the continuance of black stereotypes in popular culture, *Ring Shout, Wheel About* recognizes that American entertainment culture was largely founded and developed on negative racial imagery created and inserted into the public sphere by whites. Although the African American community holds some responsibility for the continual proliferation of racist and sexist stereotypes in the mass media, that accountability must be placed within a larger cultural and historical context. To that end, this work discussed the historical events and cultural construction that contributed to and continue to contribute to blacks' self-desecration.

Today, the proliferation of black stereotypes in popular culture simply represents a continuation of an entertainment tradition in the United States that was created intentionally to express the antiblack, prowhite ideology of America's culture. Furthermore, the perceived inferiority of blackness was actively promoted through society's folk culture. Harlem Renaissance poet Langston Hughes captured the intricacy and quandary of black performers, and furthermore the African American experience, in his prolific poem "Minstrel Man."

> Because my mouth
> Is wide with laughter
> And my throat
> Is deep with song,
> You do not think
> I suffer after
> I have held my pain
> So long?
>
> Because my mouth
> Is wide with laughter,
> You do not hear
> My inner cry?
> Because my feet
> Are gay with dancing,
> You do not know
> I die?[5]

The moral dilemmas of the African American entertainer, as articulated by Dave Chappelle, are directly related to the tradition of subjugation and negative imagery infused in popular culture that derived from the plantation society.

Racialized entertainment often constructed blackness or the black body as "other," a subordinate being who was completely incompatible with whites and just as naturally suited to serve or to amuse whites. Frantz Fanon stated, "White civilization and European culture have forced an existential deviation on the Negro. . . . [T]he black soul is a white man's artifact."[6] Throughout the foundation of North America, whites willfully negatively constructed the black body, resulting in the erroneous categorization of blackness through myths and stereotypes. Although the "black soul" was not a "white man's artifact," the public image of blackness was distorted intentionally by some whites to propagandize negative images of blacks in America.

These slave-era images were transformed after the Civil War, when some blacks began donning blackface in minstrel shows. Although the blackface performance style originated in Europe, the rise of the minstrel show in the antebellum era represented a distinctly American form of entertainment that reflected American society's collective mentality. The postbellum era witnessed the emancipation of black slaves in North America and the early roots of blacks' entrance into minstrel shows. Although there were professional black entertainers before the Civil War, such as Black Swan, Thomas J. Brown, Blind Tom, and the Whitehouse Sisters, these entertainers experienced limited success compared with those of the postbellum era, when large numbers of blacks rose in the entertainment industry.[7] Black minstrel troupes developed throughout the United States in the 1860s and gained great popularity as "authentic" darkies because they were "genuinely negroes."[8]

The popularity of black minstrel troupes in postbellum America gave some validity to the performance of blackness in blackface theater and also brought African American entertainment to the forefront of the American public sphere. However, blackface minstrelsy still represented only an imitation of an imitation, an image of a fantasy plantation life with "happy darkies" and paternal whites. The American minstrel show continued the tradition of displaying blacks "as only an irresponsible, happy-go-lucky, wide grinning, loud laughing, shuffling, banjo-playing, singing and dancing sort of being."[9] The American minstrel show contributed to the proliferation of negative stereotypes of African Americans while also ironically contributing to the professionalization of many black performers.

Although the American minstrel show was filled with negative stereotypes of black life, it also provided essential theatrical training and
experience for black actors and actresses. Blacks in the postbellum era
found popularity and fame on the minstrel stage, gaining national and
sometimes international recognition. Many black minstrel performers
were able to add diversity to characters' skin complexions, instead of the
single black complexions offered by white minstrel performers. They also
introduced cultural dance styles and new characters to their blackface
acts.[10] Black minstrel performers paved the way for the further development of black professional entertainment ventures. However, regardless
of the strides black minstrel troupes made, they still represented a "veil
of misunderstanding and make-believe" for white audiences; blacks were
continually silenced and selectively viewed by whites who were taking
this opportunity to see their "cherished fantasy made briefly real."[11]

The negative portrayal of African Americans continues today
throughout various forms of media.[12] The resurgence of negative black
stereotypes displayed through mass media has influenced and is now representative of the entertainment culture in the Unites States and several
other countries. Essentially, it must be recognized that an active part of
American culture and entertainment is grounded in racism. The collective mentality found in the United States is constructed on the premise
of whiteness and the ideals associated with whiteness in a system in
which blacks must continually contest their status.

The collective mentality present in mass media was addressed in the
controversial film *Bamboozled*, a satire about the history of black representations in television and film. Director and writer Spike Lee recreated
the blackface minstrel show in current times with African American actors in a series entitled the *New Millennium Minstrel Show*. Lee paro-
dies a network television station that, in pursuit of ratings, airs a new
comedy series created by an African American that reinvents blackface
minstrels on a plantation setting. The television series becomes a cultural
phenomenon among blacks and whites, although often falling under attack from various community activists. Lee addresses numerous controversial topics within this film in order to shed light on the degradation
of blacks throughout popular culture. He stated in an interview that the
negative images of blacks in mass media are "painful—the pain comes
from looking at the images. How people of color, in this case specifically
African-Americans, have been portrayed since the inception . . . of film,
radio and television. . . . we have to look at the way we portray black col-
lectibles . . . we're viewed as less than human, sub-human, and that stuff

is painful."[13] Lee's comments represent the turmoil many blacks face as a result of the distortions of race in American entertainment culture.

Later in the interview, Lee stated, "And film roughly is 100 years old and now we're the beginning of a new century. And what will the next hundred years bring?" This comment recognizes the persistent racism present throughout the history of film, but the characterizations that it displays have been present in American culture since its inception. The entertainment culture has centered on negative representations of blacks while placing whites and whiteness as the nonracialized, dominant representations. This study broadens the dialogue on race, racial representations, and entertainment in the culture of the United States in an effort to contribute to moving forward from the centuries of injustice in popular culture; however, there is still a need for continual scholarship, discussion, and activism.

NOTES

Introduction

1. Ray Stannard Baker, *Following the Color Line: An Account of Negro Citizenship in the American Democracy* (New York: Doubleday, Page, 1908), 28.

2. Ibid., vii.

3. Ibid., 61.

4. *Tuscaloosa Monitor*, February 23, 1869, cited in Allen Trelease, *White Terror: The Ku Klux Klan Conspiracy and Southern Reconstruction* (Baton Rouge: Louisiana State University, 1995), 253–54.

5. George M. Frederickson, *The Black Image in the White Mind: The Debate on Afro-American Character and Destiny, 1817–1914* (1971; repr., Hanover, N.H.: Wesleyan University Press, 1987).

6. Ibid, 105.

7. W. E. B. Du Bois, *The Souls of Black Folk* (1903; repr., New York: Bantam, 1989), 3.

8. This is an abridged version of Langston Hughes's "Black Clown." Langston Hughes, *The Collected Poems of Langston Hughes*, edited by Arnold Rampersad (New York: Vintage, 1994).

9. For a review of the people, events, and history of the Harlem Renaissance see David Levering Lewis, *When Harlem Was in Vogue* (New York: Oxford University Press, 1979); Ann Douglass, *Terrible Honesty: Mongrel Manhattan in the 1920s* (New York: Noonday, 1995); Samuel A. Floyd Jr., ed., *Black Music in the Harlem Renaissance: A Collection of Essays* (Westport, Conn.: Greenwood, 1990); Cary D. Wintz, ed., *The Emergence of the Harlem Renaissance* (New York: Garland, 1996).

10. Karen Sotiropoulos, *Staging Race: Black Performers in Turn of the Century America* (Cambridge, Mass.: Harvard University Press, 2008), 99.

11. Donald Bogle, *Toms, Coons, Mulattoes, Mammies and Bucks: An Interpretive History of Blacks in American Films* (New York: Continuum, 1992).

12. Robin R. Means Coleman, *African American Viewers and the Black Situation Comedy: Situating Racial Humor* (New York: Garland, 1998).

13. Ibid., 27.

14. John Straubaugh, *Black Like You: Blackface, Whiteface, Insult & Imitation in American Popular Culture* (London: Penguin, 2006), 57.

15. Ibid., 16.

16. Eric Lott, *Love and Theft: Blackface, Minstrels, and the American Working Class* (New York: Oxford University Press, 1993), 16.

17. Dale Cockrell, *Demons of Disorder: Early Blackface Minstrels and their World* (Cambridge: Cambridge University Press, 1997); Sam Dennison, *Scandalize*

My Name: Black Imagery in American Popular Music, Critical Studies in Black Life and Culture, vol. 13 (Bloomington: Indiana University Press, 1982); Mel Watkins, *African American Humor: The Best Black Comedy from Slavery to Today* (Chicago: Chicago Review Press, 2002); Mel Watkins, *A History of African American Comedy: From Slavery to Chris Rock* (Chicago: Lawrence Hill, 1994, 1999); and Michael Rogin, *Black Face, White Noise: Jewish Immigrants in the Hollywood Melting Pot* (Berkeley: University of California Press, 1996).

18. Frederick Douglass, *My Bondage and My Freedom* (New York: Miller, Orton & Mulligan, 1855), 97.

19. William L. Van Deburg, *Slavery & Race in American Popular Culture* (Madison: University of Wisconsin Press, 1984), xi.

20. Researchers such as Roger Abrahams, Jon Cruz, and Shane White and Graham White have pored over the institution of slavery from the perspective of the performing arts as a major dynamic in slaves' daily lives and as a distinct aspect of African American culture that allowed some autonomy, family, and community life while simultaneously providing an outlet for expression. Robert Abrahams, *Singing the Master: The Emergence of African-American Culture in the Plantation South* (New York: Penguin, 1992); Jon Cruz, *Culture on the Margin: The Black Spiritual and Rise of American Cultural Interpretation* (Princeton, N.J.: Princeton University Press, 1999); Shane White and Graham White, *The Sound of Slavery* (Boston: Beacon, 2005).

21. Such works as Eugene D. Genovese's *Roll, Jordan, Roll* (1972), Lawrence Levine's *Black Culture and Black Consciousness* (1977), and Sterling Stuckey's *Slave Culture* (1988); and, more recently, Peter Kolchin's *American Slavery* (1993), Philip Morgan's *Slave Counterpart* (1998), Dylan C. Penningroth's *The Claims of Kinfolk* (2002), and Ira Berlin's *Generations of Captivity* (2004) examine music and dance primarily as West African cultural continuances. Eugene D. Genovese, *Roll, Jordan, Roll: The World Slaves Made* (New York: Pantheon, 1972, 1974); Lawrence Levine, *Black Culture and Black Consciousness: Afro American Folk Thought from Slavery to Freedom* (Oxford: Oxford University Press, 1977); Sterling Stuckey, *Slave Culture: Nationalist Theory and the Foundations of Black America* (Oxford: Oxford University Press, 1988); Peter Kolchin, *American Slavery 1619–1877* (New York: Hill and Wang, 1993); Philip Morgan, *Slave Counterpart: Black Culture in the Eighteenth-Century Chesapeake and Lowcountry* (Chapel Hill: University of North Carolina Press, 1998); Dylan C. Penningroth, *The Claims of Kinfolk: African American Property and Community in Nineteenth-Century South* (Chapel Hill: University of North Carolina Press, 2002); Ira Berlin, *Generations of Captivity: A History of African-American Slaves* (Cambridge, Mass.: Harvard University Press, 2003).

22. Saidiya V. Hartman, *Scenes of Subjection: Terror, Slavery, and Self-Making in Nineteenth Century America* (New York: Oxford University Press, 1997), 17.

23. In *Laboring Women: Reproduction and Gender in New World Slavery* (Philadelphia: University of Pennsylvania Press, 2004) Jennifer Morgan explores "across time and space," recognizing that the exploitation of black women in reproduction and labor began in West Africa and continued in the Diaspora.

24. Ira Berlin, *Many Thousands Gone: The First Two Centuries of Slavery in North America* (Cambridge, Mass.: Harvard University Press, 1998); Michael Gomez, *Exchanging Our Country Marks: The Transformation of African Iden-*

ties in the Colonial and Antebellum South (Chapel Hill: University of North Carolina Press, 1998).

25. Peter Fryer, *Staying Power: The History of Black People in Britain* (Sterling, Va.: Pluto, 1984).

26. Mary Louis Pratt, *Imperial Eyes: Travel Writing and Transculturation*, 2nd edition (New York: Routledge, 2008).

27. Katrina Dyonne Thompson, "Distorted Images in Travel Literature: An Exploration of the Subjugation of Blackness in the Western World," in *America and the Black Body: Identity Politics in Print and Visual Culture*, ed. Carol E. Henderson (Teaneck, N.J.: Fairleigh Dickinson University Press, 2009), 55–74.

28. Marcus Rediker's *The Slave Ship: A Human History* (New York: Penguin, 2007) and Maria Deidrich, Henry Louis Gates Jr., and Carl Pedersen, ed., *Black Imagination in the Middle Passage* (New York: Oxford University Press, 1999) clearly illustrate the common occurrence of such performances within the international trade.

29. Eric Robert Taylor, *If We Must Die: Shipboard Insurrections in the Era of the Atlantic Slave Trade* (Baton Rouge: Louisiana State University Press, 2006).

30. Emma Christopher, *Slave Ship Sailors and Their Captive Cargoes* (Cambridge: Cambridge University Press, 2006); Stephanie Smallwood, *Saltwater Slavery: A Middle Passage from Africa to American Diaspora* (Cambridge, Mass.: Harvard University Press, 2007).

31. Scholar Saidiya Hartman's work *Scenes of Subjection* (1997) examines these "innocent amusements" to illustrate how forced music and dance were used as a form of subjugation and torture.

32. Found in Levine, *Black Culture*, 121.

33. Frederic Bancroft, *Slave Trading in the Old South* (University of South Carolina Press, 1931); Michael Tadman, *Speculators and Slaves: Masters, Traders, and Slaves in the Old South* (Madison: University of Wisconsin Press, 1996): Walter Johnson, *Soul by Soul: Life Inside the Antebellum Slave Market* (Cambridge, Mass.: Harvard University Press, 1999); Stephen Deyle, *Carry Me Back: The Domestic Slave Trade in American Life* (Oxford: Oxford University Press, 2005).

34. Robert Toll's *Blacking Up* (1977), Eric Lott's *Love and Theft* (1995), and Dale Cockrell's *Demons of Disorder* (1997) examine blackface minstrelsy as the first major form of American entertainment. Robert Toll, *Blacking Up: The Minstrel Show in Nineteenth-Century America* (Oxford: Oxford University Press, 1977).

Chapter 1. The Script

1. Jean Barbot, *Barbot on Guinea: The Writings of Jean Barbot on West Africa 1678–1712*, edited by P. E. H. Hair, Adam Jones, and Robin Law (London: Hakluyt, 1992), 563; Jean Barbot, *A Description of the Coasts of North and South Guinea; and of Ethiopia Inferior, Vulgarly Angola: Being a New and Accurate Account of the Western Maritime Countries of Africa*, cited by Awnsham Churchill in *A Collection of Voyages and Travels, Some Now First Printed from Original Manuscripts*, 6 vols. (London: 1704, 1732).

2. Jonathan E. Schroeder, "Consuming Representation: A Visual Approach to Consumer Research," in *Representing Consumers: Voices, Views and Visions*, edited by Barbara B. Stern (London: Routledge, 1998), 208.

3. Katrina Dyonne Thompson, "Distorted Images in Travel Literature: An Exploration of the Subjugation of Blackness in the Western World," in *America and the Black Body: Identity Politics in Print and Visual Culture*, edited by Carol E. Henderson (Teaneck: Fairleigh Dickenson University Press, 2009), 55–74; T. Carlos Jacques, "From Savages and Barbarians to Primitives: Africa, Social Typologies, and History in Eighteenth-Century French Philosophy," *History and Theory* 36, no. 2 (May 1997): 212.

4. The three components of the "other" come directly from the work of Perry R. Hinton, *Stereotypes, Cognition and Culture* (Hove: Psychology Press, 2000), 7.

5. Hinton, 7–12.

6. Jacques, "From Savages," 212.

7. K. H. Waters, *Herodotus, the Historian: His Problems, Methods, and Originality* (Norman: University of Oklahoma, 1985); Percy G. Adams, ed., *Travel Literature through the Ages: An Anthology* (New York: Garland, 1988), 3. Herodotus is considered the "Father of History" and was one of the earliest writers to say anything about the interior of Africa. He visited Egypt and Libya in the fifth century B.C. and recorded his experiences while also documenting the layout of the land. For several centuries there was little added to the tales of Africa reported by Herodotus.

8. Herodotus, *History*, bk. IV, chs. 171–94, trans. (Letchworth, Great Britain: J. E. P. Temple Press, 1912), 341–48.

9. Ibid.

10. Pliny, *The Natural History*, V, ch. 8, ed. and trans. (London: Bostock and Riley, 1893), 405–6, and Sorcha Carey, *Pliny's Catalogue of Culture: Art and Empire in the Natural History* (Oxford: Oxford University Press, 2003).

11. Gaius Julius Solinus, *The Excellent and Pleasant Work*, trans. (London: Golding, 1587).

12. Ibid., ch. 42.

13. Robert Lucas, "Medieval French Translations of the Latin Classics to 1500," *Speculum* 45, (1970): 226.

14. Bernard Lewis, *Race and Color in Islam* (New York: Harper and Row, 1971), 25–29.

15. Found in Natalie Zemon Davis, *Trickster Travels: A Sixteenth-Century Muslim Between Worlds* (New York: Hill and Wang, 2006), 143.

16. T. J. Bowen, *Adventures and Missionary Labours in Several Countries in the Interior of Africa from 1849 to 1856*, 2nd ed. (London: Cass, 1968), 18.

17. Ibid., 18.

18. G. R. Crone, "Notes on the Texts," in *The Voyages of Cadamosto*, ed. (London: Crone, 1937), Hakluyt Society, 2nd ser., no. 80, xliii.

19. William B. Cohen, *The French Encounter with Africans: White Response to Blacks, 1530–1880*, (Bloomington & London: Indiana University Press, 1980), 3; Humphrey J. Fisher, "Leo Africanus and the Songhay Conquest of Hausaland," *International Journal of African Historical Studies* 11, no. 1: 86–112; Davis, *Trickster Travels*.

20. Leo Africanus, John Pory, Luther Jones, *Geographical History of Africa* (Jones, 1993).

21. Ibid., 43.

22. Philip D. Curtin, *The Image of Africa, British Ideas and Action, 1780–1850*, vol. 1 (Madison: University of Wisconsin Press, 1964), 11.

23. Christopher Fetherston, *A Dialogue agaynst Light, Lewde, and Lasciuious Dauncing,* 1582 (Leicester: Guizer, 1973).

24. Benedict Anderson, *Imagined Communities: Reflections on the Origin and Spread of Nationalism* (London: Verso, 1983), 188.

25. Richard G. Cole, "Sixteenth-Century Travel Books as a Source of European Attitudes toward Non-White and Non-Western Culture," *Proceedings of the American Philosophical Society* 116, no. 1 (February 15, 1972): 59–67.

26. Marshall McLuhan, *Understanding Media: The Extensions of Man,* (Cambridge, Mass.: MIT Press, 1964), 178, and Glenn Wilmott, *Modernism in Reverse,* (Toronto: University of Toronto Press, 1996).

27. Cole, 59.

28. Norman R. Bennett, *Africa and Europe: From Roman Times to the Present* (New York: Africana, 1975), 169.

29. A copy of these paintings may be found in Peter Fryer's *Black Africans in Renaissance Europe* (London: Pluto, 1988), 36–38. There are several other paintings depicted throughout the text displaying black-skinned persons performing in music and dance.

30. Schroeder, "Consuming Representation," 21.

31. Scholarship on the fetishizing of the female body can assist in understanding the construction of race and gender. See, for example, Anne McClintock, *Imperial Leather: Race, Gender and Sexuality in the Colonial Contest* (New York: Routledge, 1995); William Pietz, "The Problem of the Fetish," *Res* 9 (1985): 5–17; Theodore Adorno, "Fetish Character in Music and Regression of Listening," in *The Essential Frankfurt School Reader,* ed. Andrew Arato and Eike Gebhardt (New York: Continuum, 1988); and Emily Apter, *Feminizing the Fetish: Psychoanalysis and Narrative Obsession in Turn-of-the-Century France* (Ithaca, N.Y.: Cornell University Press, 1991).

32. Barbot, *Barbot on Guinea,* 495–501.

33. Jacques, "From Savages," 212.

34. Winthrop D. Jordan, *White Over Black: American Attitudes toward the Negro, 1550–1812* (Chapel Hill: University of North Carolina Press 1968), 25.

35. David Wood and Robert Bernasconi, eds., *Derrida and Difference* (Coventry, England: Parousia, 1985).

36. Jean-Baptiste Labat, *The Memoirs of Pere Labat,* 1693–1705, trans. and abr. by John Eaden (London: Cass, 1970), 152–60.

37. Gabriel Almond and James S. Coleman, eds., *The Politics of the Developing Areas* (Princeton, N.J.: Princeton University Press, 1960), 278.

38. Bennett; J. Lewis Krapf, *Travels, Researches, and Missionary Labours during an Eighteen Years' Residence in Eastern Africa: Together with Journeys to Jagga, Usambara, Ukambani, Shoa, Absennia, and Khartum; and a Coasting Voyage from Mombaz to Cape Delgado* (London: Trubner/Paternoster Row, 1860). Such Portuguese missionaries who left influential travel journals include: Antonio da Coinceicao, "Tratado" and English translation, "Treatise on the Cuama Rivers," in D. N. Beach and H. de Noronha, "The Shona and the Portuguese 1575–1890," 2 vols. (Harare, 1980), 1:196–229; Francisco Monclaro, "Account of the Journey Made by Fathers of the Company of Jesus with Francisco Barretto in the Conquest of Monootapa in the Year 1569" *Theal/RSEA* 3:202–53.

39. Toyin Falola, ed., *African Cultures and Societies before 1885*, vol. 2 (North Durham, N.C.: Carolina Academic, 2000).

40. Curtin, *Image*, 327; Almond and Coleman, *Politics*, 33. Almond and Coleman provide excellent explanations of the superstitions of Africa and proclaim that "polygamy exists on every part of the coast" of Africa, contributing to the "heathenish" ideals of the region.

41. Kariamu Welsh Asante, "The Jerusarema Dance of Zimbabwe," *Journal of Black Studies* 15, no. 4 (June 1985): 381–403.

42. Cohen, *French Encounter*, 33.

43. T. J. Bowen, *Adventures and Missionary Labours in Several Countries in the Interior of Africa from 1849 to 1856*, 2nd ed. (London: Cass, 1968), 18.

44. Jordan, *White Over Black*, 21.

45. Thomas Winterbottom, *An Account of the Native Africans in the Neighbourhood of Sierra Leone: To Which Is Added an Account of the Present State of Medicine among Them*, vols. I and II (London: Cass, 1803, 1969), 351.

46. William Bosman, *A New and Accurate Description of the Coast of Guinea: Divided into the Gold, the Slave, and the Ivory Coasts* (New York: Barnes and Noble, 1704), 118.

47. Paul Belloni du Chaillu, *Explorations and Adventures in Equatorial Africa: With Accounts of Manners and Customs of the People, and of the Chase of Gorilla, the Crocodile, Leopard, Elephant, Hippopotamus, and Other Animals* (New York: Harper, 1861), 201.

48. Ibid.

49. Ibid.

50. Peter Fryer, *Black People in the British Empire: An Introduction* (London: Pluto, 1988).

51. Richard Jobson, *The Golden Trade; or, A Discovery of the River Gambra and the Golden Trade of the Aethiopians* (Teignmouth: Speight & Walpole, 1623), 105–8.

52. Winterbottom, *Account*.

53. Alphone Tiérou, *Dooplé: The Eternal Law of African Dance*, trans. Deidre McMahon (Newark, N.J.: Harwood, 1992).

54. Michel Adanson, "A Voyage to Senegal, the Isle of Goree, and the River Gambia," in John Pinkerton, *A General Collection of the Best and Most Interesting Voyages and Travels in All Parts of the World* (London: Longman, 1814), 612.

55. Barbot, *Barbot on Guinea*, 564.

56. Joan Lawson, *European Folk Dance: Its National and Musical Characteristics* (London: Pitman, 1953),163; John Playford, *The Dancing Master; or, Plain and Easie Rules for the Dancing of Country Dances* (London: Inner Temple near the Church Door, 1651–1728).

57. Wendy Hilton, *Dance and Music of Court and Theater* (Stuyvesant, N.Y.: Pendragon, 1997), 45.

58. Lawson, *European Folk Dance*, 235.

59. Mabel Dolmetsch, *Dances of England and France from 1450 to 1600 with Their Music and Authentic Manner of Performance* (New York: Da Capo, 1975), 51.

60. Hilton, *Dance and Music*, 133.

61. Ibid., 134.

62. Joseph Addison and Richard Steele, "The Spectator," vol. 1 (London: 1714), Eighteenth-Century Collections Online (Gale); James L. Clifford, *Eighteenth-Century English Literature: Modern Essays in Criticism* (New York: Oxford University Press, 1959).

63. Addison and Steele, "The Spectator."

64. Ibid.

65. Ibid.

66. Katrina Dyonne Thompson, "'Some were wild, some were soft, some were tame, and some were fiery': Female Dancers, Male Explorers, and the Sexualization of Blackness, 1600–1900," *Black Women, Gender, and Families* 6, no. 2 (Fall 2012): 1–28. This article specifically focuses on the sexualization of the black women dancers.

67. Nira Yuval-Davis and Floya Anthias, eds., *Women-Nation-State* (New York: St. Martin's, 1989).

68. Jan Janszoon Struys, *The Perilous and Most Unhappy Voyages of John Stuys through Italy, Greece, Lifeland, Muscovia, Tartary, Media, Persia, East-India, Japan, and Other Places in Europe, Africa and Asia* (Amsterdam: van Meurs, 1681), 14.

69. Paul Belloni du Chaillu, *Explorations and Adventures in Equatorial Africa: With Accounts of Manners and Customs of the People, and of the Chase of Gorilla, the Crocodile, Leopard, Elephant, Hippopotamus, and Other Animals* (New York: Harper, 1861); Charles H. Jones, ed., *Africa: The History of Explorations and Adventure; As Given in the Leading Authorities from Herodotus to Livingstone* (New York: Holt, 1875), 1, 89.

70. Chaillu, *Explorations and Adventures*, 89.

71. Judith Etzion, "The Spanish Fandango: From Eighteenth-Century Lasciviousness to Nineteenth-Century Exoticism," *Anuario musical* 48 (1993): 1–22.

72. Quoted in Etzion, "Spanish Fandango," 231.

73. Ibid.

74. Barbot, *Barbot on Guinea*, 563–64.

75. Abraham Duquesne, *A New Voyage to the East-Indies in the Years 1690 and 1691 Being a Full Description of the Isles of Maldives, Cicos, Andamants, and the Isle of Ascension . . . ; by Monsieur Duquesne; To Which Is Added, a New Description of the Canary Islands, Cape Verd, Senegal, and Gambia, &c.; Illustrated with Sculptures, Together with a New Map of the Indies, and Another of the Canaries; Done into English from the Paris Edition* (London: Dring, 1696), 92.

76. Kim F. Hall, *Things of Darkness: Economies of Race and Gender in Early Modern England* (Ithaca, N.Y.: Cornell University Press, 1995).

77. Edward Evans-Pritchard, "The Dance," *Africa* I (October 1928): 457.

78. Jobson, *Golden Trade*, 107–8.

79. Chaillu, *Explorations and Adventures*, 212.

80. Ibid., 212.

81. Edward W. Said, *Orientalism* (New York: Vintage, 1979), 49–72.

82. Duquesne, *New Voyage*.

83. Ibid., 92.

84. Ibid., 90–91.

85. Ibid., 90–91.

86. Ibid., 90–91.

87. Mungo Park, *Mungo Park's Travels in Africa*, ed. Ronald Miller (London: Everyman's, 1907, 1954, 1969).

88. Robin Hallet, ed., *Records of the African Association, 1788–1831*, Royal Geographical Society (London: Nelson, 1964), v.

89. Mary Louise Pratt, *Imperial Eyes: Travel Writing and Transculturation* (London: Routledge, 1992), 69–70, 10.

90. Park, *Travels*, 49.

91. Cole, "Travel Books," 66.

92. Olaudah Equiano, *The Interesting Narrative of The Life of Olaudah Equiano, or Gustavus Vassa, the African, Written by Himself*, ed. Robert J. Allison (Boston and New York: Bedford/St. Martin's, 2007), 41.

93. Ibid., 48; Vincent Carretta, *Equiano, the African: Biography of a Self-Made Man* (Albany: University of Georgia Press, 2005; New York: Penguin, 2007). Although Carretta challenged Equiano's origin of birth, my work recognizes that Equiano was a native-born West African who was kidnapped from the country known today as Nigeria. Carretta has challenged the abolitionist's origin of birth, arguing that Equiano may have been born in South Carolina rather than in Africa. Carretta presents archival evidence of a 1759 baptismal record and a 1773 Royal Navy muster roll, both of which mention the antislavery writer's birthplace as South Carolina. Although this evidence has not sufficiently convinced the historical community, the dispute regarding his birthplace is vitally important to his autobiography. Equiano's memories of his homeland, capture, and slave ship experience were some of the most pivotal aspects of his life that, according to many scholars, were valid and corresponded with other narratives and sources at the time. Furthermore, during his lifetime, Equiano would have encountered many African-born slaves, which would have allowed him to gain information about West African experiences and cultures, thus adding validity to his personal statements. He exposed more than simply an admiration of his homeland; Equiano's narrative reveals cultures that often were silenced and misrepresented. Equiano's firsthand account was accurate, and his assessments of West African cultures may assist in understanding an African's experience in his homeland and through the Atlantic slave trade during the eighteenth century.

94. Equiano, *Interesting Narrative*, 20.

95. Ibid., 48.

96. Eric Charry, *Mande Music: Traditional and Modern Music of the Maninka and Mandinka of Western Africa* (Chicago: University of Chicago Press, 2000), 105–7; Tiérou, *Dooplé*; Judith Lynne Hanna, "African Dance: The Continuity of Change," *Yearbook of the International Folk Music Council* 5 (1973): 165. For further reading on traditional West African dance, Judith Lynne Hanna has contributed numerous articles and books on the tradition and modern African dance and its place in society. Other scholars who have contributed to this study include Edward Evans-Pritchard ("The Dance," 446–62) and Geoffrey Gorer, *Africa Dances* (New York: Norton, 1962).

97. J. H. Kwabena Nketia, "The Interrelations of African Music and Dance," *Studia Musicologica Academiae Scientiarum Hungaricae*, T.7, Fasc. ¼ (August, 1964, 1965); and J. H. Kwabena Nketia, *The Music of West Africa* (New York: Norton, 1974).

98. Equiano, *Interesting Narrative*, 48.

99. Ibid., 61.

100. Ibid., 46.

101. Giulio Ongaro, *Music of the Renaissance* (Westport, Conn.: Greenwood, 2003), 149–71.

102. Equiano, *Interesting Narrative*, 43.

103. Betty Warner Dietz and Michael Babatunde Ojatunjii, *Musical Instruments of Africa: Their Nature, Use, and Place in the Life of a Deeply Musical People* (New York: John Day, 1965), 24–71; 84.

104. Sitki, *The Odyssey of an African Slave*, ed. Patricia C. Griffon (Gainesville: University Press of Florida, 2009).

105. Ibid., 13.

106. Douglas Anderson, "Division below the Surface: Olaudah Equiano's *Interesting Narrative*," *Studies in Romanticism* 43, no. 3 (Fall 2005): 439–60; and Louise Rolingher, "A Metaphor for Freedom: Olaudah Equiano and Slavery in Africa," *Canadian Journal of African Studies* 38, no. 1 (2004): 88–122.

107. Equiano, *Interesting Narrative*, 51–52.

108. Ibid., 51.

109. Thomas A. Hale, *Griots and Griottes: Masters of Words and Music* (Bloomington: Indiana University Press, 1998), 162–63. See also Charry, *Mande Music*; and Jan Jansen, *The Griot's Craft: An Essay on Oral Tradition and Diplomacy* (Munster, N.J.: Transaction, 2000).

110. Charry, *Mande Music*, 1. There are dozens of theories on the origin of the word *griot*, which seemed to be the most dominant manner of referring to the professional musicians of West Africa, although the term *jeli* was also used often. The most common theory is that *griot* comes from the French word *guiriot*. The professional title of *griot* ranges according to the ethnic group—for example: Wolof *guiewel*; Fulbe *gawlo*; Mande *jeli*, *jail* (Creole *djidiu*); Spanish *guirigay*; Catalan *guirigaray*; Berber and Hassaniya Arabic *iggio*, *egeum*; and Arabic *qawal* via *guewel*. The griots, or any other term used according to the geographical region, are not the only persons responsible for the music of the area; the title seemed to refer more to the profession of creating music. According to Charry, there was a distinction between jeli and non-jeli musical artists. Jelis devoted their lives to music, while non-jelis have other avenues they ventured into for an occupation, but they still were able to produce music (play musical instruments, sing, dance). In West Africa, the most common term used to identify the "musical-verbal artisan" was griot. Still, the term musician only narrowly explained the role of griot. The griots, sometimes called by other names according to the geographical region, were not the only persons responsible for the music of the area; the title seemed to refer more to the profession of creating music. Hale, *Griots and Griottes*, 162–63.

111. Equiano, *Interesting Narrative*, 48.

112. Charry, *Mande Music*, 199, 3.

113. Ibid., 233.

114. Equiano, *Interesting Narrative*, 45.

115. Pearl Primus, "African Dance," in *African Dance: An Artistic, Historical, and Philosophical Inquiry*, ed. Kariamu Welsh Asante (Trenton: Africa World, 1994, 1998, 2002), 6.

116. Charry, *Mande Music*; Nick Nesbitt, "African Music, Ideology, and Utopia," *Research in African Literature* 32, no. 2 (2001): 175–86, and Kogi Agawu, "African Music as Text," *Research in African Literatures* 32, no. 2 (2001): 8–16.

117. Hanna, "African Dance," 165–66; Nketia, *Music of West Africa*.

118. Judith Lynne Hanna, *The Performer-Audience Connection: Emotion to Metaphor in Dance and Society* (Austin: University of Texas Press, 1983), 27.

119. Hanna, *"African Dance,"* 165. Judith Lynne Hanna gives an example of the differences in dance culture among different groups/societies in Africa, stating that for Ibo, Akan, Efik, Azande, and Kamba, dance involves vocal and instrumental music, including the drum, whereas among the Zulu, Matabele, Shi, Ngoni, Turkana, and Wanyaturu, drums are not used, and sometimes the users of drums are despised.

120. Charry, *Mande Music*; Nesbitt, "African Music"; and Agawu, "'African Music as Text."

121. Equiano, *Interesting Narrative*, 11.

122. Mather, "Arrow"; Winton Solberg, *Cotton Mather, the Christian Philosopher, and the Classics* (Worcester, Mass.: American Antiquarian Society, 1987); John Phillips, *Familiar Dialogues on Dancing, between a Minister and a Dancer, Taken from Matter of Fact with an Appendix Containing Some Extracts from the Writings of Pious and Eminent Men against the Entertainments of the Stage and Other Vain Amusements: Recommended to the Perusal of Christians of Every Denomination* (New York: T. Kirk, 1798); and Ann Wagner, *Adversaries of Dance: From Puritans to the Present* (Urbana: University of Illinois Press, 1997).

123. Mather, "Arrow," 21.

124. Evans-Pritchard, "The Dance," 451.

125. D. K. Chisiza, "The Temper, Aspiration, and Problems of Contemporary Africa," Nyasaland Economic Symposium, July 18–28, 1962.

126. Nketia, "Interrelations," 91.

127. In *Jazz Dance* (New York: Schrimer, 1979), Marshall and Jean Stearns outline six characteristics of African dance: 1) African style is often flat-footed and favors gliding, dragging, or shuffling steps; 2) African dance is frequently performed from a crouch, knees flexed and body bent at the waist; 3) African dance generally imitates animals in realistic detail; 4) African dance places great importance on improvisation and satire and allows for freedom of individual expression, thus allowing for flexibility and aiding the evolution and diffusion of other African characteristics; 5) African dance is centrifugal, exploding outward from the hip with the legs moving from the hips instead of from the knees; 6) African dance is performed to a propulsive rhythm that gives it a swinging quality.

128. Equiano, *Interesting Narrative*, 56.

129. Ibid., 214.

Chapter 2. Casting

1. *Trial of Captain John Kimber for the Murder of a Negro Girl on board the Ship Recovery* (London: Symonds, 1792), 34.

2. Ibid., 12.

3. Ibid., Appendix, 1–4.

4. Sowandè Mustakeem, "I Never Have Such a Sickly Ship Before: Diet, Disease, and Mortality in 18th Century Atlantic Slaving Voyages," *Journal of African American History* 93, no. 4 (Fall 2008): 474–96.

5. *Trial of Captain John Kimber*, 8.

6. *Ibid.*, 16–18.

7. Geneviève Fabre, "The Slave Ship Dance," in *Black Imagination and the Middle Passage*, ed. Maria Diedrich, Henry Louis Gates Jr., and Carl Pedersen (New York: Oxford University Press, 1999); Lynne Fauley Emery, *Black Dance: From 1619 to Today* (Hightstown, N.J.: Princeton Book Co., 1988); and Marcus Rediker, *The Slave Ship: A Human History* (New York: Penguin, 2007).

8. *Trial of Captain John Kimber*, 41.

9. Ibid., 19–20.

10. Ibid., Appendix, 3.

11. Ibid., 3.

12. Henry Schroeder, *Three Years Adventures of a Minor in England, Africa, the West Indies, South-Carolina and Georgia 1774–1853* (Leeds: Baines, 1831).

13. Jean Barbot, *Barbot on Guinea: The Writings of Jean Barbot on West Africa, 1678–1712*, ed. P. E. H. Hair, Adam Jones, and Robin Law (London: Hakluyt, 1992); Jean Barbot, *A Description of the Coasts of North and South Guinea; and of Ethiopia Inferior, Vulgarly Angola: Being a New and Accurate Account of the Western Maritime Countries of Africa*, cited by Awnsham Churchill, *A Collection of Voyages and Travels, Some Now First Printed from Original Manuscripts*, 6 vols. (London: 1704, 1732), 675.

14. Herbert S. Klein, *The Middle Passage: Comparative Studies in the Atlantic Slave Trade* (Princeton, N.J.: Princeton University Press, 1978); Hugh Thomas, *The Slave Trade: The Story of the Atlantic Slave Trade, 1440–1870* (New York: Simon & Schuster, 1997); James Walvin, *Making the Black Atlantic: Britain and the African Diaspora* (New York: Cassell, 2000).

15. Robin Blackburn, *The Making of New World Slavery: From the Baroque to the Modern, 1492–1800*, (New York: Verso, 1997); Rediker, *Slave Ship*, 5; David Etlis, *The Rise of African Slavery in the Americas* (Cambridge: Cambridge University Press, 2000); Richard H. Steckel and Richard A. Jensen, "New Evidence on the Causes of Slave and Crew Mortality in the Atlantic Slave Trade," *Journal of Economic History* 46, no.1 (March 1986): 55–77.

16. Shroeder, *Three Years Adventures*, 26–27.

17. Joseph Hawkins, *A History of a Voyage to the Coast of Africa, and Travels into the Interior of that Country; Containing Particular Descriptions of the Climate and Inhabitants, and Interesting Particulars concerning the Slave Trade* (Philadelphia, 1797), 141.

18. Olaudah Equiano, *The Interesting Narrative of the Life of Olaudah Equiano, or Gustavus Vassa, the African, Written by Himself*, ed. Robert J. Allison (Boston and New York: Bedford/St. Martin's, 2007), 58.

19. Robert Stokes, *Regulated Slave Trade: From the Evidence of Robert Stokes, Esq., Given before the Select Committee of the House of Lords, in 1849* (London, 1851).

20. Theodore Canot, *Adventures of an African Slaver: Being a True Account of Captain Theodore Canot, Trader in Gold, Ivory and Slaves on the Coast of Guinea; His Own Story as Told in the Year 1854 to Brantz Mayer*, ed. Malcolm Cowley (New York: Boni, 1928), 70.

21. Schroeder, *Three Years Adventures*, 28.

22. Ira Berlin, *Many Thousands Gone: The First Two Centuries of Slavery in North America* (Cambridge: Harvard University Press, 1998), 17.

23. Canot, *Adventures*, 76.

24. Ibid., 72.

25. Ibid.

26. Jennifer L. Morgan, *Laboring Women: Reproduction and Gender in New World Slavery* (Philadelphia: University of Pennsylvania Press, 2004); Peter Erickson, "Representations of Blacks and Blackness in the Renaissance," *Criticism* 35 (1993): 514–15; Kim F. Hall, *Things of Darkness: Economies of Race and Gender in Early Modern England* (Ithaca, N.Y.: Cornell University Press, 1995).

27. Canot, *Adventures*, 101–2.

28. Ibid., 101–3.

29. Ibid., 102.

30. Ibid.

31. Barbot, "Description."

32. Richard Drake, *Revelations of a Slave Smuggler: Being the Autobiography of Captain Richard Drake, an African Trader for Fifty Years—from 1807 to 1857; During Which Period He Was Concerned in the Transportation of Half a Million Blacks from African Coasts to America* (New York: DeWitt, 1860).

33. Thomas Fowell Buxton, *The Atlantic Slave Trade and Its Remedy* (London: Cass, 1840), 135.

34. Canot, *Adventures*, 74.

35. Rediker, *Slave Ship*, 62–63. Detailed information on the layout and size of slave ships may be found in Stephanie E. Smallwood, *Saltwater Slavery: A Middle Passage from Africa to American Diaspora* (Cambridge, Mass.: Harvard University Press, 2007).

36. Stokes, *Regulated Slave Trade*, 12.

37. Ibid.

38. Ibid., 14.

39. Sheila Lambert, ed., *Great Britain Parliament, House of Commons Sessional Papers of the Eighteenth Century, Report of the Lords of Trade on the Slave Trade, 1789*, vol. 69 (Scholarly Resources, 1975).

40. Rediker, *Slave Ship*, 5; Eric Robert Taylor, *If We Must Die: Shipboard Insurrections in the Era of the Atlantic Slave Trade* (Baton Rouge: Louisiana State University Press, 2006); Raymond L. Cohn, "Death of Slaves in the Middle Passage," *Journal of Economic History* 45, no. 3 (September 1985): 687; Philip D. Curtin, "Measuring the Atlantic Slave Trade Once Again: A Comment," *Journal of African History* 17, no. 4 (1976): 596–605; Herbert S. Klein and Stanley Engerman, "Slave Mortality on British Ships, 1791–1797," in *Liverpool, the African Slave Trade, and Abolition: Essays to Illustrate Current Knowledge and Research*, eds. R. T. Anstey and P. E. H. Hair Historic Society of Lancashire and Cheshire Occasional Scries, vol 2, (Bristol: Western, 1976).

41. Alexander Falconbridge, *An Account of the Slave Trade on the Coast of Africa* (London: Phillips, 1788), 23.

42. Lambert, *Great Britain Parliament*.

43. Alessandro Arcangeli, "Dance and Health: The Renaissance Physicians' View," *Dance Research: The Journal of the Society for Dance Research* 18, no. 1 (Summer 2000): 11.

44. Drake, *Revelations*, 44.

45. The term "stage" in reference to the slave ship's deck was used in a narrative written by Edward Manning on the slave ship *Thomas Watson*. Found in

Edward Manning, *Six Months on a Slaver: A True Narrative* (New York: Harper, 1879).

46. Drake, *Revelations*, 44.

47. John R. Spears, *The American Slave Trade: An Account of Its Origin, Growth, and Suppression* (Williamstown, Mass.: Corner House, 1990), 78.

48. Great Britain, House of Commons, *Minutes of the Evidence Taken before a Committee of the House of Commons: Being a Select Committee Appointed to Take the Examination of Witnesses Respecting the African Slave Trade* (London, 1791), 33.

49. The "cat" refers to the cat-o'-nine-tails, which was used as a lash. See John Riland, *Memoirs of a West Indian Planter* (London: Hamilton, Adams, 1828), 46–60.

50. Bodleian Library, ed., *The Memoirs of Captain Hugh Crow: The Life and Times of a Slave Trader Captain* (Bodleian Library: University of Oxford, 2007).

51. Found in Katrina Hazzard-Gordon, *Jookin': The Rise of Social Dance Formations in African-American Culture* (Philadelphia: Temple University Press, 1990).

52. Drake, *Revelations*, 44–46.

53. Falconbridge, *Account*, 23.

54. Great Britain, House of Commons, *Minutes*, Testimony of James Arnold.

55. George Pinckard, *Notes on the West Indies*, 2nd ed. (London: Baldwin, Cradock, and Joy, 1816), 25.

56. Great Britain, House of Commons, *Minutes*, Testimony of James Arnold.

57. Ibid., Testimony of Robert Norris Esquire.

58. Ibid., Testimony of Vice Admiral Edwards.

59. Ibid., Testimony of James Penny.

60. Ibid.

61. J. R. Oldfield, "The London Committee and Mobilization of Public Opinion against the Slave Trade," *Historical Journal* 35, no. 2 (1992): 331.

62. Thomas Clarkson, *The History of the Rise, Progress and Accomplishment of the African Slave Trade by the British Parliament*, 2 vols. (London: Taylor, 1808); Roger Anstey, *The Atlantic Slave Trade and British abolition, 1760–1810* (London: Humanities, 1975).

63. Donna T. Andrew, ed., *London Debating Societies, 1776–1799* (London: Record Society, 1994).

64. Emma Christopher, *Slave Ship Sailors and Their Captive Cargoes, 1730–1807* (New York: Cambridge University Press, 2006), 52.

65. William Ray, *The American Tars in Tripolitan Slavery* (Troy, N.Y.: 1801; reprint, New York: Abbatt, 1911), 19; W. Jeffrey Bolster, *Black Jacks: African American Seaman in the Age of Sail* (Cambridge, Mass.: Harvard University Press, 1997), 70.

66. William Snelgrave, *A New Account of Some Parts of Guinea and the Slave Trade* (London, 1734), 192.

67. David R. Roediger, *The Wages of Whiteness: Race and the Making of the American Working Class* (London: Verso, 1991); Matthew Frye Jacobson, *Whiteness of a Different Color: European Immigrants and the Alchemy of Race* (Cambridge, Mass.: Harvard University Press, 1998).

68. Peter Kolchin, "Whiteness Studies: The New History of Race in America," *Journal of American History* 89, no. 1 (June 2002): 154–73.

69. David R. Roediger, "The Pursuit of Whiteness: Property, Terror, and Expansion, 1790–1860," *Journal of the Early Republic* 19, no. 4, Special Issues on Racial Consciousness and Nation Building in the Early Republic (Winter 1999): 579–600.

70. Bolster, *Black Jacks*, 32.

71. Christopher, *Slave Ship Sailors*, 56–57.

72. Bolster, *Black Jacks*, 7–43.

73. J. Franklin Jameson, ed., *Privateering and Privacy in the Colonial Period: Illustrative Documents* (New York: Macmillan, 1923); Bolster, *Black Jacks*, 34.

74. George Francis Dow, *Slave Ships and Slaving* (New York: Dover, 1970), xxiv.

75. Ibid.

76. Canot, *Adventures*, 73.

77. Dow, *Slave Ships and Slaving*, 174.

78. Drake, *Revelations*, 44.

79. Hazzard-Gordon, *Jookin,'* 9–10.

80. Drake, *Revelations*, 44.

81. Schroeder, *Three Years Adventures*, 80.

82. Dow, *Slave Ships and Slaving*, 50.

83. Schroeder, *Three Years Adventures*, 108–10.

84. Ibid.

85. Taylor, *If We Must Die*, 88.

86. Schroeder, *Three Years Adventures*, 109.

87. Taylor, *If We Must Die*, 67–84.

88. Antonio T. Bly, "Crossing the Lake of Fire: Slave Resistance during the Middle Passage, 1720–1842," *Journal of Negro History* 83, no. 3 (Summer 1998): 181.

89. Taylor, *If We Must Die*, 12.

90. Bly, "Crossing," 181.

91. Thomas Phillips, *Abstract of a Voyage along the Coast of Guinea to Whidaw, the Island of St. Thomas, and thence to Barbados, in 1693*, in Thomas Astley, *New Generation Collection of Voyages and Travels*, vol. 2: 387–416.

92. Bly, "Crossing," 182.

93. Ibid.

94. Maria Diedrich, Henry Louis Gates Jr., and Carl Pedersen, eds., *Black Imagination and the Middle Passage* (New York: Oxford University Press, 1999).

95. Barbot, *Barbot on Guinea*, 775.

96. Lambert, *Great Britain Parliament*, Testimony of James Arnold.

97. Great Britain, House of Commons, *Minutes*.

98. Amasa Delano, *A Narrative of Voyages and Travels, in the Northern and Southern Hemispheres: Comprising Three Voyages Round the World; Together with a Voyage of Survey and Discovery, in the Pacific Ocean and Oriental Islands* (Boston: House, 1817).

99. *Copies of Affidavits, Information & Certificates Rec'd by the Royal African Company of England from Abroad from January 1698 to March the 25th, 1712* PRO, T 70, 14:66–67; Taylor, *If We Must Die*, 67.

100. Jerome S. Handler, "The Middle Passage and the Material Culture of Captive Africans," *Slavery and Abolition* 30, no. 1 (March 2009): 1–26.

101. George Pinckard, *Notes on the West Indies*, 2nd ed. (London: Baldwin, Cradock and Joy, 1816), 97–103.

102. Falconbridge, *Account*, 23.

103. W. O. Blake, *The History of Slavery and the Slave Trade, Ancient and Modern* (Columbus, Ohio: Miller, 1857); Edward Reynolds, *Stand the Storm: A History of the Atlantic Slave Trade* (Chicago: Dee, 1985); David Etlis, Stephen D. Behrendt, and David Richardson, eds, *The Transatlantic Slave Trade: A Database on CD-ROM*, (New York: Cambridge University Press, 2000).

104. Schroeder, *Three Years Adventures*, 85.

105. Michael Gomez, *Exchanging Our Country Marks: The Transformation of African Identities in the Colonial and Antebellum South* (Chapel Hill: University of North Carolina Press, 1998), 28–29; Philip D. Curtin, *Atlantic Slave Trade: A Census* (Madison: University of Wisconsin Press, 1969), 156–58; David Richardson, "Slave Exports from West and West-Central Africa: New Estimates of Volume and Distribution," *Journal of African History* 30 (1989): 12–14.

106. Fabre, "Slave Ship Dance," 42.

107. *Report of the Lords of the Committee of Council, Appointed for the Consideration of All Matters Relating to Trade and Foreign Plantations*, February 11, 1788, House of Commons Papers: George III, vol. 69.

108. Eric Charry, *Mande Music: Traditional and Modern Music in the Maninka and Mandinka of Western Africa* (Chicago: University of Chicago Press, 2000), 199.

109. Philip D. Morgan, *Slave Counterpart: Black Culture in the Eighteenth Century Chesapeake and Lowcountry* (Chapel Hill: University of North Carolina Press, 1998).

110. Christopher, *Slave Ship Sailors*; Smallwood, *Saltwater Slaves*.

111. Maria Deidrich, Henry Louis Gates, Jr., and Carl Pederson, ed. *Black Imagination and the Middle Passage* (New York: Oxford University Press, 1999), 8.

112. Thomas Phillips, "Voyage Made in the Hannibal," from Churchill, *Collection of Voyages and Travels* (1732), reprinted in Elizabeth Donnan, ed., *Documents Illustrative of the History of the Slave Trade to America*, (Buffalo, N.Y.: Hein, 2002), 390.

113. Robert Harms, *The Diligent: A Voyage through the World of the Slave Trade* (New York: Basic, 2002).

114. Hannah More, *The Sorrows of Yamba; or, The Negro Woman's Lamentation* (London: Cheap Repository Tracts, 1795); William Meade and Thomas Bacon, *Sermons Addressed to Masters and Servants, and Published in the Year 1743* (Winchester, Va.: Heiskell, 1813). This quote represents only one stanza of a poem, the accurate author and publication date of which is unknown. Hannah More has been continually represented as the author, but many historians dispute this claim. Also, the original date of publication is under debate. This poem has been published in numerous works since the eighteenth century.

115. Lambert, *Great Britain Parliament*.

116. Great Britain, House of Commons, *Minutes*, Testimony of Vice Admiral Edwards.

117. Lambert, *Great Britain Parliament*, Testimony of James Arnold.

118. Barbot, *Barbot on Guinea*; Barbot, *Description*, cited by Churchill, *Collection of Voyages*, 87.

119. Falconbridge, *Account,* 253.

120. Olaudah Equiano, *Interesting Narrative,* 38.

121. Falconbridge, *Account,* 152.

122. *Revelations of a Slave Smuggler: Being the Autobiography of Capt. Richard Drake, an African Trade for Fifty Years—from 1807 to 185* (New York, 1860), found in Dow, *Slave Ships and Slaving* (New York: Dover, 1970), 253.

123. Ibid., 253.

124. Sterling Stuckey, *Slave Culture: Nationalist Theory and The Foundations Of Black America* (Oxford: Oxford University Press, 1987).

Chapter 3. Onstage

1. Solomon Northup, *Twelve Years A Slave,* ed. Sue Eakin and Joseph Logsdon (Baton Rouge: Louisiana State University, 1968), 136–39.

2. Solomon Northup was born a freeman in New York and was illegally kidnapped into the institution of slavery in the southern United States.

3. Frederick Douglass, *My Bondage and My Freedom* (New York: Miller, Orton & Mulligan, 1855), 97.

4. Saidiya Hartman, *Scenes of Subjection: Terror, Slavery, and Self-Making in Nineteenth-Century America* (New York: Oxford University Press, 1997).

5. Richard Ligon, *A True and Exact History of the Island of Barbados* (London: Cass, 1657, 1673), 46–49, 50.

6. *A Letter to the Right Reverend the Lord Bishop of London, from an Inhabitant of His Majesty's Leeward-Carribee-Islands; In Which is Inserted, a Short Essay concerning the Conversation of the Negro-Slaves in Our Sugar-Colonies; Written in the Month of June, 1727, by the Same Inhabitant* (London: Wilford, 1730); Dena J. Epstein, *Sinful Tunes and Spirituals: Black Folk Music to the Civil War* (Urbana: University of Illinois Press, 1977, 2003), 39.

7. Thomas Tryon, *Friendly Advice to the Gentlemen-Planters of the East and West Indies,* by Philotheos Phyliologus (Sowle, 1684).

8. Ibid., 146–48.

9. Charles de Rochefort, *The History of the Caribby-Islands, viz. Barbados, St. Christophers, St. Vincents, Martinico, Dominico, Barbouthos, Monserrat, Mevis* [*sic*], *Antego &c in all XXVIII . . . Rendered into English by John Davis . . .* (London: J.M., 1666), 202.

10. P. J. Laborie, *The Coffee Planter of Saint Domingo; with an Appendix. . . .* (London: Cadell and Davies, 1798), 181–83.

11. Ibid.

12. Ira Berlin, *Many Thousand Gone: The First Two Centuries of Slavery in North America* (Cambridge, Mass.: Belknap, 1998).

13. Dena J. Epstein, *Sinful Tunes and Spirituals: Black Folk Music to the Civil War* (Urbana: University of Illinois Press), 21; Lynne Fauley Emery, *Black Dance From 1619 to Today* (Hightstown, N.J.: Princeton Book Co., 1972, 1988), 15–18.

14. Peter Kolchin, *American Slavery, 1619–1877* (New York: Hill and Wang, 1993, 2003), 10–11.

15. Lerone Bennett Jr., *Confrontation Black and White* (Chicago: Johnson, 1965), 29–32.

16. John Locke, *The Fundamental Constitutions of Carolina, 1682*, Henry E. Huntington Library and Art Gallery.

17. Winthrop Jordan, *White Over Black: American Attitudes toward the Negro, 1590–1812* (Chapel Hill: University of North Carolina Press, 1968); Edmund S. Morgan, *American Slavery, American Freedom, (New York: Norton, 1975)*; Robert Olwell, *Masters, Slaves, and Subjects: The Culture of Power in the South Carolina Low Country, 1740–1790* (Ithaca, N.Y.: Cornell University Press, 1998), 1–16.

18. Thomas Atwood, *The History of the Island of Dominica* (London, 1791), 265–68, 272–74.

19. Thomas Jefferson, *Notes on the State of Virginia* (Virginia, 1853).

20. Ibid.

21. Henry C. Knight, *Letters from the South and West; by Arthur Singleton, esp. [pseud.]* (Boston: Richardson and Lord, 1824), 77. Library of Congress, *American Notes: Travels in America, 1750–1920.*

22. John F. Watson, *Annals of Philadelphia and Pennsylvania, in the Olden Time: Being a Collection of Memoirs, Anecdotes, and Incidents of the City and Its Inhabitants . . . by T. H. Mumford* (University of Michigan Library, 1870), 1:62, 2:265; Ira Berlin, *Many Thousand Gone*, 61.

23. Nicholas Cresswell, *The Journal of Nicholas Cresswell, 1774–1777* (New York: MacVeagh, Dial, 1924), 18–19.

24. Dena J. Epstein, "African Music in British and French America," *Musical Quarterly* 58, no. 1 (January, 1973): 61–91.

25. Morgan Godwin, *The Negro's & Indians Advocate, Suing for Their Admission into the Church; or, A Persuasive to the Instructing and Baptizing of the Negro's [sic] and Indians in our Plantations . . .* (London: F. D., 1680), 33.

26. John Sharpe, "Proposals for Erecting a School, Library and Chapel at New York," MS 841, Lambeth Palace Library, New York: March 11, 1712/13. New York Historical Society, *Collections*, 1880: 341.

27. Le Page du Pratz, *Histoire de la Louisiane*, 3 vols. (Paris, 1758), I:310.

28. George Whitefield, *Works of the Reverend George Whitefield . . . : Containing All His Sermons and Tracts which Have Been Already Published; With a Selected Collection of Letters Written to His Most Intimate Friends, and Persons of Distinction, in England, Scotland, Ireland, and America, from the Year 1734, to 1770; Including the Whole Period of His Ministry; Also, Some Other Pieces on Important Subjects, Never Before Printed*, vol. 4 (London: Dilly, 1772), 35–41.

29. Lerone Bennett Jr., *Before the Mayflower: A History of Black America* (New York: Penguin, 1983); Philip D. Morgan, *Slave Counterpart*: Black Culture in the Eighteenth-Century Chesapeake and Lowcountry (Chapel Hill and London: Published for the Omohundro Institute of Early American History and Culture by the University of North Carolina Press, 1998), 420–22.

30. June Purcell Guild, ed., *Black Laws of Virginia: A Summary of the Legislative Acts of Virginia concerning Negroes from the Earliest Times to the Present* (New York: Negro Universities Press 1969).

31. William D. Piersen, *Black Yankees: The Development of an Afro American Subculture in Eighteenth Century New England* (Amherst: University of Massachusetts Press, 1988); Ira Berlin, "Time, Space, and the Evolution of Afro-American Society on British Mainland North America," *American Historical Review* 85, no.

1 (February 1980): 44–78; Shane White, "'It Was a Proud Day': African Americans, Festivals, and Parades in the North, 1741–1834," *Journal of American History* 81, no.1 (June 1994): 13–50; Shane White, "Slavery in the North," *OAH Magazine in History* 17, no. 3, Colonial Slavery (April 2003): 17–21; Shane White, "Pinkster: Afro-Dutch Syncretization in New York City and the Hudson Valley," *Journal of American Folklore* 102, no. 403 (January–March 1989): 68–75.

32. Piersen, *Black Yankees*, 117–28.

33. White, "Pinkster," 68; Leslie M. Harris, *In the Shadow of Slavery: African Americans in New York City, 1626–1863* (Chicago: University of Chicago Press, 2003), 29–34.

34. George S. Roberts, *Old Schenectady* (Schenectady, N.Y.: Robson, 1904), 289.

35. Samuel E. Morison, "A Description of Election Day as Observed in Boston," Colonial Society of Massachusetts, *Transactions* 18 (February 1915): 60–61.

36. Roberts, *Old Schenectady*, 289.

37. Roberts, *Old Schenectady*, 288–90.; Shane White, ed., "Pinkster in Albany, 1803: A Contemporary Description," *New York History* 70 (April 1989): 198; White, "It Was a Proud Day," 23–24.

38. Roberts, *Old Schenectady*.

39. Berlin, "Time," 51–54; White, "It Was a Proud Day," 13–50.

40. Philip Vickers Fithian, *Journal and Letters of Philip Vickers Fithian 1773–1774: A Plantation Tutor of the Old Dominion*, ed. Hunter Dickinson Farish (Williamsburg, Va.: Colonial Williamsburg Inc., 1957), 177.

41. "Thomas Jefferson and His Unknown Brother Randolph," Thomas Jefferson to Nathaniel Burwell, March 14, 1919, quoted in Helen Cripe, *Thomas Jefferson and Music*, rev. ed. (Chapel Hill: University of North Carolina, 2010).

42. Ibid.

43. A Planter. "Notions on the Management of Negroes, &c.," *Farmers' Register* 4 (December 1836 and January 1837): 494–95, 574–75.

44. Mark DeWolfe Howe, ed., "Journal of Josiah Quincy, Junior, 1773," *Proceedings of the Massachusetts Historical Society* 49 (1916): 455–56.

45. Charles Woodson, "On the Management of Slaves," *Farmers' Register* 2 (September 1834), in James O. Breeden, *Advice among Masters: The Ideal in Slave Management in the Old South* (Westport, Conn.: Greenwood, 1980).

46. Ibid., 30.

47. John Davis, *Travels of Four Years and a Half in the United States of America; During 1798, 1799, 1800, 1801, and 1802: Dedicated by Permission to Thomas Jefferson, Esq., President of the United States* (London: 1803), I:131.

48. H., "Remarks on Overseers, and the Proper Treatment of Slaves," *Farmers' Register* 5 (September 1837).

49. James M. Townes, "Management of Negroes," *Southern Cultivator* 15 (May and June 1857).

50. N. Herbemont, "On the Moral Discipline and Treatment of Slaves," *Southern Agriculturist* 9 (February 1836): 70–75.

51. Breeden, *Advice among Masters*, 276.

52. James W. Smith, *Born in Slavery: Slave Narratives from the Federal Writer's Project 1936–1938*, WPA Slave Narrative, Texas, vol. 16, pt. 4, Manuscript Division, Library of Congress.

53. Wesley Jones, WPA Slave Narratives, Spartanburg County, South Carolina, vol. 14, pt. 3, Federal Writer's Project, Manuscript Division, Library of Congress.

54. Virginia Writers' Project, *The Negro in Virginia* (New York: Hasting, 1940), 89.

55. Breeden, *Advice among Masters*, 257.

56. John Davis, *Travels of John Davis in the United States of America, 1798–1802*, vol. 2, ed. John Vance Cheney (Boston: Bibliophile Society, 1910), 148–50.

57. Norman R. Yetman, ed., *When I Was a Slave: Memories from the Slave Narrative Collection* (New York: Dover, 2002), 5. William Wells Brown in his autobiography, *From Fugitive Slave to Free Man*, exposed the atrocities of the Midwest region. He adamantly proclaimed that slavery was often viewed as mild in Missouri when compared with slavery in the Southern states; however, he asserted that the barbarity of slavery was ever present in St Louis.

58. Virginia Writers' Project, *The Negro in Virginia*, 89.

59. A Mississippi Planter, "Management of Negroes upon Southern Estates," *DeBow's Review* 10 (June 1851): 621–27.

60. A Small Farmer, "Management of Negroes," *DeBow's Review* 11 (October 1851): 369–72.

61. Elizabeth Waties Allston Pringle (pseud. Patience Pennington), *A Woman Rice Planter, 1845–1921*, illus. Alice R. H. Smith (New York: Macmillan, 1914), 274. *Documenting the American South* (digital archive [docsouth.unc.edu]), University Library, University of North Carolina at Chapel Hill (1998).

62. Davis, *Travels of John Davis*, 143–44.

63. Saidiya Hartman, *Scenes of Subjection: Terror, Slavery, and Self-Making in Nineteenth-Century America* (New York: Oxford University Press, 1997), 22.

64. Jefferson, *Notes.*

65. Ibid.

66. Hartman, *Scenes of Subjection.*

67. Douglass, *My Bondage and My Freedom*, 97.

68. Hartman, *Scenes of Subjection.*

69. Douglass, *My Bondage and My Freedom*, 155.

70. Found in Breeden, *Advice among Masters*, 279.

71. William Byrd, *Another Secret Diary of William Byrd of Westover 1739–1741; With Letters & Literary Exercises 1696–1726*, ed. Maude H. Woodfin (Richmond, Va.: Dietz, 1942), 46, 157, 174.

72. Isabella Lucy Bird, *The Englishwoman in America* (Toronto: University of Toronto Press, 1966), 128.

73. Letitia M. Burwell, *A Girl's Life in Virginia before the War*, illus. William A. McCullough and Jules Turcas (New York: Stokes, 1895), 40.

74. Found in Hartman, *Scenes of Subjection*; Herbemont, *Moral Discipline.*

75. Nathan Bass, "Essay on the Treatment and Management of Slaves," Southern Central Agricultural Society of Georgia, *Transactions, 1826–1851*, 195–201.

76. Jacqueline L. Tobin and Raymond G. Dobard, *Hidden in Plain View: A Secret Story of Quilts and the Underground Railroad* (New York: Anchor, 1999).

77. Frances Anne Kemble, *Journal of a Residence on a Georgian Plantation in 1838–1839* (New York: Knopf, 1961), 163–64.

78. Robert Nowatzki, *Representing African Americans in Transatlantic Abolitionism and Blackface Minstrelsy* (Baton Rouge: Louisiana University Press, 2010), 82–85.

79. Alexander Barclay, *A Practical View of the Present State of Slavery in the West Indies* (London: Smith, Elder, 1826), 206–8.

80. Roger Chartier, *Forms and Meaning: Texts, Performances, and Audiences from Codex to Computer* (Philadelphia: University of Pennsylvania Press, 1995), 47.

81. Herbemont, *Moral Discipline.*

82. Breeden, *Advice among Masters*, 277–78.

83. Ibid., 278.

84. Henry C. Knight, *Letters from the South and West*, American Notes: Travels in America, 1824, Library of Congress.

85. Howard Zinn, *The Southern Mystique* (New York: Knopf, 1964).

86. John Wilson, "The Peculiarities & Diseases of Negroes," *American Cotton Planter and Soil of the South*, n.s., 4 (February, March, April, May, August, September, November, and December 1860): 79–80.

87. Harriet Jacobs, *Incidents In the Life of a Slave Girl: Written by Herself* (Boston: Published for the Author, 1861), 119.

88. Davis, *Travels of John Davis*, 2:149.

89. Ibid., 149–50.

90. Ellen Campbell, WPA Slave Narrative Project, Georgia Narratives, vol. 4, pt. 4, Federal Writer's Project, Manuscript Division, Library of Congress.

91. Edward Long, *The History of Jamaica* (London: Lowndes, 1774), 242.

92. Henry Edward Krehbiel, *Afro-American Folksongs: A Study in Racial and National Music*, 4th ed. (New York: Schrimer, 1914), 125.

93. John Blassingame, ed. *Slave Testimony: Two Centuries of Letters, Speeches, Interviews, and Autobiographies* (Baton Rouge: Louisiana State University. 1977), 228.

94. Long, *History of Jamaica*, 242.

95. Blassingame, *Slave Testimony*, 341.

96. William Howard Russell, *My Diary North and South*, ed. Eugene H. Berwanger (New York: McGraw-Hill, 1988), 176–77.

97. Ibid., 96, 135–36, 176–77.

98. Ibid., 96.

99. Davis, *Travels of John Davis*, 111.

100. Russell, *My Diary*, 96.

101. Duke of Saxe-Weimar Eisenach, Bernard, *Travels through North America during the Years 1825 and 1826*, 2 vols. (Philadelphia: Carey, Lea, and Carey, 1828); Thomas Ashe, *Travels in America, Performed in the Year 1806, for the Purpose of Exploring the Rivers Alleghany, Monongahela, Ohio, and Mississippi, Ascertaining the Produce and Condition of Their Banks and Vicinity* (London: McMillan, 1809); Reuben Gold Thwaites, ed. *Early Western Travels, 1748–1846 : A Series of Annotated Reprints of Some of the Best and Rarest Contemporary Volumes of Travel; Descriptive of the Aborigines and Social and Economic Conditions in the Middle and Far West, during the Period of Early American Settlement*, vol. 6 (Cleveland, Ohio: Clark, 1904–1907; repr. Lewisburg, Pa.: Wennawoods, 2000), 363–66; Charles Schultz, *Travels on an Inland Voyage through the States of New York, Pennsylvania, Virginia, Ohio, Kentucky and Tennessee and through the Territories of Indiana, Louisiana, Mississippi and New Orleans; Performed in the Years 1807 and 1808; Including a Tour of Nearly Six Thousand Miles; With Maps and Plates*, 2 vols. (New York: Riley, 1810).

102. *Daily Delta*, January 3, 1851.

103. Ibid.

104. Ibid.

105. Breeden, *Advice among Masters*, 260.

106. Douglass, *My Bondage and My Freedom*, 156.

107. Pringle, *Woman Rice Planter*, 274.

108. Douglass, *My Bondage and My Freedom*, 156–58.

109. Henry Wright, WPA Slave Narrative Project, Georgia Narratives, vol. 4, pt. 4, Federal Writer's Project, Manuscript Division, Library of Congress.

110. Green Willbanks, WPA Slave Narrative Project, Georgia Narratives, vol. 4, pt. 4, Federal Writer's Project, Manuscript Division, Library of Congress.

111. Douglass, *My Bondage and My Freedom*, 157.

112. Mose Davis, WPA Slave Narrative Project, Georgia Narratives, vol. 4, pt. 4, Federal Writer's Project, Manuscript Division, Library of Congress.

113. A Mississippi Planter, "Management."

114. S. D. Wagg, "Overseeing," *Farmer and Planter* 5 (June and September 1854): 141–42, 229–30.

115. Douglass, *My Bondage and My Freedom*, 156.

116. *Essential Speeches* (Toledo, Ohio: Great Neck, 2003).

117. Gerda Lerner, *The Grimke Sisters from South Carolina: Pioneers for Women's Rights and Abolition* (Chapel Hill: University of North Carolina Press, 2009).

Chapter 4. Backstage

1. Solomon Northup, *Twelve Years a Slave*, ed. Sue Eakin and Joseph Logsdon (Baton Rouge: Louisiana State University Press, 1968), 12.

2. Robert Olwell, *Masters, Slaves and Subjects: The Culture of Power in South Carolina Low Country, 1740–1790* (Ithaca, N.Y.: Cornell University Press, 1998).

3. General Oglethorpe to the Account Mr. Harman Verelst, October 9, 1739, in Candler Company, Colonial Records of Georgia, XXII, pt. 2, 232–36; William Bull Sr. to the Board of Trade, October 5, 1739, records in the British P.R.O. Relating to S.C. XX, 179–80.

4. John K. Thornton, "African Dimensions of the Stono Rebellion," *American Historical Review* 96, no. 4 (October, 1991): 111–13.

5. Oscar Reiss, *Blacks In Colonial America* (Jefferson, N.C.: McFarland, 1997), 108.

6. Michael A. Gomez, *Exchanging Our Country Marks: The Transformation of African Identities in the Colonial and Antebellum South* (Chapel Hill: University of North Carolina Press, 1998), 136–40; Thornton, "African Dimensions"; Peter H. Wood, *Black Majority: Negroes in Colonial South Carolina from 1670 through the Stono Rebellion* (New York: Norton, 1974,1996); Daniel Littlefield, *Rice and Slaves: Ethnicity and the Slave Trade in Colonial South Carolina* (Baton Rouge: Louisiana State University Press, 1981).

7. Paul Gilroy, *The Black Atlantic: Modernity and Double Consciousness* (Cambridge, Mass.: Harvard University Press, 1993), 1.

8. Le Page du Pratz, *The History of Louisiana, or of the Western Parts of Virginia and Carolina* (London: Becket, 1774), 380–87.

9. Leslie Harris, *In the Shadow of Slavery: African Americans in New York City, 1626–1863* (Chicago: University of Chicago Press, 2003).

10. David J. McCord, ed., *The Statutes at Large at South Carolina*, vol. 7, Containing the Acts Relating to Charleston, Courts, Slaves, and Rivers (Columbia, S.C.: A. S. Johnston, 1840), 397.

11. Guion Johnson, *Ante-bellum North Carolina: A Social History* (Chapel Hill: University of North Carolina Press, 1937), 599.

12. *Statutes at Large for the State of South Carolina*, vol. 6 (Columbia, S.C.: A. S. Johnston, 1839), 410. See also Katrina Hazzard-Gordon, *Jookin': The Rise of Social Dance Formations in African American Culture* (Philadelphia: Temple University Press, 1990), 33.

13. Nicholas Cresswell, *The Journal of Nicholas Cresswell, 1774–1777* (New York, 1924), 18–19.

14. Georgia Writers' Project, *Drums and Shadows: Survival Studies among the Georgia Coastal Negroes* (Athens: University of Georgia Press, 1940), 130.

15. Henry Wright, WPA Slave Narrative Project, Georgia Narratives, vol. 4, pt. 4, 200, Federal Writers' Project 1936–1938, Manuscript Division, Library of Congress.

16. William D. Pierson, *Black Yankees: The Development of an Afro-American Subculture in Eighteenth-Century New England* (Amherst: University of Massachusetts Press, 1988), 96–113.

17. Leslie M. Harris, *In the Shadow of Slavery: African Americans in New York City, 1626–1863* (Chicago: University of Chicago Press, 2003), 40–41, 49.

18. Michael A. Gomez, *Exchanging Our Country Marks: The Transformation of African Identities in the Colonial and Antebellum South* (Chapel Hill: University of North Carolina Press, 1998), 136–40; Thornton, "African Dimensions"; Peter H. Wood, *Black Majority: Negroes in Colonial South Carolina from 1670 through the Stono Rebellion* (New York: Norton, 1974, 1996); Littlefield, *Rice and Slaves*.

19. Green Willbanks, WPA Slave Narrative Project, Georgia Narratives, vol. 4, pt. 4, Federal Writer's Project, Manuscript Division, Library of Congress.

20. John Finnely, "When I Was a Slave: Memoirs from the Slave Narrative Collection," WPA Narratives, Fort Worth, Texas, Federal Writers Project 1936–1938, Manuscript Division, Library of Congress, 39–42.

21. Roger D. Abrahams discusses the corn-shucking festival in *Singing the Master: The Emergence of African American Culture in the Plantation South* (New York: Pantheon, 1992).

22. Willbanks, WPA/Georgia Narratives, 136–47.

23. Charles L. Perdue Jr., Thomas E. Barden, and Robert K. Phillips, eds, *Weevils in the Wheat: Interviews with Virginia Ex-Slaves* (Charlottesville: University of Virginia Press, 1976, 1992), 278.

24. Estella Jones, WPA Slave Narrative Project, Georgia Narratives, vol. 6, pt. 2, Federal Writer's Project, Manuscript Division, Library of Congress.

25. Ibid., 348.

26. Debra G. White, *Ar'n't I a Woman? Female Slaves in the Plantation South* (New York: Norton, 1985).

27. Jones, Georgia Narratives, 348.

28. Sallie Paul, interviewed by Annie Ruth Davis, WPA Slave Narrative Project, South Carolina Narratives, vol. 4, pt. 4, Federal Writer's Project, Manuscript Division, Library of Congress, 242–43.

29. Christopher J. Gill, "A Year in Residence in the Household of a South Carolina Planter: Teachers, Daughters, Mistress, and Slaves," *South Carolina Historical Magazine* 97, no. 4 (October 1996): 304–5.

30. Roscoe Lewis, *The Negro in Virginia* (New York: Arno, 1969), 87.

31. Old Mary of the Roof Plantation, Interview, WPA Slave Narrative Project, Georgia Narratives, vol. 4, pt. 4, Federal Writer's Project, Manuscript Division, Library of Congress, 334–35

32. Jones, Georgia Narratives, 346.

33. Frederick Douglass, *My Bondage and My Freedom* (New York: Miller, Orton, & Mulligan, 1855), 154.

34. Pearl Randolph, WPA Slave Narrative Project, Florida Narratives, vol. 3, Federal Writer's Project, Manuscript Division, Library of Congress, 212–13.

35. Jones, Georgia Narratives, 347.

36. Clement Bethel, "Junkanoo in the Bahamas," *Caribbean Quarterly* 36, no. 3/4, Konnu and Carnival-Caribbean Festival Arts (December 1990); Rosita M. Sands, Maureen "Bahama Mama" DuValier, and Ronald Simms, "Junkanoo Past, Present, and Future," *Black Perspective in Music* 17, no. 1/2 (1989).

37. Harriet Jacobs (Linda Brent), *Incidents in the Life of a Slave Girl*, ed. Lydia Maria Child (New York: Harcourt Brace Jovanovich, 1973).

38. Janet DeCosmo, "Junkanoo: The African Cultural Connection in Nassau, Bahamas," *Western Journal of Black Studies* vol. 27, no. 4 (Winter 2003): 246.

39. Jacobs, *Incidents*, 51.

40. Ibid.

41. Gomez, *Exchanging*.

42. JBHE Foundation, "The Origin of the Cake Walk," *Journal of Blacks in Higher Education* 35 (Spring 2002): 134.

43. Tom Felcher, *The Tom Felcher Story: 100 Years of the Negro in Show Business* (New York: Burdge, 1954), 19.

44. Sterling Stuckey, *Slave Culture: Nationalist Theory and the Foundations of Black America* (London: Oxford University Press, 1987), 66.

45. JBHE Foundation, "Cake Walk," 134.

46. Jones, Georgia Narratives, 348.

47. Lynne Fauley Emery, *Black Dance From 1619 to Today* (Hightstown, N.J.: Dance Horizons/Princeton Book Company, 1972, 1988), 91.

48. Paul A. Cimbala, "Black Musicians from Slavery to Freedom: An Exploration of an African-American Folk Elite and Cultural Continuity in the Nineteenth Century Rural South," *Journal of Negro History* 80, no. 1 (Winter 1995): 15–29.

49. Ibid., 15.

50. Northup, *Twelve Years a Slave*, 149.

51. George P. Rawick, ed., *American Slave*, supp. series 2, vol. 16: *Maryland Narratives*, pt. 8, 66.

52. George P. Rawick, ed., *American Slave*, supp. series 2, vol. 7: *Texas Narratives*, pt. 6, 2469.

53. George P. Rawick, ed., *American Slave*, supp. series 2, vol. 13: *Georgia Narratives*, pt. 3, 206.

54. A. J. H. Christensen, *Afro-American Folk Lore Told Round Cabin Fires on the Sea Islands of South Carolina* (Boston: Cupples, 1892), 3.

55. Northup, *Twelve Years a Slave,* 137.

56. Fannie Fulcher, WPA Slave Narrative Project, Georgia Narratives, vol. 4, pt. 4, Federal Writer's Project, Manuscript Division, Library of Congress.

57. Willbanks, WPA/Georgia Narratives, 136–48.

58. Melinda Mitchell, WPA Slave Narrative Project, Georgia Narratives, vol. 4, pt. 4, Federal Writer's Project, Manuscript Division, Library of Congress, 336.

59. The folktale of Uncle Dick, the slave musician, comes directly from George P. Rawick, ed., *American Slave,* supp. series 2, vol. 16, no. 11: *Kentucky Narratives,* 68–73, 95–99.

60. Eric Charry, *Mande Music: Traditional and Modern Music in the Maninka and Mandinka of Western Africa* (Chicago: University of Chicago Press, 2000).

61. Henry Wright, WPA/Georgia Narratives, 200.

62. George P. Rawick, ed., *American Slave/Georgia,* pt. 3, 219.

63. Bilal Abdurahman, *Traditional African Musical Instruments* (New York: Ethno Modes, 1987), 1.

64. Georgia Writers' Project, *Drums and Shadows,* 148.

65. Guion Johnson, *Ante-bellum North Carolina,* 599.

66. Charry, *Mande Music*; Jan Jansen, *The Griot's Craft: An Essay on Oral Tradition and Diplomacy* (Munster, N.J.: Transaction, 2000).

67. G. C. Rankin, *The Story of My Life, or More Than a Half Century as I Have Lived It and Seen It Lived Written by Myself at My Own Suggestion and That of Many Others Who Have Known and Loved Me* [electronic edition]. This work is the property of the University of North Carolina at Chapel Hill.

68. Ibid., 17–19.

69. Wilbur J. Cash, *The Mind of the South* (New York: Vintage, 1941), xi.

70. Robert B. Winans, "Black Instrumental Music Traditions in the Ex-Slave Narratives," *Black Music Research Journal* 10, no. 1 (Spring 1990), 53.

71. Ibid., 51.

72. Ibid.

73. Edward Thorpe, *Black Dance* (Woodstock, N.Y.: Overlook, 1989), 27.

74. Hazzard-Gordon, *Jookin',* 19–20.

75. Georgia Writers' Project, *Drums and Shadows,* 115.

76. Doris Green, "Traditional Dance in Africa," in *African Dance: An Artistic, Historical and Philosophical Inquiry,* ed. Kariamu Welsh Asante (Trenton, N.J.: Africa World, 1994, 1998, 2002), 16.

77. Hazzard-Gordon, *Jookin',* 18.

78. Ibid., 186–87.

79. Emery, *Black Dance,* 120–21.

80. Ibid., 92.

81. P. Amaury Talbot, *The Peoples of Southern Nigeria* (London: Oxford University Press, 1926), 804; Stuckey, *Slave Culture,* 10–12.

82. E. E. Evans-Pritchard, "The Dance," *Africa: Journal of the International African Institute* 1, no. 4 (October 1928): 446–62.

83. Hazzard-Gordon, *Jookin',* 18–53.

84. John Davis, *Travels of John Davis in the United States of America, 1798–1802,* vol. 2, ed. John Vance Cheney (Boston: Bibliophile, 1910), 149.

85. Hazzard-Gordon, *Jookin',* 15–53.

86. Emery, *Black Dance,* 122.

87. John Spencer Bassett, *Slavery in the State of North Carolina*, (Baltimore, Md.: Johns Hopkins Press, 1899), 92–93; Dena J. Epstein, "African Music in British and French America," *Musical Quarterly* 59, no. 1 (January 1973): 61–91.

88. Dena J. Epstein, *Sinful Tunes and Spirituals: Black Folk Music to the Civil War* (Urbana: University of Illinois Press, 1977, 2003), 71; Clement Caines, *The History of the General Council and General Assembly of the Leeward Islands, Which Were Convened for the Purpose of Investigating and Ameliorating the Condition of the Slaves throughout These Settlements and of Effecting a Gradual Abolition of the Slave Trade* (Basseterre, St. Christopher: R. Cable, 1804), 110–11.

89. Caines, *History*.

90. Epstein, "African Music in British and French America."

91. John Blassingame, ed. *Slave Testimony: Two Centuries of Letters, Speeches, Interviews, and Autobiographies* (Baton Rouge: Louisiana State University Press, 1977).

92. Lawrence Levine, *Black Culture and Black Consciousness: Afro-American Folk Thought from Slavery to Freedom* (New York: Oxford University Press, 1977); Eugene Genovese, *Roll, Jordan, Roll: The World the Slaves Made* (New York: Pantheon, 1974), George Rawick, *From Sundown to Sunup: The Making of the Black Community* (Westport, Conn.: Greenwood, 1972); Sterling Stuckey, *Slave Culture*.

93. Douglass, *My Bondage*, 64–65.

94. Ibid.

95. Ibid., 64–65.

96. All of the information pertaining to Susan Snow appears in Rawick, *American Slave/Maryland*, pt. 5.

97. W. E. B. Dubois, *The Souls of Black Folk* (New York: Bantam, 1903, 1989), 3.

98. Northup, *Twelve Years a Slave*.

99. Blassingame, *Slave Testimony*, 615–16.

100. Ibid., 616.

101. Fulcher, WPA/Georgia Narratives, 336.

102. Roger D. Abrahams, *Singing the Master: The Emergency of African American Culture in the Plantation South* (New York: Penguin, 1994).

103. Chris Franklin, WPA Slave Narrative Project, Texas Narratives, vol. 16, pt. 2, Federal Writer's Project, Manuscript Division, Library of Congress, 57.

104. Federal Writers' Project, *Slave Narratives: A Folk History of Slavery in the United States From Interviews with Former Slaves*, 17 vols. (Washington, D.C.: Federal Writers' Project, 1936–1938), XVI, pt. 2, 137.

105. George P. Rawick, ed., *American Slave/Texas*, pt. 8, 3520.

106. Ibid., pt. 4, 1448.

107. Lewis, *Negro in Virginia*, 93; See also, Stuckey, *Slave Culture*, 370.

108. Stuckey, *Slave Culture*, 67; Lewis, *Negro in Virginia*, 93.

109. James B. Cade, "Out of the Mouths of Ex-slaves," *Journal of Negro History* 22 (April 1935): 328–29.

110. Allen Dozier, WPA Slave Narrative Project, Georgia Narratives, vol. 4, pt. 4, Manuscript Division, Library of Congress.

111. Benjamin Russell, WPA Slave Narrative Project, South Carolina Narratives, vol. 14, pt. 5, Federal Writer's Project, Manuscript Division, Library of Congress.

112. *Folklore Slaves* (Dillon), Federal Writers Project, Northwestern State University of Louisiana, Watson Memorial Library, Cammie G. Henry Research Center.

113. George Womble, WPA Slave Narrative Project, Georgia Narratives, vol. 4, pt. 4, Federal Writer's Project, Manuscript Division, Library of Congress, 182.

114. W. L. Bost, interviewed by Marjorie Jones in *When I Was a Slave: Memoirs from the Slave Narrative Collection*, ed. Norman R. Yetman (New York: Dover, 2002), 17.

115. "Slavery and the Bible," *DeBow's Review* 9 (September 1850): 281–86.

116. Ella Alford of Bastrop, quoting Frank Roberson in John B. Cade, "Out of the Mouths of Ex-slaves," 329.

117. Willbanks, WPA/Georgia Narratives, 143–44.

118. Ruby Lorraine Radford, *Slavery*, 30 interviews, WPA Slave Narrative Project, Georgia Narratives, vol. 4, pt. 4, Federal Writer's Project, Manuscript Division, Library of Congress

119. *True American*, January 1, 1839.

120. Cade, "Out of the Mouths of Ex-slaves," 328–29.

121. Thomas Jefferson, *Notes on the State of Virginia* (Richmond, Va.: Randolph, 1853).

122. Willbanks, WPA/Georgia Narratives, 143–44.

123. Old Tim, WPA Slave Narrative Project, Georgia Narratives, vol. 4, pt. 4, Federal Writer's Project, Manuscript Division, Library of Congress.

124. Cade, "Out of the Mouths of Ex-slaves," 323.

125. Willbanks, WPA/Georgia Narratives, 143.

126. Lyle Saxon, Edward Dreyer, Robert Tallant, eds., *Gumbo Ya-Ya: A Collection of Louisiana Folk Tales* (Gretna, La.: Pelican Publishing Company, 2006), 240.

127. Wright, WPA/Georgia Narratives, 200.

128. Rawick, *American Slave/Maryland*, pt. 8, 45–48.

129. Within these meetings, various events occurred, from plans of rebellion to religious celebration and the continuation of West African traditions. Frolicking was just one of the many activities that took place in private among the slaves.

130. Cade, "Out of the Mouths of Ex-slaves," 331.

131. Jake Green, WPA Slave Narrative Project, Alabama Narratives, vol. 1, 168, Federal Writer's Project, Manuscript Division, Library of Congress.

132. "Anthony Dawson," *Voices from Slavery: 100 Authentic Slave Narratives*, ed. Norman R. Yetman (New York: Holt, Rinehart, Winston, 1970, 2000), 25.

133. *Folklore: Terrebonne Stories and Legends*, Houma Section—Nacogdoches records, collected by August Coxen-Schiriever, Northwestern State University of Louisiana, Watson Memorial Library, Cammie G. Henry Research Center.

134. Levine, *Black Culture*, 121.

135. Ibid.,122.

136. Genovese, *Roll, Jordan, Roll.*

137. Epstein, *Sinful Tunes*, 244–47, 363.

138. Eugene D. Genovese, *From Rebellion to Revolution: Afro-American Slave Revolts in the making of the Modern World* (Baton Rouge: Louisiana State University Press, 1979); Stephen B. Oates, *The Fires of the Jubilee: Nat Turner's Fierce Rebellion* (New York: Harper & Row, 1975).

139. Stuckey, *Slave Culture*, 24.

140. Charley Williams, WPA Slave Narrative Project, Oklahoma Narratives, vol. 13, Federal Writer's Project, Manuscript Division, Library of Congress.

141. "Henry Bibb," *Puttin on Ole Massa: The slave narratives of Henry Bibb, William Wells Brown, and Solomon Northup,* ed. Gilbert Osofsky (New York: Harper & Row, 1969), 66.

Chapter 5. Advertisement

1. George Featherstonhaugh, *Excursion through the Slave States from Washington on the Potomac to the Frontier of Mexico; With Sketches of Popular Manners and Geological Notices* (New York: Harper, 1844; reprint, New York: Negro Universities Press, 1968), 36–38.

2. Ibid., 37.

3. *Christy's Plantation Melodies, Godey's Lady's Book* 50, no. 2 (February 1855).

4. Featherstonhaugh, *Excursion,* 37.

5. Peter Kolchin, *American Slavery 1619–1877* (New York: Hill and Wang, 1993).

6. R. C. Simmons, *The American Colonies: From Settlement to Independence* (New York: McKay, 1976).

7. Donald L. Robinson, *Slavery in the Structure of American Politics, 1765–1820* (New York: Harcourt Brace Jovanovich, 1971); Paul Finkelman, *Slavery and the Founders: Race and Liberty in the Age of Jefferson,* 2nd ed. (Armonk, N.Y.: Sharpe, 2001).

8. Robert McColley, *Slavery and Jeffersonian Virginia,* 2nd ed. (Urbana: University of Illinois Press, 1973), 164–65.

9. Jeremiah Taylor, "'Sold Down the River': The Rise of Kentucky's Slave Trade with the Lower South," *Upsilonian,* Cumberland College Department of History and Political Science, vol. 10 (Summer 1998).

10. Thomas Jefferson Randolph, Speech in the House of Delegates of Virginia, on the Abolition of Slavery (Richmond: White, 1832).

11. *New Orleans Courier,* February 15, 1839; William Jay, *Miscellaneous Writings on Slavery,* vol. 3 (Boston: Jewett; Cleveland: Jewett, Proctor, and Worthington; London: Sampson Low, 1853), 273.

12. Michael Tadman, *Speculators and Slaves: Masters, Traders, and Slaves in the Old South* (Madison: University of Wisconsin Press, 1989), 70.

13. John Blassingame, ed. *Slave Testimony: Two Centuries of Letters, Speeches, Interviews and Autobiographies* (Baton Rouge: Louisiana State University Press, 1977), 705.

14. Sam T. Stewart, WPA Slave Narrative Project, North Carolina Narratives, vol. 11, pt. 2, Federal Writer's Project, Manuscript Division, Library of Congress.

15. Mary Gaines, interview from Arkansas Narratives, vol. 2, pt. 3, *Born in Slavery: Slave Narratives from the Federal Writers' Project, 1936–1938*; Sophie Word, WPA Slave Narrative Project, Kentucky Narratives, vol. 7, Federal Writer's Project, Manuscript Division, Library of Congress.

16. "Interview with Fannie Moore," in *When I Was a Slave: Memories from the Slave Narrative Collection,* ed. Norman R. Yetman (Mineola: Dover, 2002), 90.

17. Betty Guwn, interview from Indiana Narratives, vol. 5, Negro slaves in Delaware County, in *Born in Slavery: Slave Narratives from the Federal Writers Project, 1936–1938*, 99.

18. Yetman, *When I was a Slave*, 66–67.

19. "The Story of Mrs. Julia King of Toledo, Ohio," WPA Narratives, Lucas County, Toledo, Ohio, Ohio Narratives, vol. 12.

20. William Goodell, *American Slave Code in Theory and Practise: Its Distinctive Features Shown by Its Statutes, Judicial Decisions, and Illustrative Facts*, 1853, p. 31, available at HeinOnline.org (accessed July 6, 2013).

21. Charles Ball, *Slavery in the United States: A Narrative of The Life and Adventures of Charles Ball, A Black Man* (Lewistown, Pa.: Shugert, 1836), 267.

22. Frederick Douglass, *My Bondage, My Freedom* (New York: Miller, Orton & Mulligan, 1855), 116–17.

23. Isaac Johnson, *Slavery Days in Old Kentucky: A True Story of a Father Who Sold His Wife and Four Children* (Ogdensburg, N.Y.: Republican & Journal, 1901).

24. John Blassingame, ed. *Slave Testimony: Two Centuries of Letters, Speeches, Interviews, and Autobiographies* (Baton Rouge, Louisiana State University, 1977), 705.

25. William Gilmore Simms, *The Pro-Slavery Argument: As Maintained by the Most Distinguished Writers of the Southern States, containing the Several Essays on the Subject of Chancellor Harper, Governor Hammond, Dr Simms, and Professor Dew* (Charleston, S.C.: Walker, Richards, 1852), 57.

26. Thomas H. Jones, *Experience and Personal Narrative of Uncle Tom Jones: Who Was for Forty Years a Slave; Also the Surprising Adventures of Wild Tom, of the Island Retreat, a Fugitive Negro from South Carolina* (Boston: Skinner, 185-?); Harriet Beecher Stowe, *Key to Uncle Tom's Cabin* (New York: Arno, 1968), 305; and Blassingame, *Slave Testimony*, 347.

27. Word, WPA Slave Narrative Project/Kentucky, vol. 7.

28. William Wells Brown, *My Southern Home; or, The South and Its People* (Boston: Brown, 1880), 143–44.

29. Letter from Thomas Jefferson to Bowling Clarke on selling slaves, Monticello, September 21, 1792. Located in the "Domestic Slave Trade" section, Schomburg Center for Research in Black Culture, New York; *In Motion: The African American Migration Experience*, available at http://www.inmotionaame.org/migrations (accessed August 13, 2013).

30. Strait Edge, "Plantation Regulations," *Soil of the South* 1 (February and May 1851): 20–21, 68; James O. Breeden, ed., *Advice among Masters: The Ideal in Slave Management in the Old South* (Westport, Conn.: Greenwood, 1980), 228–29.

31. H., "Remarks on Overseers, and the Proper Treatment of Slaves," *Farmers' Register* 5 (September 1837): 301–2; Breeden, *Advice among Masters*, 35.

32. An Overseer, "On the Conduct and Management of Overseers, Driver and Slave," *Southern Agriculturist* 9 (May 1836): 225–31 and Breeden, *Advice among Masters*, 34.

33. Nathaniel Southgate Shaler and Sophia Penn Page Shaler, *The Autobiography of Nathaniel Southgate Shaler* (New York: Houghton Mifflin, 1909), 36.

34. "Interview of Eliza Washington" (Slave memories - birth, mother, father, separation house), WPA Slave Narrative Project, Arkansas Narratives, vol. 2, pt. 7, Federal Writer's Project, Manuscript Division, Library of Congress, 52.

35. Sam T. Stewart, WPA Slave Narrative Project, North Carolina Narratives, vol. 11, pt. 2, 317–18, Federal Writer's Project, Manuscript Division, Library of Congress.

36. Originally in *Western Luminary*, Lexington, October 4, 1826. Quoted in John Winston Coleman, *Slavery Times in Kentucky* (Chapel Hill: University of North Carolina Press, 1940; reprint 1970), 144.

37. Frederick Law Olmstead, *A Journey in the Seaboard Slave States: With Remarks on Their Economy* (New York: Mason, 1861), 45.

38. George Tucker, *Letters from Virginia*, trans. F. Lucas (Baltimore: J. Rubinson, 1816), 31–33.

39. Ibid.

40. Wilson Armistead, *A Tribute for the Negro: Being a Vindication of the Moral, Intellectual, and Religious Capabilities of the Coloured Portion of Mankind: With Particular Reference to the African Race* [electronic edition] (Manchester: William Irwin, 1848), 542; located in *Documenting the American South*, University Library, University of North Carolina at Chapel Hill (available at http://docsouth.unc.edu/neh/Armistead; accessed November 2012).

41. William Goodell, *The American Slave Code in Theory and Practice: Its Distinctive Features Shown by Its Statutes, Judicial Decisions, and Illustrative Facts* (New York: American and Foreign Anti-Slavery Society, 1853), 53.

42. Robert H. Gudmestad, *A Troublesome Commerce: The Transformation of the Interstate Slave Trade* (Baton Rouge: Louisiana State University Press, 2004), 171.

43. Featherstonhaugh, *Excursion*, 37.

44. Philo Tower, *Slavery Unmasked: Being a Truthful Narrative of a Three Years' Residence and Journeying in Eleven Southern States; To Which Is Added the Invasion of Kansas, Including the Last Chapter of Her Wrongs* (Rochester, N.Y.: Darrow, 1856).

45. Brown, *My Southern Home*, 143–44.

46. Featherstonhaugh, *Excursion*, 38.

47. Thomas Dwight Weld, *American Slavery As It Is: Testimony of a Thousand Witnesses* (New York: American Anti-Slavery Society, 1839).

48. Shaler, *Autobiography*, 36.

49. Levi Coffin, *Reminiscences of Levi Coffin, the Reputed President of the Underground Railroad; Being a Brief History of the Labors of a Lifetime in Behalf of the Slave, with the Stories of Numerous Fugitives, Who Gained Their Freedom Through His Instrumentality, and Many Other Incidents*, 2nd Edition (Cincinnati: Clarke, 1880), 12–13.

50. Breeden, *Advice among Masters*, 277.

51. The story of Edmondson was detailed in Stowe, *Key to Uncle Tom's Cabin*, 323.

52. Tyrone Power, *Impressions of America during the Years 1833, 1834, and 1835* (London: Bentley, 1836).

53. Dorothy Schneider and Carl J. Schneider, eds., *Slavery in America*, 2nd ed. (New York: Facts on File, January 2007), 220.

54. Jethro Rumple, *A History of Rowan County, North Carolina, Containing Sketches of Prominent Families and Distinguished Men, with an Appendix* (Salisbury, N.C.: Bruner, 1881, 323–24; repr. Salisbury, N.C.: Elizabeth Maxwell Steele Chapter, Daughters of the American Revolution, 1916).

55. Featherstonhaugh, *Excursion*, 37.

56. J. Winston Coleman Jr., "Lexington's Slave Dealers and Their Southern Trade," [Louisville, Kentucky] *Filson Club History Quarterly* 12 (January 1938): 7.

57. Lincoln to Mary Speed, September 27, 1841, in John G. Nicholsy and John Hay, *Complete Works of Abraham Lincoln* vol. 1 (New York: Tandy, 1905), 177.

58. Ibid.

59. Frederic Bancroft, *Slave Trading in the Old South* (Baltimore: Furst, 1931; reprint, Columbia: University of South Carolina Press, 1996), 100.

60. Charles H. Corey, *A History of the Richmond Theological Seminary with Reminiscences of Thirty Years' Work among the Colored People of the South* (Richmond: Randolph, 1895), 46–48.

61. Coleman, "Lexington's Slave Dealers," 9–10.

62. Edward E. Baptist, "'Cuffy,' 'Fancy Maids,' and 'One-Eyed Men': Rape, Commodification, and the Domestic Slave Trade in the United States, *American Historical Review* 106, no. 5 (2001): 55.

63. *Free Trader* and *Concordia Intelligencia*, October 15, 1852. Newspaper cited in Stowe, *Key to Uncle Tom's Cabin*, 338.

64. *Daily Enquirer*, June 27, 1853.

65. Bancroft, *Slave Trading*, 156–57.

66. John A'Becket, "Blind Tom as He Is Today (1898)," *Black Perspective in Music* 4, no. 2 (July 1976).

67. Olmstead, *Journey*, 310.

68. "Interview, Jennie Kendricks," WPA Slave Narrative Project, Georgia Narratives, vol. 4, pt. 3, Federal Writer's Project, Manuscript Division, Library of Congress.

69. Solomon Northup, *Twelve Years a Slave*, ed. Sue Eakin and Joseph Logsdon (Baton Rouge: Louisiana State University, 1968), 51.

70. William Wells Brown, *Narrative of William W. Brown, an American Slave; Written by Himself* (London: Gilpin, 1849), 41–42.

71. Louis Alexis Chamerovzow, ed., *Slave Life in Georgia: A Narrative of the Life, Suffering, and Escape of John Brown, a Fugitive Slave, Now in England* (London: Watts, 1855), 112–13; *Documenting the American South*, 2001, University Library, University of North Carolina at Chapel Hill (available at http://docsouth.unc.edu/neh/jbrown/jbrown.html, accessed November 2012).

72. Brown, *My Southern Home*, 111, 192–93

73. Henry Clay Bruce, *The New Man. Twenty-Nine Years a Slave, Twenty-Nine Years a Free Man*, (York, Pa.: Anstadt, 1895), 47–49.

74. Ms. Martin, WPA Slave Narrative Project, Georgia Narratives, vol. 4, pt. 4, Federal Writer's Project, Manuscript Division, Library of Congress.

75. Chamerovzow, *Slave Life in Georgia*, 112–18.

76. Joseph Sturge, *A Visit to the United States in 1841* (London: Hamilton, Adams, 1842; repr. New York: Kelley, 1969).

77. Chamerovzow, *Slave Life in Georgia*.

78. Walter Johnson, *Soul by Soul: Life Inside the Antebellum Slave Market* (Cambridge, Mass.: Harvard University Press, 1999.

79. William Wells Brown, *Narrative of William W. Brown, an American Slave: Written by Himself* (London: Gilpin, 1849), 44.

80. Olmstead, *Journey*, 40.

81. Chamerovzow, *Slave Life in Georgia.*

82. Ibid., 116.

83. Ira Berlin, *Generations of Captivity: A History of African American Slaves* (Cambridge, Mass.: Belknap, 2004).

84. Brown, *My Southern Home*, 143–44.

85. "Interview with W. L. Bost," in Yetman, *When I Was a Slave*, 16.

86. Peter Randolph, *Sketches of Slave Life; or, Illustrations of the "Peculiar Institution"* [electronic edition] (Boston: 1855), 8–10, Special Collections, University of Virginia Library, *Documenting the American South*, Electronic Collection the University of North Carolina at Chapel Hill.

87. "Interview with Delicia Patterson," in Yetman, *When I Was a Slave*, 101

88. Ruth Galmon, Personal Records, December 2001.

89. Orland Kay Armstrong, *Ole Massa's People: The Old Slaves Tell Their Story* (Indianapolis: Bobbs-Merrill, 1931), 261.

90. Randolph, *Sketches.*

91. Steven Deyle, *Carry Me Back: The Domestic Slave Trade in American Life* (Oxford: Oxford University Press, 2005), 243.

Chapter 6. Same Script, Different Actors

1. Richard L. Klepac, *Mr. Matthews at Home* (London: Society for Theater Research, 1979), 49–50.

2. Francis Hodge, "Charles Matthews Reports on America," *Quarterly Journal of Speech* 36 (1950): 492.

3. Klepac, *Mr. Matthews at Home*, 98–120.

4. Robert Toll, *Blacking Up: The Minstrel Show in Nineteenth Century America* (New York: Oxford University Press, 1974), 26–27.

5. Klepac, *Mr. Matthews at Home*, 106.

6. *National Advocate*, August 3, 1821, 2.

7. Errol G. Hill and James V. Hatch, *A History of African American Theater* (Cambridge: Cambridge University Press, 2003), 25–28.

8. *National Advocate*, May 8, 1824.

9. Marvin McAllister, *White People Do Not Know How to Behave at Entertainments Designed for Ladies and Gentlemen of Colour: William Brown's African and American Theater* (Chapel Hill: University of North Carolina Press, 2003), 159.

10. Sam Dennison, *Scandalize My Name: Black Imagery in American Popular Music* (New York: Garland, 1982).

11. Several scholars have illustrated varying sections of these lyrics with some alteration. See Dennison, *Scandalize My Name*, 20–21 and Appendix 1.

12. Aaron, a Slave, *The Light a Truth of Slavery, Aaron's History* (Worcester, Mass.: 1845), 15–16.

13. Ira Berlin, *Many Thousand Gone: The First Two Centuries of Slavery in North America* (Cambridge, Mass.: Belknap, 1998); Leon Litwack, *North of Slavery: The Negro in the Free States, 1790–1860* (Chicago: University of Chicago Press, 1961).

14. "Mr. Rantoul's Connexion with Town and Parochial Affairs—His Views of Religion," *Historical Collections of the Essex Institute* 6 (April 1864): 85; Shane

White, "The Death of James Johnson," *American Quarterly* 51, no. 4 (December 1999): 755–59.

15. Leslie Harris, *In the Shadow of Slavery: African Americans in New York City, 1626–1863* (Chicago: University of Chicago Press, 2003), 69.

16. William Torbert Leonard, *Masquerade in Black* (Metuchen, N.J.: Scarecrow, 1986), 9.

17. Lawrence Levine, *Highbrow/Lowbrow: The Emergence of Cultural Hierarchy in America* (Cambridge, Mass.: Harvard University Press, 1988), 50.

18. Toll, *Blacking Up*, 25–30.

19. Dennison, *Scandalize My Name*, 20.

20. Toll, *Blacking Up*, 26–27.

21. *Songster's Repository*, The Songsters Repository (New York: Nathaniel Dearborn, 1811).

22. Bruce Laurie, *Artisans into Workers: Labor in Nineteenth Century America* (Urbana: University of Illinois Press, 1997).

23. Charles Sellers, *The Market Revolution: Jacksonian America, 1815–1846* (Oxford: Oxford University Press, 1994); Sean Wilentz, *Chants Democratic: New York City and the Rise of the Working Class, 1788–1850* (New York: Oxford University Press, 1984), 266.

24. George Rogers Taylor, *The Transportation Revolution, 1815–1860* (Armonk, N.Y.: Sharpe, 1977).

25. Wilentz, *Chants Democratic*, 5.

26. W. E. B. Dubois stated that "nineteen million immigrants entered the United States" in the nineteenth century. W. E. B. Dubois, *Black Reconstruction In America: An Essay Toward a History of the Part Which Black Folk Played in the Attempt to Reconstruct Democracy in America, 1860–1880* (New York: Atheneum, 1935, 1962).

27. Leonard Dinnerstein and David M. Reimers, *Ethnic Americans: A History of Immigration and Assimilation* (New York: Harper & Row, 1975).

28. Michael Chevalier, *Society, Manners and Politics In the United States: Being a Series of Letters on North America* (Boston: Weeks, Jordan, 1839), 341.

29. Dinnerstein and Reimers, *Ethnic Americans*, 12; Theodore Allen, *The Invention of the White Race* (New York: Verso, 1994), 186.

30. Hodge, "Charles Matthews Reports," 493.

31. Ibid., 498.

32. See Dennison, *Scandalize My Name*, 513.

33. The information pertaining to the stage performance comes directly from Francis Hodge and Mrs. Charles Matthews's publication of Charles Matthews's memoirs.

34. Hodge, "Charles Matthews Reports," 497.

35. Matthew Frye Jacobson, *Whiteness of a Different Color: European Immigration and the Alchemy of Race* (Cambridge, Mass.: Harvard University Press, 1999).

36. J. B. D. DeBow, *Statistical View of the United States* (Washington: Nicholson, 1854), 192.

37. Michael Kaplan, "New York City Tavern Violence and the Creation of a Working-Class Male Identity," *Journal of the Early Republic* 15, no. 4 (Winter 1995): 595.

38. Chevalier, *Society, Manners and Politics*, 347.

39. David R. Roediger, *The Wages of Whiteness: Race and the Making of the American Working Class* (New York: Verso, 1991), 71.

40. Ibid., 23.

41. W. T. Lhamon Jr., *Jump Jim Crow: Lost Plays, Lyrics, and Street Prose of the First Atlantic Popular Culture* (Cambridge, Mass.: Harvard University Press, 2003), 95–98.

42. Dale Cockrell, "Jim Crow, Demon of Disorder," *American Music* 14, no. 2 (Summer 1996): 161–84.

43. *Boston Post*, July 22, 1838. Quoted in Cockrell, "Jim Crow," 161.

44. Cockrell, "Jim Crow," 162–63.

45. "Stephen C. Foster and Negro Minstrelsy," *Atlantic Monthly* 10 (November 1867).

46. Toll, *Blacking Up*, 2.

47. James Weldon Johnson, *Black Manhattan* (New York: Knopf, 1940); Dale Cockrell, *Demons of Disorder: Early Blackface Minstrels and Their World* (Cambridge: Cambridge University Press, 1997); George F. Rehin, "Harlequin Jim Crow: Continuity and Convergence in Blackface Clowning," *Journal of Popular Culture* 9 (Winter 1975): 682–701; Alexander Saxton, "Blackface Minstrelsy and Jacksonian Ideology," *American Quarterly* 27, no. 1 (March 1975): 3–28; and William J. Mahar, *Behind the Burnt Cork Mask: Early Blackface Minstrelsy and Antebellum American Popular Culture* (Urbana: University of Illinois Press, 1999). This brief review of scholarship on the American minstrel show does not fully reflect current and past work on the subject.

48. Leonard, *Masquerade in Black*, 227.

49. Ibid., 227–42.

50. Ibid., 241–47.

51. Eileen Southern, *The Music of Black Americans: A History*, 2nd ed. (New York: Norton, 1983), 92.

52. Ibid.

53. Toll, *Blacking Up*, 46–47.

54. Frederick Buckley, George F. Harris, and Stephen Collins Foster, *The Christy's Minstrels' Song Book: Sixty Songs with Choruses and Pianoforte Accompaniments* (London: Boosey, 1857).

55. Roediger, *Wages of Whiteness*, 76–77.

56. American Minstrel Show Collection, 1823–1947 (MS Thr 556). Harvard Theatre Collection, Houghton Library, Harvard University, Cambridge, Mass.

57. Scott Herring, "Du Bois and the Minstrels," *MELUS*, 22:2, Popular Literature and Film, (Summer 1997): 8.

58. Susan Key, "Sound and Sentimentality: Nostalgia in the Songs of Stephen Foster," *American Music* 13, no. 2 (Summer 1995), 145–66.

59. Uncle Tom's Cabin and American Culture, University of Virginia: A Multi-Media Archive.

60. Robert Nowatzki, *Representing African Americans in Transatlantic Abolitionism and Blackface Minstrelsy* (Baton Rouge: Louisiana State University Press, 2010).

61. Steven Deyle, *Carry Me Back: The Domestic Slave Trade in American Life* (Oxford: Oxford University Press, 2005), 242–44.

62. Isabella Lucy Bird, *The Englishwoman in America* (London: Murray, 1856; Toronto: University of Toronto Press, 1966), 129–30.

63. Jon Cruz, *Culture on the Margins: The Black Spiritual and the Rise of American Cultural Interpretation* (Princeton, N.J.: Princeton University Press, 1999).

64. Eric Charry, *Mande Music: Traditional and Modern Music of the Maninka and Mandinka of Western Africa* (Chicago: University of Chicago Press, 2000).

65. Robert Winans, "The Folk, the Stage, and the Five String Banjo in the Nineteenth Century," *Journal of American Folklore* 89 (October 1976): 407–37.

66. Robert B. Winans and Elias J. Kaufman, "Minstrel and Classic Banjo: American and English Connections." *American Music* 12, no. 1 (Spring 1994), 2–10.

67. Toll, *Blacking Up*, 44.

68. Ibid.

69. Lott, *Love and Theft: Blackface Minstrelsy and the American Working Class*, Race and American Culture (Oxford: Oxford University Press, 1995), 52.

70. Carl Wittke, *Tambo and Bones: A History of the American Minstrel Stage* (Durham, N.C.: Duke University Press, 1930).

71. Cornel West, *Race Matters* (New York: Vintage, 1993), 157; Benedict Anderson, *Imagined Communities: Reflections on the Origin and Spread of Nationalism* (New York: Verso, 1991).

72. McAllister, *White People*, 1.

73. *National Advocate*, August 3, 1821.

74. George Odell, *National Advocate*, September 21, 1821.

75. Shane White, *Stories of Freedom in Black New York* (Cambridge, Mass.: Harvard University Press, 2007), 93.

76. McAllister, *White People*, 360.

77. Thomas Birch, *Zip Coon* (New York: Atwill's Music Saloon, 1834), digitized by Nathan Piazza at the Digital Media Center, Clemons Library, University of Virginia.

78. David R. Roediger, *Wages of Whiteness*, 13.

79. The Library Company, Philadelphia, 1844.

80. Mahar, *Behind the Burnt Cork Mask*, 210.

81. Cockrell, *Demons of Disorder*, 92.

82. Toll, *Blacking Up*, 69.

83. Ibid.

84. Robert Winans, *The Early Minstrel Show*, New World Records, 1985, 1998, digitized by Adam Soroka at the Digital Media Center, Clemons Library, University of Virginia.

85. Berlin, *Many Thousand Gone*, 98.

86. Charles Reagan Wilson and William Ferris, eds., *Encyclopedia of Southern Culture* (Chapel Hill: University of North Carolina Press (used by permission of the publisher); Leah Rawls Atkins, "High Cotton: The Antebellum Alabama Plantation Mistress and the Cotton Culture," *Agricultural History* 68, no. 2 (Eli Whitney's Cotton Gin, 1793–1993: A Symposium) (Spring 1994): 93.

87. John Pendleton Kennedy, *Swallow Barn; or, A Sojourn in the Old Dominion*, 2 vols. (Philadelphia: Carey & Lea, 1832), 28. This work is the property of the University of North Carolina at Chapel Hill, *Documenting the American South* (online database).

88. Wilson and Ferris, *Encyclopedia of Southern Culture*. Used with permission of the publisher.

89. Richard J. Calhoun, Review of *From Nationalism to Secessionism: The Changing Fiction of William Gilmore Simms*, by Charles S. Watson, *South Atlantic Review* 60, no. 1 (January 1995): 149–51; Lucinda MacKethan, "An Overview of Southern Literature by Genre," North Carolina State University, originally published in *Southern Spaces*, accessed February 17, 2007.

90. William Gilmore Simms, *Richard Hurdis; or, The Avenger of Blood, A Tale of Alabama* (Philadelphia: Carey & Hart, 1838), vol. 1, ch. 9.

91. Caroline Howard Gilman, *Recollections of a Southern Matron* (New York: Harper, 1838), 102. This work is the property of the University of North Carolina at Chapel Hill, *Documenting the American South* (online database).

92. Harriet Beecher Stowe, *Uncle Tom's Cabin* (Cutchogue, N.Y.: Buccaneer, 1852).

93. Information on Stowe's work *Maya* can be found in Jeanette Reid Tandy, "Pro-Slavery Propaganda in American Fiction of the Fifties," *South Atlantic Quarterly* 21 (1922): 41–50, 170–78.

94. Stowe, *Uncle Tom's Cabin*, 25–26.

95. Ibid.

96. William Torbert Leonard, *Masquerade in Black* (Metuchen, N.J.: Scarecrow, 1986), 164.

97. Toll, *Blacking Up*, 28.

98. Saxton, "Blackface," 8.

99. William L. Van Deburg, *Slavery & Race in American Popular Culture* (Madison: University of Wisconsin Press, 1984), 47–48.

100. *Early in de morning*, comp. and arr. by Thomas Comer (Boston: Reed, 1852), LOC American Memory, African American Sheet Music, 1850–1920.

101. *History of the Theater Royal, Dublin* (Dublin, 1870), 100. See Douglass C. Riach, "Blacks and Blackface on the Irish Stage, 1830–1860," *Journal of American Studies* 7, no. 3 (December 1973): 231.

102. McAllister, *White People*, 176.

103. Ibid.

104. Lott, *Love and Theft*, 46; Nicholas M. Evans, "Ira Aldridge: Shakespeare and Minstrelsy," *The American Transcendental Quarterly* 16, no. 3 (September 2002).

105. Patricia Turner, *Ceramic Uncles and Celluloid Mammies: Black Images and Their Influence on Culture* (New York: Anchor, 1994).

Epilogue

1. The information concerning the *Oprah Winfrey Show* and her interview with Dave Chappelle comes directly from the archives of *The Oprah Winfrey Show*.

2. Michael Eric Dyson, *Debating Race with Michael Eric Dyson* (New York: Basic Civitas, 2007).

3. Michael Richards, comedian and actor, commonly known as Cosmo Kramer from the television series, *Seinfeld*. In November 2006, Richards sparked national controversy when he shouted racial epithets at black hecklers in a Los Angeles

comedy club. Don Imus, controversial radio host, made negative racial and sexual comments toward the Rutgers female basketball team on April 4, 2007.

4. Kathryn Stockett, *The Help: A Novel* (New York: Berkley, 2009).

5. Langston Hughes, Arnold Rampersad, and David Roessel, *The Collected Poems of Langston Hughes* (New York: Knopf, 1994).

6. Frantz Fanon, *Black Skin, White Masks*, trans. Charles Lam Markmann (New York: Grove, 1967), 14.

7. Henry T. Sampson, *Blacks in Blackface: A Source Book on Early Black Musical Shows* (Metuchen, N.J.: Scarecrow, 1980), 1.

8. Robert C. Toll, *Blacking Up: The Minstrel Show in Nineteenth-Century America* (New York: Oxford University Press, 1974), 262; Karen Sotiropoulos, *Staging Race: Black Performers in Turn of the Century America* (Cambridge, Mass.: Harvard University Press, 2006), 3.

9. James Weldon Johnson, *Black Manhattan* (New York: Arno, 1968), 93.

10. Sampson, *Blacks in Blackface*; Tom Fletcher, *One Hundred Years of the Negro in Show Business* (New York: Da Capo, 1984).

11. Scott Herring, "Du Bois and the Minstrels," *MELUS* 22:2, Popular Literature and Film (Summer 1997): 10.

12. Robin Means Coleman analyzed the history of African American representations in mass media for more than fifty years. She reviewed the various trends and portrayals of blacks, determining that the minstrel show was active in the foundation of mass media and has presently resurged in what she labels the Neo-Minstrel Era. This revival of minstrelsy was also mentioned by mass media scholar J. Fred MacDonald in his work on the history of television. He referred to the displays of blacks in television shows in the 1990s as a new form of minstrelsy, with blacks performing negative stereotypes of themselves instead of whites in blackface promoting these stereotypes.

13. Interview with Spike Lee, http://www.bamboozledmovie.com (accessed May 10, 2007).

INDEX

KATRINA DYONNE THOMPSON is an assistant professor of history and African American studies at St. Louis University.

The University of Illinois Press
is a founding member of the
Association of American University Presses.

Composed in 9.5/12.5 Trump Mediaeval
by Lisa Connery
at the University of Illinois Press
Manufactured by Sheridan Books, Inc.

University of Illinois Press
1325 South Oak Street
Champaign, IL 61820-6903
www.press.uillinois.edu